ELEGANCE

ELEGANCE

A Guide to Quality
in Menswear

G. BRUCE BOYER

ILLUSTRATIONS BY TONY KOKINOS

W · W · NORTON & COMPANY · NEW YORK · LONDON

The text of this book is composed in Electra, with display type set in Stark Debonair.
Composition and Manufacturing by Maple-Vail Book Manufacturing Group.
Book design by Antonina Krass

First Edition

Library of Congress Cataloging in Publication Data
Boyer, G. Bruce.
Elegance: a guide to quality in menswear.

1. Men's clothing.   I. Title.
TT617.B69   1985   646'.32   84–27271

ISBN 0-393-01878-4

W. W. Norton & Company, Inc., 500 Fifth Avenue, New York, N.Y. 10110
W. W. Norton & Company Ltd., 37 Great Russell Street, London WC1B 3NU

For my wife, Pam,
and my mother, Betsy

CONTENTS

FOREWORD | 9

ACKNOWLEDGMENTS | 13

FOREWORD

I first began writing about men's clothing a dozen years ago in the pages of *Town & Country*. The Duke of Windsor had just passed away, and I thought it fitting to pay some tribute to a man who for the better part of a half century had so elegantly influenced what men wore. Windsor's passing ironically coincided with the considerably less mourned death of the "denim decade" in American fashion and with the rise of the menswear designer. The phenomenon of the designer collection in menswear had been born in 1966 when Pierre Cardin launched his first line of men's clothing, and the ensuing years have witnessed the burgeoning of this aesthetic and retailing force in our lives. In 1968 Bill Blass won the first Coty Award for men's fashion design, and by 1973, when Ralph Lauren won a "Return Award" for his men's clothing collection, it became perfectly clear that a trend had become an established phenomenon in contemporary life: that men's attire was to be accorded as much attention, talent, and publicity as had traditionally been devoted to the design of women's fashions.

One reason the clothing designer has flourished is that we are so highly tuned to visual images, and whether it be a museum exhibition devoted to the costumes of a bygone era, a TV program about the lifestyles of the rich and famous, or any one of a number of creamy-

9

complexioned magazines, there is ample evidence that dress is considered an important aspect of our lives. Social philosophers have waxed both eloquent and tedious on the subject, but the point is that fashion designers have garnered celebrity, wealth, and status in amounts to make rock stars, gourmet chefs, and prime-time actors pea-green with envy. They have, as the phrase goes, high social identity.

Social identity, interestingly enough, is what clothing is all about anyway. The clothes we wear offer the first sign as well as the most continuing reminder of who we are. What we believe to be the truth of other people's appearances is likely determined by what they wear—and for many of our relationships that is quite enough. "Do not enquire too deeply into the truth of other people's appearances," wrote the cynical and worldly-wise Lord Chesterfield in one of the many epistles framed for his son's edification. "Life is more sociable if one takes people as they are and not as they probably are."

Those whose appearances we admire wear their clothes with a certain sense of comfort and propriety of style we often call elegance, a word variously defined but always including, even centering on, the idea of gracefulness, the skillful ease with which something is done. And that ease, I think, is generally a quality one develops from an intelligent familiarity with the endeavor.

In the several decades since World War II we have seen a number of approaches to dress for men: the casual California Look of the 1940s (based on the leisure-time life-style of country club, barbecues, and recreational sports); the Ivy League outfit of the 1950s (that softly-constructed business dress of the Eastern Establishment); the Continental Look of the early 1960s (which arrived from Rome with the films of Fellini and Visconti); the Roughwear Approach of the mid-1960s to early 1970s (an anti-elitist look in which prole gear rose the the top of the social scale and fashion was set in the streets).

Since 1973, or thereabouts, the past has played a dominant role in men's clothing, a return to more traditional business wardrobes often hailed in the fashion media as a "return to elegance"—a return to the glory that was Grant and the grandeur that was Astaire. At the same time, designers are also reconsidering the several other genres of dress we've come through since the 1940s. Today, whether in designer clothes, custom-tailoring, the established haberdashery, or the new boutique, men have choices undreamt of a generation ago, choices that are often confusing and frustrating. My aim in this book is to discuss the proprieties and possibilities of men's attire by considering its history and contemporary applications, and to provide information related to quality in purchasing and maintaining a good wardrobe. Some insightful person (I haven't been able to track down the source in my Bartlett, but my guess would be either Mark Twain or William James) opined that being properly dressed can confer a peace of mind often not attained even from prayer. In a sense, this book is a footnote to that elegant and perceptive thought.

ACKNOWLEDGMENTS

Some of these essays appeared first in *Town & Country*, and I should particularly like to thank editor-in-chief Frank Zachary. Several others appeared in *Diversion*; thanks to editor David Walker.

A special thanks to Brooks Brothers for supplying the clothing for the illustrations.

ELEGANCE

ACCOUTREMENT

S ome men take clothing too seriously. They are intimidated by the subject and afraid to stray from the unspoken yet rigidly prescribed rules of business and professional wear. They are always seen in their dark gray suits, white or blue shirts, and terribly discreet navy foulard neckties. You know without looking that they are wearing dark gray or navy hose and black plain oxfords as well. Others, who unfortunately know themselves even less, don't take their appearance seriously enough, and their sad sartorial philosophy usually falls into one of two camps: they will either tell you that clothes really don't matter anyway, or they buy their clothing on the theory that it should be amusing. I may be wrong, but I've come to the conclusion that in both cases we are dealing with someone who is very much afraid of clothing—and, by extension, has trouble dealing with his appearance. Well, these are deeper waters, Watson, than we need dive into. This latter ocean of rampant let's-dress-any-old-way-we-want-to individualism does seem to have ebbed a bit since its high tide in the mid-1970s, so perhaps we may rest a little easier on that score. Those attempts at wardrobe whimsy rarely result in anything more than public spectacle anyway.

The truth is, though, that we must look on both of these types more in sadness than derision, because they are both slaves of a sort, locked in their prison of extremes. The one is afraid to even whisper his uniqueness, while the other feels compelled to shout his individuality. Someone—me, at the moment—should point out to these fellows that it isn't necessary to dress completely in gray to be taken seriously, any more than it is necessary to wear tattered jeans to the office to proclaim you are your own man. What I am getting at is that the trick, it seems to me, is to first understand that there are rules. Like social discourse, dress has its proprieties—because of course, dress *is* social discourse; it speaks for us and about us. And, as we were all taught in English 101, it is necessary to understand the rules before breaking them. The man who, as is often said, "can get away with" wearing his trenchcoat over his dinner jacket, or an old school tie for a belt, is the one who in fact understands best the rules of proper dress and can bend them to suit his own personality and requirements. He is perfectly accustomed to playing within the rules of the game, but he is not blind to the creativity, exuberance, and freedom within the rules, either. It's a good thing to remember what Alexander Pope said: "Those move easiest who have learned to dance." We could all look silly and disheveled, or dull and boring. Some men choose not to.

When you stop to consider it, individuality in dress almost always presents itself in terms of accessories rather than basics. The Fred Astaires and Dukes of Windsor and Douglas Fairbankses of this world would never think of wearing anything but the most proper gray flannel suits and navy blazers. Not for Cary Grant are the Day-Glo bow tie, fruit-salad jewelry, or lime green tuxedo. But who would disagree that each man possesses a singular, fashionable aura?

Sartorial distinction requires an understanding and approach to accoutrement, to those furnishings that proclaim the style of the man, just as the basics of dress proclaim his sense of propriety. Consider jewelry, for instance, which is perhaps the most difficult accessory category for a man to understand—difficult because there is so much of it around, and in such variety: everything from Cartier tank watches and simple gold wedding bands to Roman coin cuff links, ankle bracelets, and chest medallions that resemble gilded pepperoni pizzas. There is no need for the confusion, however, when the rule of jewelry is a veritable maxim of style: Keep it simple and wear it sparingly. Cuff links, collar bar, wristwatch, and wedding ring are usually all the jewelry a gentleman wears, and they should be all relatively simple. This is not to say you shouldn't wear a fancy western belt buckle or one of those incredibly intricate sports wristwatches that seems to record every changing facet of the environment. Fine. But unless one is either in show business or India, where there is a strong tradition of carrying one's wealth on one's person, don't load up. Ostentation in dress began to disappear in the seventeenth century, with the exception of court ceremony. The French Revolution took care of even that, and Beau Brummell instituted the elegance of simplicity and fit in its stead.

With clothing, on the other hand, the trick to using accessories is often to play against form, to mix the images a bit by combining a few lighter elements into an otherwise sedate and serious picture. This kind of thing, you may remember, was practiced with a vengeance a few years ago, when some otherwise sane citizens were seen wearing their dinner jackets with fatigue pants and sneakers, and other studied combinations too precious to recount. All of which proved once again that a good thing can be carried too far. Wearing a mink-lined denim cowboy jacket may be whimsical, but it is also vulgar and ostentatious—the antithesis of style.

The principle and tradition of playing against form are, nevertheless, legitimate and useful both in the articles of clothing themselves and in the demeanor with which they are worn. Some designer once pointed out that the trick to dressing was to wear a mink coat like a cloth one and vice versa, and the principle—mink coats aside—applies to men as well as women. I'm sure I'm not the first to conclude that the reason Fred Astaire looked so marvelous in tails is that he played against that stuffed-sausage look that so predominates when one wears a terribly formal getup. In all of those wonderful films he always looks so much at ease, so comfortable and casual; more as though he were wearing terribly elegant pajamas, rather than white tie, top hat, and tails. Edward VII, the fashionable monarch who gave his name to an age, often enjoyed the exuberance of playing against form in dress— and no one before or since knew the proprieties better than he. Once, while awaiting a friend at a railway station in Marienbad, he caused considerable astonishment by appearing on the platform wearing a pink tie and bright green cap with his otherwise somber and discreetly cut tweed suit. That's style.

When it comes to business wear, a suit of conservative hue and cut is hard to surpass, but there's no reason why it mightn't be enlivened with a pair of tastefully resplendent suspenders—perhaps in old school colors and with fine pigskin tabs—and a discreet paisley pocket square. Not something that looks as though an ice cream cone had exploded in your chest pocket, nor one that perfectly matches the tie (a common mistake that creates a much too studied look), but one that just picks up and accents the suit with color. A pocket square should, by the way, be easily folded and tucked neatly into the chest pocket of the jacket so that only about three-quarters of an inch rises from the welt all the way across. The point of accessories is that they should complement the basics and each other, but should not match or imitate. The word for basics with matching accessories is "uniform," and when your shirt and your handkerchief and necktie match, people tend to mistake you for an airline employee.

Footwear is another area of business attire that is thought by some to be sacrosanct but that realistically offers considerable leeway these days. Ever since the mid-1950s, in fact, when Dr. Aldo Gucci revolutionized the shoe industry by designing a sophisticated slip-on that combined good looks with comfort and durability, the casual shoe has been more and more accepted into the business wardrobe. It is no longer a strict rule that town shoes must be lace-ups. The clunky, brown penny loafer of campus fame is still off-limits with pinstripes, but a streamlined pair of black slip-ons with a discreet snaffle bit or tassels is perfectly acceptable and makes a comfortable alternative, particularly for travel, when a light shoe that does double duty is an advantage, as is one that slips on and off easily during tiresome, leg-cramping flights.

Small leather goods as business accessories are perhaps the most ignored area for stylish attention. This is rather odd, because while businessmen are sometimes reluctant to discuss the subject, few items come in for more scrutiny than the "ol' leather lunch pail." The rule here is to go either one way or the other. For the man who is genuinely secure, or really doesn't care, or just wants to give the impression of being one of the boys, something like L.L. Bean's woodsy haversack, a canvas book bag, or even an old fishing creel will work. Even in stuffy conference rooms, these outdoors bags speak of cool, gurgling streams, green meadows, and trout flies. Coming at it from the other

side, nothing creates quite the murmur of approval from the members of the board as a sleek-and-sybaritic, state-of-the-art briefcase that proclaims the mettle of its owner. I'm thinking, for example, of a case like the Mark Cross Envoy Deluxe, a superior pigskin attaché completely leather-lined, with a triple-file compartment and dual interior pockets, brass hinges and combination locks, and a contoured pigskin handle. Costing about $550 or so, it is a tad steep, but mighty prestigious. Another eye-catcher that is highly serviceable is the Zero Halliburton, with its distinctive aluminum shell. It's a bit on the heavy side (about seven pounds), and not exactly inexpensive (about $300), but doubles as an overnight case better than most.

The same principle holds for toilet and medical kits and other grooming aids: it's best to go either with something completely functional and perhaps fun, like those brightly-colored nylon wet packs found in almost every men's store and mail-order catalogue, or with something elegant and distinctive. Stores like Brooks Brothers and Paul Stuart provide that extra measure of style with toiletry bags of rep silk, leather-trimmed and vinyl-lined, which nicely hold the necessities for an overnight business trip or a weekend jaunt. An important point to keep in mind concerning such small extras as grooming kits, wallets, eyeglass cases, and even luggage is that they need not be of a set. Sales clerks will tell you that everything must match or your status in society will never rise above racetrack tout—and why shouldn't they tell you that; their job is to sell as many of these items as they possibly can. And the Victorians of course were fond of that sort of thing, suites of furniture, matching luggage, parlors awash with furbelows and antimacassars. But the notion that billfold and briefcase and checkbook must all match up is an idea whose time is well passed. If you like Louis Vuitton, don't worry to buy the whole line, or wonder whether the key ring will blend with your canvas bag . . . of course it will.

Grooming aids themselves are fascinating and important accessories because they are so personal, yet many men overlook them. Some men think that because no one really sees their toothbrush, they might just as well keep on using the one they picked up several years ago at a drugstore sale for twenty-nine cents and which bears a strong resemblance to a caterpillar on a stick. There's nothing wrong with buying a toothbrush for twenty-nine cents, mind you, but one should be as attentive to the smaller items as to the larger and more expensive ones. This is the real importance of accessories: they are the surest indicators of a person's style, precisely because style is not something that is turned on or off depending on the circumstance. A person's style should reflect what and who he is all the time, so that everyone—including himself—has the same image of him. The style and the man are as inseparable, in this life anyway, as the mind and the body.

Consider colognes for a moment. Our olfactory sense is quickly evoked and tenacious, and scents are among the first kinds of information we communicate to others. How absurd, then, to believe, as some men still do, that any old after-shave lotion is fine for them. The sensible man here is the one who realizes that it's necessary to pick and choose among an ever-growing array of scents available, and the appropriateness is the key. Without going into all the "chemistry" business of the thing—much of which I suspect is a great steaming pile of advertising hype anyway—there are a few guidelines. Heavy scents ("You can smell him before you see him" colognes) are generally to be avoided, especially during the day and particularly during warm weather. For business, one wants to give the impression of merely being clean and fresh, and so a light scent, such as citrus, is recommended. For the evening and for cooler climes, more assertive fragrances—the herbal and spiced varieties—are appropriate.

Granted that one must do a bit of experimenting here, it isn't all that necessary to be continually trying every new scent that comes on the market. Find one you like and stick to it, making it your signature. It's also a good idea to first consider the reputable brands, those that have been in business for a long time, know what they are doing, and have an elegant selection from which to choose. Caswell-Massey carries a fine range of colognes and after shaves (some of which they have been making for over two hundred years), as do Roger & Gallet, Crabtree & Evelyn, Guerlain, and several other firms. The differences between after shaves and colognes are, by the way, often misunderstood, not surprisingly since the cosmetics industry has few guidelines and fewer government regulations to dictate how scents should be labeled. Generally, however, in terms of strength of scent (determined by the amount of scent-producing essence used), from weakest to strongest, fragrances are labeled after shave, cologne, toilet water, or perfume. Additionally, after-shave products customarily contain various emollients to help lubricate the skin after it has been scraped by a razor.

Choices of scents include everything from brisk Indian limes and verbenas to spicy bay rums and the more delicate yet perfectly masculine lavender and orange waters. Fine clothing stores also carry house-brand toiletries—small ranges, perhaps four or five, of different colognes and after shaves—and these are generally of good quality and trustworthy. I particularly like them for being identified usually either by number or by their basic scent, rather than by some obvious macho name like "Trucker," "Saddle Sore," or "Locker Room." I know that that kind of thing strikes a reverberating note in the hearts of juveniles everywhere, but surely the rest of us do not have to take it seriously.

This business about having a signature is, by the way, a good approach to accessories. Along with the other considerations already suggested, may I make a special plea for finding something one particularly likes and having the courage to stick to it. Tom Wolfe has his high starched collars and his white suits, Rex Harrison and Daniel Moynihan their

tweed hats, Woody Allen his square, black-framed glasses, so why shouldn't you have your trademark? Of the dozen pairs of shoes I've got, only two are not brown suede. I've rationalized this with myself by arguing that brown suede shoes complement just about every outfit and clean up easier than other shoes, but the truth is I just like brown suede shoes—and over the years everyone who knows me knows it. The man who insists on wearing his pink oxford button-downs, red suspenders, canary yellow socks, or brightly checked golf hat, regardless of the trendy winds of fashion or the impersonal machinations of the garment industry, is the man whose style bespeaks courage and a sense of tradition, discipline, and indelible individuality—from all of which a certain personal integrity tends to accrue.

So, when it comes to accoutrement, go ahead: swagger with that malacca cane, sport that English bowler you've always admired, don those crimson hose and Donegal plus fours—in short, be yourself, and be proud of it!

THE ASCOT

I t is an unfortunate truth that most American men have no idea what to do with their necks. When not safely ensnared in a necktie, they seem to forego all other options and literally stick their necks out. Some actually fold their open shirt collars down over their jackets, exposing not only their necks, but a slice of their chests as well: call that the Sicilian Solution, which is no solution at all. Nor is the California Solution, a collection of chain and ceramic clutter slung across the sternum, producing a look that accords better with snakeskin bomber jackets, tight velvet jeans, silk Romeo shirts, and sequined cowboy hats than with normal sports clothes.

I remember too that about a decade ago the turtleneck sweater made one of its periodic returns to the sartorial scene as a *deus ex machina* for the exposed gullet, and many—too many—men absolutely dove into it with a passion usually reserved for the hopelessly desperate. Whole squadrons of otherwise sane gentlemen would arrive at a cocktail party sporting their navy double-breasted blazers with white turtleneck jerseys. Clustered on the patio, they resembled nothing so much as a cast of movie extras between takes of *Sink the Bismarck*.

There is really no need for all the confusion over the matter of the neck when the perfect solution has for so long been at hand, if you'll pardon that mixed anatomical metaphor: the comfortable, jaunty, and ancient tradition of the scarf. Call it what you will—ascot, cravat, stock—the scarf at the throat is the tried and tested answer to the naked neck. It is also the answer for those baffling dress up but "dressed down" occasions when a coat and tie are too stuffy and slacks and a polo shirt are too scruffy. Nothing so exactly strikes the air of casual elegance, of sporty self-confidence, as a mannerly fold of fine silk with an open collar.

The historical precedent alone, you would think, would cause men to look in that direction, as the history of neckwear has, in one form or another, been the history of the scarf. By the middle of the seventeenth century a separate neckcloth began to replace the spreading lace-edged collar that one sees in so many Dutch portraits of the period. This neckcloth (in imitation of the collar it was replacing in popularity) was also lace-edged, so that when wrapped around the neck and tied in front, the lace cascaded down the shirt bosom and gave a handsome touch of decoration when the coat was left open.

Over the years different names have been given to this piece of cloth. The general term up to the nineteenth century was simply "neckcloth," which could take two different forms: the cravat, a long strip of cloth wound around the neck and tied in front; and the stock, a band of fabric that passed around the neck and was fastened in back at the nape with a knot, and later a buckle or hook-and-eye arrangement.

At first the cravat held fashionable sway. Some say the idea was first brought home to France about 1640 by French officers who had fought beside troops of Croatian mercenaries against the German emperor in the Thirty Years War. These Croats were known to tie their collars together with long flowing strips of cloth, and "cravat" is the French word for Croat. At any rate, evidence of this style can be clearly found in paintings after 1650. Seen on monarchs and subjects alike, cravats were either lace-trimmed or, more expensively, all lace, and became as popular in America as in Europe. Fine sheer cotton cravats were advertised in the *Boston Evening Post* as early as 1735.

During the eighteenth century, the stock came to dominate neckwear. This is in the main attributed to the increased popularity of the waistcoat, which tended to hide the decorative front of the cravat. Ladies and gentlemen of the hunt still wear a modified version of this eighteenth-century stock today. Usually made in pique, linen, silk, or fine cotton, the hunting stock is always white, tied in a prescribed manner, and fastened with a gilt safety pin about three inches long. Novice riders like to joke that learning to tie a stock properly is only slightly more difficult than learning to ride itself. There's a buttonhole in the middle of the stock, which attaches to a button on the front of the shirt; then the stock is wound front to back, one end is passed through a loop of material on the stock band, then both ends are brought to the front again and tied in a square knot. The pin is used to secure the long ends flat in front and keep them from flapping in the face.

This stock is the only neckwear that is still really functional. It not only provides protection for the neck—from the sun in the summer, and cold in winter—but is used as an emergency bandage or sling in the field should there be an accident to either man or horse.

After 1760 waistcoats came to be worn open again, as a deshabille approach to dress gained popularity for both men and women, and gentlemen of fashion often tied a ruffle of fabric around the stock to flow over the shirt front. This accommodation was called a "jabot," and it was in effect a two-piece cravat and signaled the demise of the stock.

In the early nineteenth century, the Regency period, the cravat may, in fact, be said to have come into the full flush of its popularity. The French Revolution, with its *liberté, egalité,* and *fraternité,* had swept away the silk and satin exuberances of the court, and the Industrial Revolution quickly stepped in to replace them with a decidedly more democratic and sober approach. As the great French author Honoré de Balzac pointed out, when the French gained equal rights they simultaneously acquired sameness of dress. And while there were no longer great differences of style to distinguish between classes, a gentleman's cravat was a peculiarly telling feature of his wardrobe. The elegantly tied and starched neckcloth became the hallmark of the true gentleman of refinement. He was called a dandy. Some dandies so voluminously exaggerated their cravats that they rose up over their chins and all but concealed their mouths, all of which made turning the head a bit tricky and accounted for the dandy's classic imperturbability and hauteur.

Interestingly enough, Balzac himself is the reputed author of an extensive manual on neckwear. (He never actually acknowledged authorship of the volume, but it is assumed that the name on the cover, H. Le Blanc, is a pseudonym.) There are lessons given on thirty-two different ways to tie a cravat: a style for every mood and occasion.

And lest you think this matter of tying a cravat is a minor point, it is well to remember that George "Beau" Brummell's reputation as a leader of society was in considerable measure based on his finesse with his neckwear. He had literally made it the focal point of a gentleman's appearance—in somewhat of a stroke of sartorial genius—and it was quite the thing at the time to spend one's entire morning achieving the proper arrangement. As Max Beerbohm explained, the dandy was a painter whose canvas was himself. There is a story of a visitor calling on Brummell in the middle of the morning, and finding him and his valet in his dressing room, knee-deep in discarded cravats. When the visitor inquired what they were, the valet replied, "Oh, sir, those are our failures."

In the mid-nineteenth century we meet the term "necktie" for the first time. The cravat had come to be wound around the neck once, and tied in front with either a large bow (and thus the "bow tie"), or with a small knot with the long ends left to hang down the shirt front (the predecessor of our contemporary necktie). Neckwear thereafter came to be known by the manner in which it was tied or arranged: the four-in-hand (our contemporary tie, named after the manner in which the reins of a four-horse team are held in the hand, and thus a "four-in-hand" knot); the bow tie; and the famous ascot itself, in which the long blades of the scarf were folded across the shirt front and fixed with a pin—but not, originally, tucked in.

The latter style is of course named after the most fashionable event of the London Season—the annual race meeting held, as it has been for almost three hundred years now, at Ascot Heath in June. The Ascot has always been the most dressy event of the English sporting season as well, and a broad silk neck scarf fastened with a pin became de rigueur for the occasion. The name took. As early as 1908, in a short story entitled "The Gentle Grafter," the American writer O. Henry mentioned a fellow as wearing a "white flannel suit and a pink ascot tie."

It's a shame that the only heartily surviving member of this august triumvirate is the necktie. Why should the others, if you will allow me another mixed metaphor, be endangered species? Why should the bow tie be left to languish around the necks of a few magazine editors, eccentric lawyers, or Ivy League profs? And why should the ascot be proscribed to all but a select natty few?—the Astaires, Cary Grants, and Douglas Fairbankses of the world.

Actually, that, I think, is precisely the rub. The jaunty scarf at the neck has been so associated with aristocratic dress that few men believe they can carry it off well. This casually romantic and slightly flamboy ant accessory does not sit easily with some who must dress for their business in a more sober manner, although why an accountant or postal clerk, milkman or bank president, should not be accorded the right to a bit of romance and flamboyance I do not understand.

And the fact is that no one has come up with a better method of covering the neck for those occasions when a tie is not wanted. The scarf allows for tremendous variety in design, color, and style. There are, for example, any number of ways of tying the scarf. It used to be that ascots were designed in the Edwardian manner, in which the center section—that which wound round the neck itself—was a narrow, pleated band, while the blades were considerably wider, and often pointed. The idea was that the narrow band around the neck would fit more comfortably under the shirt collar and would be less bulky, while the wider blades in front would provide a suitably puffy effect to fill in the shirt opening. This type of ascot is still the one typically sold in men's shops.

A similar effect, however, can be got by other methods. One can use either a square scarf of about thirty-two inches, or a long band of about six inches wide and a yard long. The scarf should be folded cornerwise to form a triangle, then rolled apex toward base until a long band results. In the other case, the band is simply folded until an appropriate width is formed. Both methods are good because they're simple and accommodating.

The other point is that a scarf folded in these ways is easy to fix at the front of the neck. The Duke of Windsor used to simply and elegantly thread the long ends of the scarf through a finger ring and let them hang down the shirt front. Astaire has been known to favor a small tie clip to secure the ends, in the original Ascot fashion. An antique stickpin, Art Deco jewelry, or perhaps a miniature gold clothespin would all be perfect. On the other hand, simplicity—the greatest of virtues—would recommend a mere knot. Actually, by passing one blade under the knot and then over it, making a flap, it is possible to achieve the appropriate puffiness without the bulk.

Well, there is really no end to the possibilities here. This is one of those nice places where one can indeed be an individual. A man can devise his own way of wearing a scarf, have his own special knot and make it his signature. There's a chap I know who, when he's not wearing a necktie, always wears a navy-and-white polka dot scarf, double-knotted. It's his trademark of sorts, and it serves and suits him well.

One of the simplest solutions to this look within memory was a sports shirt with an attached ascot done up by Brooks Brothers about a dozen years ago or so. The "Brooks-Clarney" shirt it was called (after the fellow who designed it), a lovely flannel checked affair, with an ascot of the same material attached to the neckband. Perfect for informal entertaining, cocktail parties at the club, that sort of thing. Unfortunately Brooks no longer makes this item, although the firm still does something similar for the ladies. Perhaps if enough interest were shown it might be revived.

Especially in this day and age when causal dressing is so much a part—perhaps the largest part—of our lives, is there any reason why it should degenerate into ragged denims, sweat shirts, and jogging shoes? Just as there are levels of speech, there are levels of dress. And correctness in both would seem to depend on appropriateness: to the purpose, the audience, and the occasion. While a pair of cut-offs may be perfectly appropriate on a deserted beach (as nothing at all might be), they hardly seem the thing for a cocktail party. But, to bring us full circle, neither do a tie and dress shirt. With a cashmere cardigan, tweed jacket, navy blazer, or summer sports coat, a scarf at the neck provides the right accoutrement.

And the other point about this style of neckwear is that it never changes: the same proportions, the same fine silks, even the same classic designs—paisleys, polka dots, geometric prints—so that you end up buying a new one simply for color's sake. There is no reason to presume that the ascot will ever be out of fashion.

BLAZERS

A part from clothing associated with the horse, has any type of attire been as evocative of function, yet so terribly natty, as sailing clothes? Of social distinction and historic association? Of easy style yet correct deportment? The romance and adventure of the sea and faraway places with strange-sounding names, of sailors with rugged faces and sou'westers staring into the gray and misty sou'west, or of a yacht skimming across the sparkling waves with signal flags fluttering in the breeze, are glowing images often conjured up by the merest glimpse of sailing garb. Those striped jerseys, white ducks, and navy blazerrs have an emotional appeal that even the most confirmed landlubber recognizes and appreciates. For many of us it is a summer approach to dress, mingled with seaside vacations, tangy salt air, and white wicker furniture. When the poet John Masefield says, "I must down to the seas again, to the vagrant gypsy life," some undoubtedly think of St. Tropez, others of Atlantic City. These associations are not to be denied.

But much of nautical wear's allure and cachet comes from its military background. Consider the blue and white colors that we now automatically associate with nautical dress, a product of the traditional navy uniform. Other colors have at various times been used for naval attire—

the Tudor monarchs of the English Renaissance favored green and white, and green was also the color worn by the officers and sailors of the late nineteenth-century Russian fleet—but blue has been the prime color for naval uniforms in the English-speaking world (as well as France, Holland, and Germany) since the eighteenth century. Britain's George II put his naval officers into blue and white uniforms in 1748, and the United States Navy has been wearing dark blue coats ever since Secretary of War James McHenry issued orders in 1797 that "a perfect uniformity of dress . . . be obtained by officers, marines, and others, on board the Ships of War which may be employed in the service of the United States." Officers and midshipmen wore blue coats (with distinguishing buttons, epaulets, and cuffs) and either blue or buff breeches. Interestingly enough, the noncombatant status of certain members of the ship (such as medical officers) was clearly defined by the color of their uniforms: they wore green coats, rather than dark blue.

Today that dark blue jacket, having been a staple for so many years, is internationally civilized, equally at home in the board room as on board, and its versatility and classic lines make it the perfect jet-age jacket, even though it was born on the sailing ships of the North Atlantic. It is such a correct and traditional component of a gentleman's wardrobe that we tend to take it for granted. Everyone's list for a basic wardrobe includes a blazer, as surely as it includes a gray flannel suit and plain black oxfords. And everyone has undoubtedly heard the apocryphal story of the fastidious captain of the H.M.S. *Blazer*, a frigate in the British Navy, and how he was so embarrassed by the disreputable appearance of his crew that, for the coronation of Queen Victoria in 1837, he ordered them into dark blue serge jackets with gleaming brass buttons. All of which, so the legend has it, not only dramatically improved the aspect and morale of the crew, but so impressed Victoria that she instituted the jacket as naval uniform.

It's a charming tale to be sure, but there appears to be not much truth in this oft-repeated history. The nineteenth-century captain and his famous ship seem to be more ghostly than the *Flying Dutchman*. In fact, short blue jackets had been worn by midshipmen since the 1820s; they were called "reefers," after the slang expression for the men who took in the reefs, or sails—and they still are. The blazer, as we think of it today, is really a stylized reefer jacket, but it is the word itself that causes the problem. The term "blazer" originates in the late nineteenth-century version of the traditional sports jacket. At first worn for cricket, later for boating, tennis, and other sports, it was a short coat usually boldly colored and accompanied by flannel trousers and straw boater hat. Originally the term had come from the particular jacket worn by the members of the Lady Margaret Boat Club of St. John's College, Cambridge. To distinguish themselves from other college boat clubs, members wore a bright red flannel sports jacket, which undoubtedly led to not a few stares and several remarks along the lines of, "Good Lord, Wilfred, did you see the jacket on that chap? Bit of a blazer, what?" In short, the derivation of the term "blazer" as it applied to sports jackets is found in the bright color, rather than any naval associations.

As it happens, this distinction between the blazer and reefer jackets is still maintained in Britain: technically, on the reefer all three right-side buttons are buttoned, while on the blazer the top-side button is there merely for the sake of symmetry (as it is on the double-breasted suit jacket) and is never functional. But why the navy blue jacket came to be called a blazer in common parlance rather than a reefer is more difficult to say. It appears that on the one hand, the term "reefer" was always strictly reserved for navy jackets, while on the other hand, all casual boating jackets came to be called blazers in the early years of this century—even when the darker reefer jacket became popular with white flannels for boating; that it did not fulfill the original requirements of the term, that is, to blaze with vibrant color, seems not to have mattered. And, actually, these past several years have witnessed something of a return to the original meaning of the term, with blazers shining forth in crimson, plum, billiard-table green, and other bright hues.

What *is* known is that boating jackets that did blaze forth with color were first seen in number during the 1880s, when in an orgiastic assault on somber city garb, gentlemen punters on England's civilized waterways preened themselves in boldly striped jackets of red and orange, lavender and black, powder blue and cream, scarlet and canary, and other shades, one of which the incomparable Edwardian humorist Jerome K. Jerome forbore to name in his *Three Men in a Boat:*

George has brought some new things for this trip, and I'm rather vexed about them. The blazer is loud. I should not like George to know that I thought so, but there is really no other word for it. He brought it home and showed it to us on Thursday evening. We asked him what colour he called it, and he said he didn't know. He didn't think there was a name for the colour. The man had told him it was an oriental design. George put it on, and asked us what we thought of it. Harris said that, as an object to hang over a flower-bed in early spring to frighten the birds away, he should respect it.

This tradition of brightly colored boating jackets is still with us, and in both England and the States the university rowing blazers are the most colorful of all. Both the reefer and the blazer had rather remained distinctly British institutions until the 1920s, when a wave of anglophilia swept across the Atlantic. English university sports teams came to visit (and compete in everything from polo to boat races), and it was the universities, particularly Oxford, that set the fashion trends that reverberated around the world: wide-legged "Oxford bags" trousers, plus fours, Fair Isle pullovers, bright tweeds, and blazers were among the many new styles emanating from the High Street of Oxford. And the dashing Prince of Wales completed three smashingly successful tours of the States (1920, '24, and '27), introducing English styles at every media-covered appearance. The empire's greatest salesman, as he was aptly dubbed, was very much appreciated by British clothing manufacturers.

Until then American men had been fairly content to wear white flannel "extra" trousers with their blue serge suit jackets as standard resort wear. Although the 1915 Brooks Brothers catalogue does list a "single-breasted flannel Blazer for tennis, cricketing, etc.," it was not until after 1920, when the regatta fashions of the English undergraduates began to spread to American campuses and resorts, that the blazer became popular over here. The campus and the resort in most instances went hand-in-hand when the campus was a large eastern one such as Harvard, Yale, or Princeton, and it was quite natural that the blazer should have materialized at both places simultaneously. The navy version was first seen at this time in Newport and a few other yachting hunts and was taken up by college men on vacation, who continued

to wear it when they returned to campus. J. Press, that reputable cyno-sure of Ivy League clothing from New Haven, began selling volume orders to the various schools in the east (St. Mark's, St. Paul's, and so on) beginning in the late 1920s, and there was a tremendous upsurge in the blazer in the 1930s after the Yale College plan came into effect. The navy blazer had become a uniform and many colleges—Dart-mouth may have been the first—outfitted the junior class in blazers with the graduating year on a breast-pocket shield.

Today the navy blazer is considered to be perhaps the most essential article of dress clothing a man can own, and as such it has a tradition-ally prescribed, straightforward look that should not be tampered with. Ultimately the quality of a blazer rests on pristine cut, traditional fab-ric, and good buttons. The single-breasted version, with ventless, cen-ter, or side vents, and with either a two-or three-button front, has its historic antecedents and makes a serviceably handsome addition to the wardrobe. But the classic cut for a blazer is double-breasted, with six buttons, of which the lower two right ones are functional (the rest are merely for show); additionally, the double-breasted blazer has side vents, two side pockets and a breast pocket (but no ticket pocket), and peaked lapels cut straight, with a buttonhole in *each* lapel (curved lapels are considered a trifle too studied). Over the years manufacturers, tailors, designers, and others of an interfering nature have sought to improve the blazer by tarting it up with a western yoke or cuffs, by changing the button stance or adding a half-belt, or by giving it a shawl collar or bi-swing back. These innovators should not necessarily be hanged, but one should for self-protection cross the street whenever they come into view.

There is some slight leeway in choice of fabrics. For warm weather dressing, lightweight hopsack or doeskin flannel are correct (and trop-ical worsted, linen, or blended fabric acceptable). Otherwise, wool serge, flannel, or cashmere are appropriate cloths. Buttons are gener-ally of metal—the only sports jacket to use them—either brass, silver, or gold. These may be plain and unadorned, simply decorated (which usually means initialed or with a simple pattern such as a scroll or basket-weave design), or crested (to indicate a particular interest or affiliation). Occasionally they are smoked or enameled, as is now cus-tomarily found with university buttons. Blazer buttons are considered jewelry and can obviously be quite costly. The caution here is that in contrast with women's dress, in which the clothing is often a foil for the jewelry, the blazer is never a foil for its buttons. If the cut and fit of the blazer are not there, and if the fabric is not of good quality, no expensive button can help. Expensive buttons are of the least importance.

While I'm on this matter of buttons, I want to point out that there is a particular way in which metal buttons are attached to a jacket that differs from buttons of horn or plastic or shell. On a blazer, the show buttons (that is, those buttons that are not actually buttoned) are fastened to the inside of the jacket by cutting a hole in the fabric, inserting the metal loop on the underside of the button through it, and either sewing it to the inner lining or tying it off with a short piece of fabric to prevent it from falling from the hole—the latter being the most usual since expensive buttons are removed before dry cleaning.

The blazer leads a very established life, sharing its time with a handful of trusting and gregarious companions. Pastel oxford-cloth buttondowns are perfect, and polo shirts—with or without an ascot—casually reliable. Back in the sartorially regrettable 1960s there was a somewhat misguided vogue—I seem to remember it was started by Lord Snowden, of all people—for white turtleneck sweaters, which are not bad in themselves, but when they are worn with navy blazers en masse they do suggest a convention of German U-boat commanders. Boldly striped broadcloth shirts are also particularly appealing, especially in summer months when the stripes can be either of vibrant or delicate hue—and coupled with a polka dot silk bow tie.

One of the nice things about a navy blazer is that it can securely be accompanied by such a variety of trousers: tan cavalry twills, gray flannels, or even wool tartans for winter; neutral shades of tropical worsted, linen, or white flannels for summer. But the authentic nautical look dictates white ducks. The word "duck" as it is used here derives from the Dutch "doek," meaning canvas. In the seventeenth century, Holland was the great seafaring nation and developed this tightly woven and durable fabric for both clothing and sails. Today canvas has become a broad term often used interchangeably with duck, but traditionally and technically canvas is made of linen or flax, while duck is made of cotton fibers and is therefore a bit lighter in weight and not as stiff.

White, or even beige or gray, linen trousers are just as appropriate as duck, but linen is both heavier and wrinkles easier; this is one of those places where a blended fabric is preferable to a 100 percent natural one: a blend of linen and polyester will be both lighter in weight and more wrinkle-resistant and still have all the characteristic texture of fine linen.

White summer-weight flannels are another alternative trouser to accompany a navy blazer for warm-weather wear and are slightly dressier in a South-of-France sort of way. But white flannels are tricky, and something of a misnomer. They should not in fact be dead white—as should ducks—since one of the nice qualities of a good English flannel is that it will have a kind of Devon cream color about it. The proper white flannels look as though they's been stored away in the bottom of a trunk for fifteen or twenty years to age and mellow them. They should have a soft color as well as a soft hand to them.

Finally, for summer wear there are the striking red cotton trousers worn originally by the Breton fisherman. The cloth is technically called "Bretagne," the French designation for Brittany, and was originally a bleached linen fabric of ecru and blue as well as the vibrant red. But today it is the latter version that presents the really snazzy alternative to white, beige, and gray.

BROOKS BROTHERS

W hen it phased out its custom tailoring department, the story
was carried on the front page of the *New York Times*. The
Daily News Record has called it the greatest men's store in
the world. It has a history going back over a century and a half and is
in fact not so much a clothing store as an institution of American life.
There is really nothing to compare with Brooks Brothers.

And of course, it is not just a men's store any longer. In fact, it was
something of a sociological event when Brooks, the bastion of masculine conservatism, opened a women's department back in 1976. Not
that women and Brooks discovered each other then for the first time,
you understand, since the ladies had been lurking about the store for
years, making off with raincoats and Shetland sweaters, ordering Bermuda shorts and polo shirts from the boys' department. In 1949 *Vogue*
photographed a woman in a pink Brooks Brothers button-down shirt.
The decision to start a women's department simply reflected an awareness of the arrival of the businesswoman and Brooks Brothers' deter-
mination to accommodate her. After all, the firm has dressed her
husband since the beginning of the nineteenth century.

Long before a Mary McCarthy heroine, in her short story "The
Man in the Brooks Brothers Shirt," picked up such a gentleman on a

train ride, the relaxed Establishment Brooks look had more than a whiff of the right stuff. One suspected an old school tie stuffed in the pocket, a library crammed with well-thumbed English essayists, and possibly a full-bent briar. Nothing outré, nothing exaggerated or self-conscious. The Brooks Brothers suit seemed to peg a man somewhere between Wall Street and his country house, by way of the Ivy League.

Interestingly enough, people who customarily shop at Brooks aren't really clotheshorses and don't like to spend time worrying about how they look, which is of course the ideal. They let Brooks worry for them, and Brooks has always worried wonderfully. There is the story about a customer who phoned up to ask if the store sold nightcaps. The unflappable salesclerk calmly asked, "With or without tassel, sir?"

Brooks Brothers is the fortress of sartorial sensibility for Establishment clothing. Back in 1818 when Henry Sands Brooks, the son of a Connecticut physician, first opened a clothing store at the southeast corner of Catherine and Cherry Streets in lower Manhattan, things were perhaps different, but not that much different. Then as now, the store was situated in the center of New York's thriving business district and sold its quality clothes to the gentry, the prosperous, and the professional.

Henry Brooks acquired his new premises at an auction sale held at the Tontine Coffee House in Wall Street. He had bid the considerable sum of $15,250 for the building and grounds, and at the age of forty-six he embarked on his determined career to sell quality men's clothing. It was his plan (as stated in an advertisement he ran in the *Morning Courier*) to "have on hand a very large stock of ready-made clothing, just manufactured with a due regard to fashion, and embracing all the various styles of the day." While Henry Brooks made clothing to measure as well, he should rightly be considered the pioneer of ready-made clothes, an innovation of great historical importance.

The building at Catherine and Cherry Streets served Henry Brooks well. After his death in 1833, it was refurbished and enlarged by his sons Henry, Daniel, John, Elisha, and Edward—who adopted the name "Brooks Brothers" in 1850—and two new stores were opened: one large four-storey building at Broadway and Grant Street in 1858, and another in South Union Square in 1869. The Broadway store became the principal place of business for the firm during the Civil War years, and it was probably from this store that Abraham Lincoln ordered his frock coats—one of which he was wearing when he was assassinated at Ford's Theatre on that fateful April evening in 1865, just a few days after Robert E. Lee had surrendered to Grant at the Appomattox Court House. The Brooks Brothers label on the inside of the coat was embellished with an embroidered design of a bald eagle, holding in its beak a flowing pennant inscribed "One Country, One Destiny."

During the War between the States, Brooks made uniforms for the Union Army and numbered Generals Grant, Sherman, Hooker, and Sheridan among its customers. Grant was probably wearing a Brooks Brothers suit at Appomattox, and he continued to to be dressed by the firm when he became president. In fact, practically every president since Lincoln (and several before) has worn clothes from Brooks Brothers, including both Roosevelts, Wilson, Hoover, Kennedy, Nixon, and Ford. Other famous customers have included the Duke of Windsor, Cary Grant, Fred Astaire, F. Scott Fitzgerald, Rudolph Valentino, Clark Gable, John O'Hara, Andy Warhol, J.P. Morgan, and most of the Rockefellers, Astors, and Vanderbilts. Morgan in fact bought his clothes from Brooks his entire life, and even as a mature and awesomely remote man he was called "Jack" by the saleman who had known and dressed him since he was a tot. Hard to imagine, that.

As the center of commerce and business moved farther and farther north in Manhattan, so did Brooks Brothers: to Broadway and Bond Street in 1874, to Broadway and 22d Street in 1884, and finally, in 1915, to 44th and Madison. This present flagship store was specifically designed for the firm by the architects LaFarge & Morris and is still considered a fine example of quiet elegance in commercial design, perfectly in keeping with its very proper product and service.

The firm grew and prospered, with the late-nineteenth-century industrial elite as favored customers, and continued to grow as New York became the business mecca of the early twentieth century. Its customers included politicians and generals, old-guard bankers, and nouveau-riche manufacturing barons. In 1903, with four of Henry Brooks's grandsons and six employees as principals, the firm incorporated. Six years later the first branch store was opened at Newport, Rhode Island, the glittering summer resort of the epoch. By the time another branch store opened in Boston in 1928, Brooks Brothers was already a venerable institution, with a copious general catalogue that included such items as vicuña overcoats ($45), silk top hats ($8), tweed shooting capes ($35), and Russian leather brogues ($10), as well as complete outfits for sport, day wear, and evening wear. The firm also offered a complete range of uniforms for army and navy officers and complete outfitting for chauffeurs, butlers, footmen, and pages.

Since then Brooks has solidified its image as outfitters to democracy's ruling classes, the managerial elite. In 1946, coincident to the passing of the last member of the Brooks family, a great-great-great grandson of Henry Sands Brooks, the firm was taken over by Garfinkel, the retailing corporation in Washington, D.C. Some customers, apprised of the change, feared the worst—that the store's traditional and personal quality might suffer under the thumb of a large, impersonal corporation. But as it turns out, Brooks is allowed to go its merry way, dressing gentlemen as it always has. One reason, one may conjecture, is that it works. Brooks's annual sales in the past thirty years have risen from $5.6 million to over $140 million at the end of 1980. And the firm has expanded to include in addition to its main store in Manhattan twenty-four branches in this country. Additionally, in 1980 the first foreign branch opened in Tokyo, with a projection of eight more to open in Japan within the next half-dozen years.

One particularly interesting aspect of this expansion is that whether the store is in Tokyo, Dallas, or Scarsdale, there is no concession made to regional taste whatever. Of course, there's no need to stockpile Harris tweed overcoats in Ft. Lauderdale, but apart from the dictates of climate, each Brooks store carries identical merchandise. The Brooks Brothers man is the same the world over, and it is an approach to dress that is basically American.

The line, whether for jackets or shirts, is freer flowing, more natural and loosely cut, than European clothing, which is generally more shaped and contoured. A Brooks jacket is often said to be not felt on the body, since it falls easily from the shoulders and has as little padding as a jacket can have and still have a constructed appearance. This look solidified in the 1940s, and Brooks has stuck with it and promoted it through all the ups and downs of masculine fashion trends, including the great Mod Moment of the late 1960s, which swamped any number of lesser outfitters and left little but jeans shops in its wake.

While Brooks can honorably be called a bastion of full-fig conservatism, it cannot be considered either reactionary or blindered to trends itself. The fact is, if the trend survived to become a cherished fixture of the successful man's wardrobe, Brooks probably started it. In its role as tasteful innovator, Brooks is perhaps the greatest single influence on American menswear. During its formative years, there were undoubtedly dozens of styling and merchandising innovations of consequence that have not been documented for posterity. But after 1890, we are on sure and safe ground. Brooks Brothers, probably the first clothing store in the States, and the first to offer ready-to-wear clothing, was also the first to introduce: the foulard tie (from England, in the 1890s); the Shetland sweater (from England, about 1904); madras fabric (pre-1900); Harris tweed (from Scotland, about 1900); the polo coat (from England, about 1910); coconut straw hats (1928); seersucker and cotton cord suiting (1930); and lightweight Dacron-cotton washable suiting (1955).

In the matter of shirting the firm has given particular pleasures. In 1900 Mr. John Brooks, who had retired as president of the firm in 1896, vacationed in England. At a polo match he noticed the players wearing shirts on which the collar points were buttoned to the shirtfront (it was explained to him that this technique kept the collar points from flapping into the face), and he sent one of these shirts back home, where it was introduced by Brooks. The firm still refers to it as their "polo" collar. It was, half a century later, the shirt chosen by Du Pont to initiate the wash-and-wear concept of clothing they had invented with their Dacron-cotton blended fabric; it was clear to Du Pont that only Brooks could give this fabric the prestige and credibility needed to put it across. And in these days, when the change-for-the-sake-of-change approach of fashion is more and more being questioned, prestige is what Brooks has most of.

There was a great story in Lawrence Van Gelder's Metropolitan Diary in the *New York Times* a couple of years ago about an important-looking, white-haired, well-dressed gentleman standing on a Park Avenue corner, talking with a friend and waiting for the light to change. The white-haired fellow could be heard talking proudly about his first grandson—his first, apparently, after a succession of granddaughters.

"Can't wait to get him into Brooks Brothers," he said.

"Why haven't you?" the friend asked.

"I will, I will," came the reply, "just as soon as he stops wetting his pants."

A charming story based not only on the history of Brooks, but on the fact that until World War II all men's clothing stores were boy's outfitters as well, both because styling did not differ very much and because an establishment endeavored to keep a customer for life. Now Brooks is one of a very few clothiers who follow this tradition. And since there are more than one or two salesmen who have been "on the floor" for over thirty years, many a child has been taken from short pants to maturity by the same clerk. This illustrates one or two outstanding features about the firm, to my mind: that there is a consistent image of styling and quality that a man can learn and build on, and that salesmen and customers can develop good working relationships over a long period of time. Loyalty and integrity form the two sides of this relationship, and of course both sides profit. This seems to be a difficult lesson for others to learn, living as we do in a world of fast cars, fast food, fast marriages, trade up, trade in, and move on.

The other feature that is unique to Brooks is the "Own Make" designation, which means exactly what it says: manufactured in Brooks's own three factories, which together employ about eight hundred people. The shirt factory is in Paterson, New Jersey; the neckwear plant and tailored-clothing plant are both in Long Island City, New York. The lamentable decision to end bespoke tailoring was made in 1976, attributed to a difficulty in securing enough qualified tailors. In reality the custom-work never did account for more than one percent or two of business, but it was symbolically considered by many to mark the passing of an era as sadly and surely as the passing of great men. There is still the special order department, in which a jacket, trousers, or shirt can be individually made from a standard pattern altered to fit the customer.

Considering the well-established Brooks Brothers image and the legendary loyalty of its customers, the curious thing is why the firm bothers to advertise at all. Indeed, many years ago there was a president of the firm who did look askance at advertising in general, on the grounds, as he put it, that "we don't want the kind of trade that has to be enticed with sales and flashy goods." Then again, not to advertise might seem that bit standoffish, and the Brooks ads are so discreet anyway that they seem merely to serve as gentle reminders that the season has changed and perhaps we may be wanting to brighten the coming days with a new necktie or something. Absolutely civilized.

Which is finally what Brooks is about. Civilized is their bottom line, and that means proper and responsible. Which calls to mind another little anecdote. After Lindbergh's famous flight across the Atlantic, he was welcomed to New York by the greatest ticker-tape parade in the city's history. The tailoring department at Brooks worked all through the night making the suit that he would wear in the parade. This had been arranged by the mayor of New York, "Gentleman Jimmy" Walker, a good Brooks Brothers customer himself. When the suit was delivered to Lindbergh, the mayor suggested to the firm that the publicity should be adequate payment for the clothing. The company replied that publicity was not in its area of interest, and the matter of the bill remained.

BUSINESS ATTIRE

T he reality is, theories about protection from the elements and modesty notwithstanding, that the main purpose of clothing is adornment, and those fashion accoutrements that are the least utilitarian are in fact the most important. For male attire, the necktie is the perfect paradigm of this sartorial irony: it is precisely because it is so obviously inessential that it is so endowed with significance. Despite its history, the necktie today serves no other purpose than pure decoration. There are of course reasons why men wind decorative strips of cloth around their necks—psychological, historical, cultural reasons—but there is no practical necessity to it apart from subtle social dress codes: no physical, sanitary, medical, or even aesthetic compulsion. It is something of a higher need, a spiritual one, if you will. The necktie is pure symbol, a badge slung round our necks and emblazoned on our chests for all to behold and interpret. Sometimes it is an albatross, telling of our past sins (in his *Notebooks*, F. Scott Fitzgerald condemned a man by saying that "when he buys his ties he has to ask if gin will make them run"); sometimes a medal of honor, or stamp of entry and privilege (or what else are old school ties all about?). It is, in short, a personal flag that signals to friend and foe alike who we are.

There are men who will spend as much time selecting a new tie as they would a new car, which is excessive perhaps, but understandable. A tie can tell as much about a man as a whole battery of personality tests; it can enlighten and inform us about his background, his habits, his vocation and standing in the community, even his dreams and his image of himself. Brillat-Savarin, had he been an astute dandy rather than an astute gourmand, might well have said, "Show me a man's tie, and I'll tell you who he is."

And because it is so expressive, the necktie offers a good place to show one's individuality. Actually, the necktie and the shirt should be considered as a unit of dress, because a business shirt perforce is accompanied by a necktie, and a tie usually is worn with a business shirt. Further, sartorial distinction requires an understanding and approach to the accessories, those furnishings that proclaim the style of the man, just as the basics of the wardrobe affirm his sense of decorum. Of the items of haberdashery, none are more important than the shirt and tie. They are the focal points of business attire, and our grandfathers were quite correct in their precept that "a clean collar and a decent tie will see a man through."

Next to its being clean, it is the style of the collar that should be considered, for there are only half a dozen collar styles considered safe for business wear, and the differences are subtle but telling. The button-down collar is at the casual end of the business-shirt spectrum and is the jauntiest collar that one can wear in the office or board room. Its purposefully nonchalant roll acts as a counterpoint to an otherwise sedate outfit and tends to give the impression of dressed-down and approachable respectability; figuratively as well as literally, it softens the stiff edges of the appearance. The space at the top of the collar points (where the collar is buttoned on the neckband) is wide enough to accommodate a full-Windsor or half-Windsor knot for the necktie, as well as perfectly receptive to bow ties. It is the most American of collars, and its intent—which is also the great virtue of American clothing generally—is to relax the appearance, to bring a touch of deshabille to the formality of business garb.

The rounded collar (usually called a club collar) is the next least formal in the spectrum. Equally at home with a bow tie as the button-down, it is not constructed to accept a full-Windsor knot since the

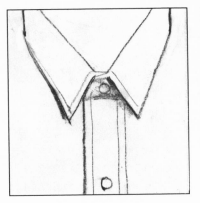

SPORT POINT COLLAR

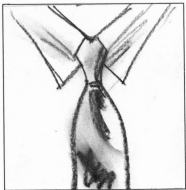

TAB COLLAR

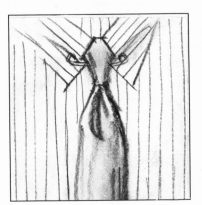

PIN COLLAR

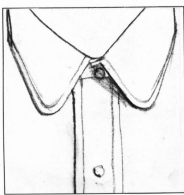

CLUB COLLAR

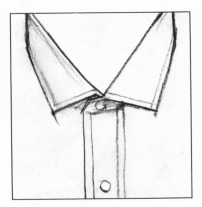

SPREAD COLLAR

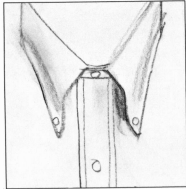

POLO, OR BUTTON-DOWN, COLLAR

amount of space between the front flaps of the collar (the space is called "spread," and the flaps are usually referred to as "points," whether they are actually pointed or not) is small and would be overpowered by a large knot. The effect of an ample knot in a small spread is to buckle the points of the collar, causing them to bulge. The design and line of the collar is then destroyed, and if the collar itself is comparatively small (which is often the case with club collars), the relationship between tie and collar is completely unbalanced and disproportionate. A simple four-in-hand knot tends to nicely moderate the distinctive contours of the club collar and balance its proportions. Since the club collar finds its heritage in the celluloid collars worn by Edwardian school boys, it suggests youthful charm, while remaining neat and unobtrusive.

Today the short point is the standard and most versatile collar for business wear. It too is unsuitable for a large knot, which bends the points that should rest smoothly on the collar bones, but its great virtue is that it has no other restrictions: it is direct, simple, and always appropriate. It is the *juste-milieu* of collars, neither flamboyant nor austere.

Tab- and pin-collared shirts, however, are another matter. Both restrict the spread dramatically to achieve a slightly exaggerated neatness and sense of formality. Both collars work best with smaller knots, a simple four-in-hand for example, which accord with the proportions of the smaller spread. In the spectrum of the business collar, we have now crossed the neutral median of the short-point collar and have entered the realm of conscious formality. The pin collar—which may be either rounded or pointed—also affords men the opportunity to wear jewelry without resorting to stringing gilded hubcaps across their sternums.

The spread collar (often called an English collar since it was first popularized in England in the 1930s by the Duke of Windsor to accommodate the larger knotted neckties he favored—and that bear his name) is at the opposite end of the spectrum from the button-downs. If the button-down is consciously casual and cavalier, the spread collar is purposefully elegant and dressy. It is happiest with the larger knot of the full- or half-Windsor with which it was originally paired and with suits of impeccable shape and cut. It is meant to be serious and perhaps a bit autocratic, and its sangfroid is completely destroyed by a bow tie.

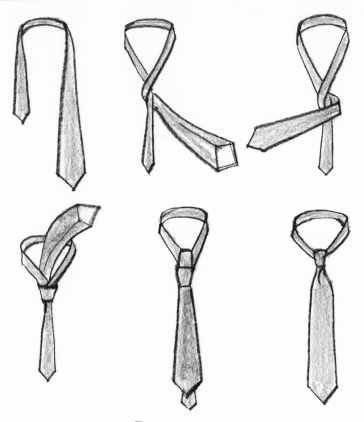

FOUR-IN-HAND KNOT

Of making rules about which men should wear what collar styles there is no end, and much study of them is an exercise in futility. The only rule that makes any sense at all about the shirt collar is that it should correspond to the proportions of the neck that wears it: the longer the neck, the longer the collar; the shorter the neck, the lower the collar. That only a very large man should wear a very large collar would seem not to need saying, and foregoing all the hype about wide faces and high foreheads and prominent cheekbones and God knows what, the truth is that any of these collar styles can be worn by anyone—that's the point of business attire! It is not so much a question of physiognomy as it is a matter of character. Different collar styles and shapes, like clothing generally, tend to convey or suggest different moods (from the breezy to the very proper). In selecting a collar style, the

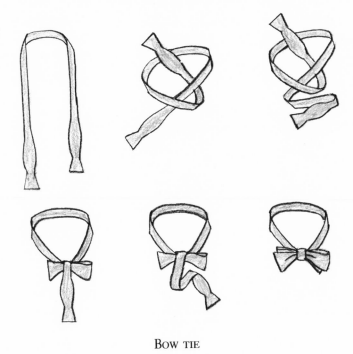

BOW TIE

question should be, Will the moods that its design suggests accord with the personality of the man who wears it? The idea that some men shouldn't wear a certain style because of their physical appearance—apart from proportionate concerns—is rather nonsensical. Clothing changes one's appearance—that is its function—and the question is whether or not a man's personality fits the appearance his clothes create for him.

Business shirts are traditionally restricted to light colors or plain white (historically, a white shirt indicated that the wearer was above manual labor and had the wherewithal to maintain a delicate wardrobe) and simple patterns. White and pale blue are the safest, with ivory and pale gray following in favor. Pale pink is not unacceptable, nor are shirts with white collars and cuffs and colored bodies. The latter two categories, however, call for an added confidence and sense of color coordination, since deviation from the tried-and-true hues always carries the double risk of appearing too studied and of clashing with the jacket and tie.

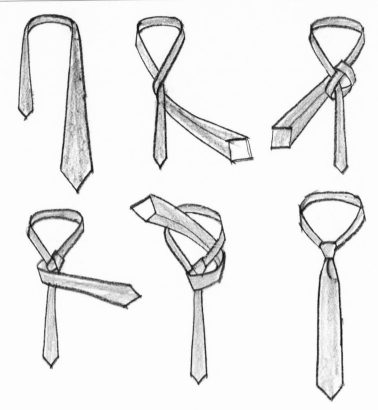

HALF-WINDSOR KNOT

Actually, it isn't color so much as pattern that provides the pitfalls to trap the unwary. After all, it is difficult to go far wrong with a white shirt or pale blue one, regardless of the tie or jacket, but when it comes to mixing checks with stripes and dots, the men and the boys must part company. The safest, but also most boring, approach is to stick to solid shades and forego any decoration: dark gray suit, light blue shirt, dark blue tie. Very proper, always acceptable, usually dull. Another approach, some argue, is to reduce the risk of error by allowing no more than two components of the visual field (shirt, tie, jacket) to be patterned: if the shirt and tie are striped, keep the jacket plain; if suit and tie are patterned, the shirt should be plain; if shirt and jacket are patterned, keep the tie simple. This formula is an improvement over the all-solids

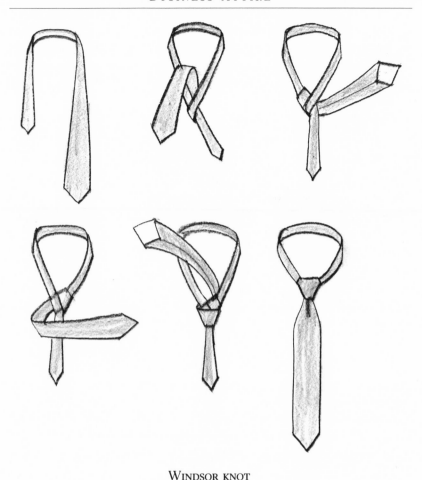

WINDSOR KNOT

approach and can undoubtedly protect some men from wearing those dizzying combinations customarily reserved for circus barkers, while at the same time allowing for considerable variety and scope for individualism. It is a fair approach to the problems of pattern mixing.

But the most practical rule—commonsense observation, really—is simply to avoid overpowering one's appearance, which is the raison d'être of business attire in the first place. The business wardrobe is meant to comprise an interchangeable series of garments that allow for subtle variation and yet produce a discreet uniformity. Too much color, too many patterns, or too bold or discordant a combination of elements in an ensemble acts like too much wattage on a fuse box. If you plug in all the appliances at the same time, you can expect to overload the system.

Shirting patterns have for the past hundred years or so been relegated to a limited array of stripes (hairline, pin, pencil, shadow, and bengal denote the accepted thicknesses), multi-striped blendings, and checks (box, tattersall, miniature, and pin-check are standard). As with unpatterned business shirts, colors that are too bright, dark, or bold run the risk of being thought too fancy and self-conscious. Patterns of neckties are myriad, and yet here too there are only a handful that have won long-standing places of correctness and affection in the gentleman's office wardrobe, and each has its particular appeal: polka dots are fastidious, foulards reliable, and stripes authoritative. The maxim that seems to work best with any of these patterns is, the bolder the tie the more prudent the jacket and shirt. Combining a patterned suit, shirt, *and* tie is not impossible, but the man able to carry that sort of thing off has exceeded the bounds of propriety and snatched a grace beyond the reach of art. There are those who are able to combine checks and stripes and dots with a sure touch that passeth all understanding. With others the touch is none too sure and all too understandable, and it would have been much better to let one item lead and have the others follow.

This approach, of allowing one item prominence in an outfit, also has the advantage of promoting a sense of individual style. Some men choose one item and repetitively give it a certain prominence, so that it becomes a signature of sorts for them. The familiar pink shirt, or the bow tie, or the tweed hat are small but telling signs that these men recognize convention but insist on their individuality as well, as we all should—and know the satisfaction of finding something they particularly like and sticking to it regardless of the trendy whims of fashion and the impersonal machinations of the garment industry.

BUYING A SUIT

M any men never feel comfortable buying a suit. Some begrudge themselves the time, others think it's effeminate to be concerned with one's appearance. There are those whose mothers picked out their clothes when they were boys, and when they grew up their wives simply inherited the task. The fact is, of course, that many men were never taught what to look for in a suit, never instructed about fit, fabric, color, styling, or anything else, and they are consequently slightly embarrassed, even defensive, because they realize they should know more. Maybe it's one of those little nagging aspects of modern life, like changing a tire, fixing a dripping faucet, or poaching an egg, that was overlooked in high school while we were being taught medieval European history and English literature.

Not that there's necessarily anything wrong with that. Some of one's best friends may be medieval Europeans. And most American men do tend to pick up a good deal of information about fixing their cars. But most of them know precious little about the clothes they wear every day. Correction: they know precious little about the clothes they *ought* to wear. This regrettable situation wasn't quite so terrible in the distant past when a suit cost $40 or $50 (twenty-five years ago it was possible to get one custom-made for $100 or so). The clothing salesman and

57

the tailor were devoted to their calling, you could put yourself safely and securely in their time-honored hands and come away looking fairly respectable, even if you didn't know your Inverness cape from your instep. Every town had its share of reliable clothing stores, haberdashers, or campus shops, family-owned and with two or three trusty salesmen who knew their clientele from head to toe. Even the least dandified among us felt comforted by a casual chat with one of these esteemed gentlemen of the cloth. We knew they would not steer us wrong just to make a quick sale, and we looked forward to years of association with them. They were, in short, knowledgeable and helpful, and they helped us—sartorially at the very least—to know ourselves better.

Things are considerably different today. Many of these small shops have, almost overnight it seems, become pizza parlors and jeans outlets. Some areas are serviced only by large chain department stores, with impersonal clerks and no desire to take orders if your size is not in stock. Many a department store clerk, in fact, who is selling trousers this week will move on to garden equipment or insurance or major appliances the next, and he simply cannot be counted on for the expert advice necessary to the purchase, however nice a chap he may be. And then the price of a decent suit has, along with everything else decent, soared beyond the imagination, to the point where buying one calls for decidedly serious outlays of money—which should be accompanied by serious outlays of time and deliberation. Today, good clothing constitutes a major investment.

Finally, the waters have been made all the murkier by the incredible proliferation of brand and designer names infiltrating the clothing market these past several years. There are perhaps in excess of half a hundred American, European, and Oriental designer labels around just now— many with unpronounceable names affixed to garments faintly resembling open cans of tunafish—making designer clothing the most lucrative of bandwagons and our fastest growing glamour industry. Time was when a raincoat was a raincoat was a raincoat, and the only question was whether or not your local haberdasher had your size in stock at the moment, and if not how long it would take him to order it. Today it is almost impossible to even find a clothing store where you can order anything. It's enough to put one in—using the current jargon—a long-faced situation to be sure.

But let us not dwell on the darker side. It is still possible not only to find one's way in the maze of quilted, iridescent bomber jackets, snakeskin tennis shorts, and sequined cowboy hats, but to emerge better dressed in the bargain. And without taking your mother along, either. To begin, there are a number of general caveats. First, stores that specialize in selling clothing are to be recommended above those in which the sports jackets are on a rack next to the plumbing supplies, particularly those clothing stores that have been in business for a while. Even if this means traveling to another town, or even a city some distance away. Selection will be better, salesmen will be more knowledgeable, and tailors will be more skilled. It pays off in the long run to develop a good relationship with reliable clothing stores.

Second, the matter of designer labels. A designer label indicates not only a certain approach to style and a level of taste, but an added cost value as well—and of course in not a few instances the level of taste is so questionable as not to warrant the additional cost. Do not be taken in by a name; the clothing must stand on its own feet. Some designers are marvelously creative and are committed to taste and quality. Others should simply be committed. And sadly, I am afraid awards are not the uniformly best indication of a designer's talent either. I can think of several designers who richly deserve their fashion awards, but I know many others whom I would not trust to design a funeral suit for a dead goat. Many designer clothes are rather extreme in fit and styling and are specifically designed for the virgate figure of the youth market. If you try on a European-style "fitted" jacket and suddenly have the sensation that your circulation has stopped, you're probably not having a coronary; the jacket is merely cut closer to the body than any pattern to which American men are accustomed. Confusingly enough, there is also a fashionable tendency to oversized clothing at the moment, which creates rather the opposite sensation of being imperceptibly shrunk by some malevolent witch doctor.

Finally, poor quality, regardless of the imprimature, is no bargain. Designer suits are like anything else: a matter of expectations and priorities, both of which revolve around life-style, economic status, interests, and professional and social activities just as much as physique and upbringing. Undoubtedly a fellow midway up the corporate ladder would find a Claude Montana concoction slightly bizarre, just as a continental restaurateur would think a Brooks Brothers sack-cut suit drab and formless. And they would both be perfectly correct, for even in these advanced days of *laisser-aller*, propriety is still something with which to reckon. And just as there are levels of usage in language—depending upon the purpose, occasion, and audience, as we used to say in English class—there are proprieties of dress. Clothes talk; in fact they never shut up, and it makes sense to have them say what you want them to. And propriety is perhaps more important than ever. It is safe to say that of late, clothing has begun to take a conservative turn, and that clothing in the coming decade will be more "classic" than in the preceding decade, certainly more staid than in the 1960s. One does tend to hear that word "classic" more than a bit—applied to everything from suits to salads to southern vacations—but the necessary result of inflation is that belts are tightened, not traded in for new models.

I think we are, in a sense, returning to pre-World War II days, when buying a suit was a solemn and weighty occasion and not something done every season. Styles will no longer change with the foliage, and men will once again have to pay close attention to the finer points of fit and fabric, tailoring and style. The carefree days of unbridled consumption are fast running out, and purchases will increasingly be treated as investments, and the person who realizes this is very much one up. To consider the initial outlay of money is not enough. It is also necessary to consider the longevity of the garment, the cost of maintenance, long-term style, and adaptability to repair and alteration. The wise dresser is he who appreciates the maxim that it is very expensive to buy cheap. Three good pairs of shoes are better than six cheap ones: they'll fit more comfortably and last longer; good shoes look good even when they're old, but cheap shoes look shoddy even when they're new. A fine custom-tailored suit can now cost in excess of $1,000, but if it helps you to look well-attired for ten, fifteen, or twenty years, what is the real worth of that suit?

The cardinal rule is: If it doesn't fit, don't buy it! Even if it's on sale. *Especially* if it's on sale, because then you can't return it should you be dissatisfied after the purchase. Fit is the top priority, because while a great variety of colors and fabrics are usually at least acceptable if the fit is good, a person looks terrible in even the poshest cloth if the fit is a poor one. In other words, never sacrifice fit to color or cloth. Never buy a cheaply cut garment just because it's made up in the snappy and fashionable color of the moment. In the past, women have perhaps been the more prone to this fault, but it is now as full-blown a problem for men.

Rule two: Never allow yourself to be talked into extensive alterations. Any tailor worth his salt will be most reluctant to drastically alter a garment, not because he's inherently lazy but because he knows that the line and balance can only be tampered with minutely. A good tailor, as I have said before, and may say again, measures in quarter-inches. For your part, you must absolutely insist on service and proper fit, even if it means returning the garment half a dozen times to the shop. In fact, clothing should be broken in a bit—I think it was Thoreau who pointed out that new clothing belonged to nobody, literally and figuratively—and the knowing tailor will assume that some adjustments may be necessary after the suit is worn.

Rule three: The suit must be made to conform to you, not you to the suit. While you are being fitted before the triplex mirror—you will want to see all sides of you, so never settle for a single-view mirror—don't try to stand ramrod straight unless that is your normal posture. Put on the new suit and walk about a bit, sit down, cross your legs, and fold your arms. Put in the pockets what you normally carry: wallet, eyeglasses, mini-calculator, address book, dog's leash. If you intend to wear a sweater under the jacket, wear a sweater at the fitting. Appropriate shoes should be worn, too, because heel height has a great deal to do with where the trouser leg "breaks" over the shoe. Don't go shopping for a suit wearing sneakers, unless for some reason you intend to wear sneakers with the suit. Don't wear sneakers with the suit.

Examine yourself critically in the fitting mirror. The collar of the jacket should hug the neck without pulling, gaping, or riding up, and the lapels should drop straight down the chest when the jacket is buttoned. This area—the chest and collar—is crucial because very little here can be effectively corrected if it is not proper at the outset. If the chest and lapels tend to buckle, the jacket is simply too small and no amount of alteration will correct the problem because the chest of a jacket, once it is cut, cannot effectively be made larger. You don't get more doughnut by cutting a larger hole in it. If the suit is from a ready-made line, you must either move up to the next larger size, try another style, or (since all manufacturers cut their suits to slightly different proportions and patterns depending on the styling of the garment) find a brand of suit that is cut with a larger chest.

The back of the jacket, on the other side of things, can more easily be adjusted. If there is a tension crease running horizontally across the shoulder-blade area, the back is too small and must be eased; if there is a "hollow"—a slack, concave area—the back is too large and must be tightened. The back of the jacket should sit like a still pond. It must rest lightly over the shoulders, fall without a crease down the upper back, gently follow the curve of the lower back, and break easily over the hips and derriere. The only thing that can be said about the proper jacket length is that the jacket should cover the seat entirely, and even that is more a matter of style and fashion than strict propriety. In the 1920s, men wore "bum freezers," that is, ventless jackets that extended only halfway down their buttocks; while in the 1960s, very long hacking-style jackets with deep fourteen-inch vents were the dernier cri (better left unmentioned the zoot suits of the 1940s, with the one-button, rolled-lapel jackets that reached almost to the knee). These are fashionable extremities. It is often stated—even by tailors who should know better—that the bottom edge of the jacket should be long enough to reach the bend in your fingers when your hand is cupped at your side. How this nonsensical concept got started is something of a mystery, since the length of one's arms plays no role at all in relation to the length of the jacket. What does, however, affect that length is the length of the legs, and the rule here is: short legs, short jacket. If your legs are short, ask for a "short" fitted jacket; if long, ask for a "long" fitted one; average leg lengths take a "regular" jacket. These length fittings are noted on the jacket size-tag either by the words themselves or by the letters S and L (a size 38 short fitting will be seen as a 38S; a 38 long fitting as a 38L; and a regular 38 simply as 38). Any clothing store that doesn't stock long and short fittings in addition to the regular ones is not a good clothing store. Spend your money elsewhere and get a proper fit. Even if you believe you take a regular fitting, it's a good idea to try on a longer or shorter jacket just for comparison's sake. You never can tell; a bit shorter jacket, for example, just might make you look taller, thinner, and younger.

Jacket sleeves generally end not where the hand meets the wrist—

which is where the shirt sleeve would normally fall—but about a half-inch above, at the middle of the wrist bone when the arm is at rest. This allows for a quarter- to half-inch of shirt cuff to extend beyond the jacket sleeve end. The jacket sleeve itself should not be so tight that it grabs the forearm or upper arm when the arm is bent. A tight sleeve is not only uncomfortable, it wrinkles a great deal more, resulting in the old accordian-arms syndrome. It's a good idea to wear the jacket around the house a bit before having the sleeve length adjusted, because sleeves tend to ride up slightly, sometimes as much as half-inch, when they are being broken in. At the other end of the sleeve, armholes should be as high as possible without binding. High armholes (technically called "scyes" by the tailor) are not only neater in appearance, but they are actually much more comfortable because they allow for freer movement; a low-cut armhole tends to pull the back of the jacket with it when the arm moves, giving the sensation of having half the jacket move forward with the arm. The high armhole allows the sleeve to move more independently of the jacket body itself.

The waist of the jacket should sit close to the wearer's actual waist without producing any horizontal tension lines. A loose or tight jacket waist can be corrected—but it is a major alteration, to be entrusted only to a competent tailor. If the waist is off by more than an inch, don't have the alteration done, since the line of the jacket will be ruined. A half-inch alteration at both sides is as much as the balance of the jacket will tolerate. Additionally, button stance (the number and position of buttons on the front of the jacket) is of importance when considering the waist. There is always much ado about the number of buttons on a jacket: whether two buttons are better than three; whether more than one is really necessary anyway; how many buttons should actually be buttoned; should the placement of them be high, low, or at the natural waist; and where, pray tell, is the natural waist anyway? These are matters more of sensibility than of sense, more in the realm of discretion, fashion, and taste. If you favor a three-button jacket, by all means stick to it. If the salesman tells you that you'd look better in a two-button one, he is most likely saying that he doesn't stock any three-button jackets anyway and that if you insist, he's going to lose a sale. Let him lose the sale. On the other hand, it is my strong belief that a high or a low button stance can considerably change a physique for better or worse. Men with large chests tend to look better in a jacket with a lowered button stance, large-stomached men with a higher one.

Today, jackets have three types of backs: single-vented, double-vented (also called side-vented), and ventless. Here again, some of the distinction is merely a matter of fashion or individual preference, but there are other considerations that should enter into the choice about which style of back to wear. A ventless jacket gives the more elegant, uncluttered line, but you must be slim of hip and slight of derriere to wear this style. Otherwise it looks as though you were poured in and forgot to say "when." The double-vented jacket is preferable for the man with the fuller derriere because the part of the jacket below the waist (technically called by tailors the "skirt" of the jacket) is actually cut fuller; there is more material there to give a bit of flair to the jacket, a skirting away over the hips in a hacking jacket silhouette. Nothing, when it comes to vents, looks worse—or, one might add, is more commonly seen—than a gaping center-vented jacket with the trouser seat and perhaps just an indiscreet soupçon of shirttail on public view. If the vent doesn't overlap by a generous three-fourths inch or more, there's either not enough jacket or too much you. One or the other should be changed.

Shoulder design (such as natural, rope, concave, full English), pockets (such as besom, patch, ticket, chest, bellows, flapped), and other stylistic matters are best left to individual discretion. Now for the trousers. The first rule is that trousers should never be tight or short. If there is horizontal creasing across the front of the trousers—the lap or abdomen area—they are too tight. A fellow with a bit of a tummy would do wisely to consider wearing pleated trousers, which not only help disguise fullness (paradoxically), but are more comfortable as well.

Trousers, by the way, sit over the hips, never below them. If your trousers do not reach your hips, it is because the "rise"—the distance between the base of the crotch and the waistband—is too short. You must ask for a trouser with a higher rise. If the salesman tells you there is no such thing, he is either ignorant or untruthful. In either case you have no need to ever speak to him again; he is not interested in your welfare or your appearance, and you owe him nothing. To keep the trousers at their proper height on the waist, waistbands are designed either with belt loops, self-supporting tabs of one kind or another, or buttons (sewn to the inside) for suspenders—you can use all three if you are feeling insecure. There is a vogue on at the moment for suspenders—part of the 1930s nostalgia style—but the choice depends more on comfort and style than other considerations. My experience has been that they do tend to hold the trousers better, but some men find them more cumbersome than either a belt or tabs.

The seat of the trouser may easily be altered to make it either fuller or tighter, and this alteration will also tend to raise or lower the crotch. Only very snug-fitting trousers need provision for what is called "dress." Dress refers to the side on which a man places the more intimate parts of his anatomy; he is said accordingly to "dress left" or "dress right." Since—and again we are dealing here in mysteries—most men dress left (but please don't consider yourself abnormal if you don't), the fork

of the left trouser leg is conveniently made to account for this phenomenon. Dressing right—an ironic turn of phrase—is a problem that can be dealt with, if one wants to deal with it, simply by changing over.

The trouser leg should fall straight—a crease should run down the center of the leg front and back—and although there have been rages within memory for both exaggeratedly flaired and tapered trousers, the average trouser leg of conservative cut has remained surprisingly stable over the years: about nineteen inches at the knee, seventeen and a half inches at the bottom. Cuffs go in and out of fashion—at the moment they're in, but should this book go to a second edition, this is one of the sentences that will have to be reconsidered—and while the width has varied from one to two inches, the average cuff has a depth of one and a half inches, regardless of the length of the legs wearing them. Whether cuffed or plain-bottomed, trouser legs should reach the top of the shoes, preferably breaking slightly over the instep and dropping to within an inch of the top of the heel in back. Because some men tend to be bowlegged, this effect can only be achieved by slanting the trouser bottom slightly downward toward the rear, making the trouser leg a half-inch or so longer in the back than in front. This little tailor's trick keeps the trousers from flying away behind as though the shoe heels had semaphore flags attached.

Now for the third part of the suit: the vest. In pre-World War II days it was not unusual to find suits with vests; it was in fact typical for all single- as well as double-breasted ones, with the sometime exception of summer suits. Today most double-breasteds are vestless, and perhaps only about a third of the single-breasted models come with a vest. Any tailor will tell you that the vest is in fact the most difficult part of the suit to make because it sits closest the body (and as it happens, there are very few good custom vestmakers around today, it being a specialized craft within the tailoring realm). Fortunately, there are not as many parts to a vest that must be got right: the front must be long enough to cover completely the trouser waistband, so that no part of the shirt shows, and not so tight that creases form horizontally at the buttonholes; as opposed to the jacket, vest armholes should be low and certainly not binding; and the back should be provided with a tab-and-buckle so that a snug fit can be assured through slight variations in weight.

There is also some confusion about the bottom button on the vest, whether it should be left undone or not. Britain's Edward VII started the fashion of leaving the button undone—some say because he grew too fat to button it—and English tailors still consider it properly left that way; Savile Row tailors in fact construct the vest so that it is not to be buttoned at the bottom. Most ready-made vests, however, are cut so that the button actually works, and so it becomes a matter again of style, with nothing much lost or gained one way or t'other. And oh yes, be sure that the blade end of the necktie does not dangle out below the vest, as this tends to provide an unnecessary point of focus.

Now for a few shopping suggestions. Never buy impulsively. When you're in a hurry, things often look very nice in the shop simply because you didn't take the time to examine them carefully enough, or to worry about fit, or to consider whether the item conforms to the scope of your wardrobe. It's far better to have something specific in mind when you enter the shop, rather than this deplorable mania for "just going shopping" which leads to the most regrettable examples of impulse buying imaginable. But going out for a specific item doesn't mean you shouldn't look around—in fact, you should, because when there's no pressure on you from either a sales clerk or necessity, you have an excellent opportunity to educate yourself about items you well may want or need in the future. And if the clerk or tailor is agreeable, ask questions: What's the difference between flannel and worsted? When's the best time to order a seersucker sports jacket? Are their khakis 100 percent cotton? What's the weight of their tropical wool suits?

Buy the absolute best you can afford. Fine clothes will last ten times longer than cheap, shoddy merchandise, will feel and fit better, and of course will look better. A cheap suit looks cheap even when it's brand new, while a good one retains its appearance after years of wear. A good raincoat, tweed jacket, and flannel slacks actually improve with age and wear. It's a matter of quality.

To help determine the quality, read the fiber-content label affixed to the jacket sleeve and trouser waistband. This label is required by law on ready-made clothing and will inform you whether the garment is made of 100 percent natural fibers, a blend of natural and synthetic, or all synthetic. Natural fabrics—wool, cotton, linen, and silk—in their pure forms, or blended with each other, cannot be exceeded for appearance and comfort. The reason that synthetics are used more and more in clothing is that they are cheaper to produce. Synthetic-fiber manufacturers spend millions on advertising to convince people that their products are superior. Their pitch is that synthetics are wrinkle-free, which is true. But then, so is sheet metal. In the past, synthetic fabrics tended to have a shiny look and a slick hand, they tailored badly, had little porosity, and tended to pill after being worn for a period of time (those that were blended with natural fabrics). While these problems are being seriously addressed by the synthetic-fiber industry, solutions are apparently still in the future. All in all, synthetics are not yet to be recommended.

While you're looking at the fiber-content label, inspect the inside of the jacket and trousers. Better jackets have full linings, which add longevity and help the jacket retain its shape longer. The lining should have a pleat down the center of the back, and there should be a small fold of hem along the bottom edge; these extra folds allow for expansion when you move, while the lining itself prevents the jacket from bunching up or clinging, enhances movement, and discourages wear-and-tear to the outer cloth itself. In the trousers there should be take-out seams of at least one and a half inches in the waist, seat, and legs, to allow for a maximum one-inch expansion should you put on a pound or two over the years—which does seem to be the way of all flesh. More than an inch and you'll have to either go on a diet or move up to the next size suit.

It need hardly be said that loose threads and buttons indicate shoddy workmanship, but few men take the trouble to look. Tug gently at a button, any button on the suit, and if it comes away, place it quietly in the salesman's hand, give him a sympathetic pat on the shoulder, and saunter out the door. When it comes to construction, though, there is a far more serious problem to recognize than a dangling button or two. Better suits are stitched together, and the best ones are done by hand. Cheap ones, funny though it may sound, are literally glued together in a process called "fusing." Fused suits can easily be detected because they have a decidedly stiff feel, not unlike cardboard, in those areas (the chest, lapels, pockets, and collar) where the material is joined. Stiffness is not, however, the major drawback of the fused suit. The real problem is that after some wear, and cleaning, and time—often less than a year—the glue begins to dry out and the layers of the fabric start to "bubble," pulling apart in spots. This deterioration creates a stunning visual effect not unlike blistered paint on an old barn wall. And nothing can be done to prevent, correct, or reverse this process. You are stuck with it, and it will only get worse as time goes by, whether you wear the suit or not. Fused construction is, as you might expect, much cheaper for the manufacturer but much more expensive for the customer in the long run. A $200 fused suit that lasts a year is just twice as expensive as an $800 hand-stitched one that lasts eight years— even without considering fit or appearance or comfort. Unless you think looking like old paint is great fun, avoid the fused suit.

Coordinate. Stick to the colors that you like and are best for you, the ones that complement your wardrobe, and don't worry about what particularly nifty shades are being touted at the moment. This means that you can avoid buying a complete set of accessories every time you get a new suit. Completely coordinated outfits that cannot be broken up and worn with other aspects of the wardrobe are just sales gimmicks anyway and are about as fashionable as complete suites of furniture. Interestingly enough, when you buy fine clothes the problem of coordination usually takes care of itself, for fine clothes have a marvelous way of complementing each other. If you must buy a shirt and tie to complement your new suit, you are buying the wrong suit: if you've nothing to wear with it, it perforce has nothing to do with your wardrobe. And if you buy a tie that only can be worn with one shirt or one suit, you've bought an expensive tie no matter what it cost!

Accessories should do double and triple duty and should therefore be pretty much of a piece, as should the essentials of the wardrobe. For the truth is that while fashion changes, style remains the same, because as Georges-Louis LeClerc pointed out so long ago, "le style est l'homme même." Understand yourself and your needs, and fit your clothing to your life-style. And don't let anyone tell you otherwise. If you wear a dinner jacket only once every three or four years, there is little reason to buy one; find a reputable rental shop. Conversely, if you are in black tie once a month or so, you may need two good ones. A white raw-silk suit is wonderfully elegant, but unless you've got a dozen more serviceable ones in your wardrobe, stay away from it; a white suit must be cleaned all the time, and if you wear it more than four times a year, people will think you live in it. This goes for deafening plaids as well and is of course the reason sensible businessmen who must wear a suit every day usually stick to gray or tan shades, letting a touch of color come from the tie.

To add just a brief fillip to the Socratic admonition "Know thyself," try to dress the part. Inasmuch as clothing is still the most obvious sign of one's identity, a man should dress in accordance with his profession and standing in the community. This may sound too Victorian and confining for some, but the social reality is that credibility is still based in large measure on consistency. If a man changes his style too often, we feel he is insecure and trying very hard to impress us. Particularly after the blush of youth has passed. A man should find his style and develop it, should have done his experimenting when young, we feel. A banker who chooses to dress like his sixteen-year-old son, and who turns up at the First National one morning wearing topsiders without socks, fatigue pants, and a neon-enscrawled T-shirt, is not a man to be trusted with your money or mine. And incidentally, his son will not respect him either. Tight jeans and ten yards of gold chain and ceramic clutter on a middle-aged, slightly paunchy, but otherwise solid citizen are embarrassing because they tend to indicate an identity crisis. In this case, psychiatric help is probably a better investment than an extensive new wardrobe.

The wardrobe should develop over the years. Don't throw anything out. This advice always tends to cause a lot of flak from wives who have an obsessive itch to clean out closets and "throw out all those old things you haven't worn in years." Don't do it. Stand up for your rights as a dues-paying member of the household and cart the stuff right back to your closet—be sure to hang it up properly. Too many women, sad to say in this day and age, are still manipulated by rapidly changing fashion scenarios. But if you bought good clothes to begin with, you will always be in style, something that goes far beyond the frivolities of trendy fashions. The decision to throw things away should be predicated on whether or not they fit, and indeed here your partner may well be the better judge of that than you. The rule is: if it doesn't fit, don't wear it; but if you keep your figure, keep your clothes. Time is very gentle with quality clothing. The classic navy blazer has been in style for better than half a century and will be for another fifty years.

A good blazer, that is. The Duke of Windsor—a natty and fastidious dresser if ever there was one—wore his suits for years and years, including several he had inherited from his father and calculated to have lasted for more than sixty years!

Finally, keeping one's clothes implies keeping them in good repair. This advice is bound to sound rather trite to a throw-away-oriented person, but since we've already agreed, haven't we, that we are going to buy quality clothing that is made to last, it makes perfect sense. Suits should be brushed (with soft bristles) not only before but after being worn. Otherwise, accumulated dirt and dust will set in the fabric, causing abrasive wear as well as deterioration of color. A good suit should always be hung on a sturdy hanger—a substantial wooden one, for example, not one of those flimsy wire things—and dry cleaned by a reliable establishment that knows something not only about cleaning but about pressing a good suit. A dependable dry cleaner and competent alterations tailor will double the life of your suit. If you don't know any, ask at the clothing store if they can recommend someone. Or ask your mother—just because you don't need her anymore to select your clothes doesn't mean she doesn't know a lot of things you may not.

CASHMERE

S ince the virtual disappearance from the world markets of vicuña—usually considered to be the finest of all animal fibers—cashmere is undoubtedly the ultimate luxurious fabric. There is no question that anything cashmere today costs a packet. A custom-made topcoat from a reputable tailor would easily exceed $2,000, a superior sweater upwards of $400, and even a pair of socks might cost $75 or $80. Tidy sums indeed.

The fact is, there exists today a classic case of limited supply and high demand for cashmere cloth and garments. The amount of cashmere in the world has always been extremely small. Even with all of our technological expertise, less than four million pounds of cashmere are produced annually, compared with twenty-five billion pounds of synthetic fibers. Moreover, the differences in production costs are as enormous. The true source of cashmere is a nimble little mountain goat, who lives in the inaccessible and barren high plateaus of the Himalayas. Because the goat's habitat is so remote, the most primitive methods still must be used to obtain the fiber—it is an arduous trip from goat to sweater.

Once a year nomadic herdsmen remove the cloud-soft fleece that grows under the goat's thick outer coat of coarse hair as an insulation against the severe climate. The fleece is not sheared away; it is removed with large handmade combs. Each goat grows only four ounces of usable cashmere fiber a year, which means that the total annual output of three goats is needed to produce enough yarn to knit one sweater. To make a topcoat, it takes the fleece of twenty-seven goats.

After the fleece has been combed from the goats and collected together, it is baled and carried by porters (as well as yaks, horses, and camels when and where available) down the precipitous mountain passes to various coastal ports. This is only the beginning of a journey that will last several months. In Mongolia, from which comes the world's best raw cashmere, the precious cargo is then transported on rafts and sampans to Kwangchow (formerly known as Canton) in the People's Republic of China. The Kwangchow Export-Import Commodities Fair, the largest cashmere market in the world, is the international marketplace for the purchase of raw cashmere. Western producers must come here if they want the best.

The obvious question that must arise when one is confronted with this situation is: why aren't the cashmere goats raised and bred in more accessible places like Florida, Michigan, or Vermont? And the answer, unfortunately, is that the fine undercoats of the cashmere goats don't appear to grow in Florida or Michigan or Vermont, or anywhere at all except their native habitat high in the Himalayas. Over the years, many attempts have been made to augment the supply of cashmere by building up herds elsewhere. One of the first recorded attempts was made by a squire in Sussex, England. He transported a herd of goats to his home, Weald Hall, in 1823 at no little expense. Turned loose on the grounds, they grazed, romped, cavorted, reproduced, and thoroughly enjoyed themselves. All they didn't do was grow that wonderful downy coat. Thoroughly disappointed, the squire made the herd a gift to King George IV, and their descendants can still be seen grazing in the Great Park at Windsor Castle—and still minus their luxurious undies.

Today raw cashmere fiber costs in excess of $100 the kilo in China; a dozen years ago it was $15 a kilo. Furthermore, import duties on cashmere cloth and finished garments virtually double the price of cashmere in the U.S.A. And then of course there are the costs of production to consider.

The raw cashmere must be made into fabric of some sort before it

can be manufactured into clothing, that is, the cashmere hair must be painstakingly processed before it can be woven or knitted. Much of this processing is handwork done by highly skilled workers. First, sorters must grade and mix the shades of hair—which vary in their natural state from almost pure white to dark brown—to prevent variations in the yarn and thus ensure standardization. The blended cashmere must then be scoured, to remove grease and dirt, and then dried. Next, the coarser hairs, some of which are inevitably combed out with the finer ones of the undercoat, must be separated and removed. This "de-hairing" process, as it is called, was first developed in Bradford, England, by two brothers, Benjamin and Allon Dawson, in the 1890s. In fact, when the Dawson brothers successfully developed a machine capable of de-hairing cashmere, Bradford became the center of the British cashmere operation, and even today Dawson's is the world's largest user of high-quality raw cashmere and still produces what the textile trade considers the highest quality woven cashmere cloth.

Once the coarse hair has been removed, the fine hair is again combed, then carded, carefully inspected, and packed off to fabric manufacturers who will make it into yarn or woven cashmere cloth. The production of cashmere cloth is still very much a craft. The finishing process alone takes three weeks of careful, meticulous work: the cloth must be brushed and steamed and combed several times over to raise the fiber and ensure the luxurious handle and soft glow we associate with the cloth. And this procedure is not something that is written down in a textbook somewhere. You can't just take a course in this sort of thing at your local community college. Like all true crafts, it's a combination of knowledge and skill and a feeling for the work, which is passed down from father to son, from master to apprentice. It is very much a hands-on learning experience and occupation. A fine cloth finisher, for example, may have worked at his craft for over fifty years, and most of them are the sons of finishers.

There are many reasons given to explain why the British produce what is generally considered the best cashmere knitwear and cloth. Much has been said over the years about the clarity of the River Tweed, for example, which courses through romantic, Sir Walter Scott country, and the river's relationship to the successful cashmere industry in Scotland. The water, according to textile industry experts, does play a part: because it has been free from pollutants and hard mineral deposits, it can help soften the hair at various stages of production.

But the best reason for the industry's success there, in the Scottish Border towns of Hawick, Selkirk, and Galashiels, is that they have got the *craft*—a system of handworked production that is learned and built up slowly over the years, generation by generation. It is the epitome of, one could say, a way of life that is alien to fast food, instant replays, prioritized printouts, and mini-series. Even the dyeing process is a special skill that has been practiced for generations in Scotland. The cashmere hair (as with most animal hair that can be dyed) may be dyed at any one of three stages: before it is made into yarn, after it is made into yarn, or after it is made into cloth, which is called "piece-dyeing." Good knitwear is never piece-dyed, while good cloth may be. The Scottish have developed the art of producing colors as subtle as can be imagined, and as deep and vibrant as can be had—and without any harshness.

Throughout history cashmere has been a luxury cloth, prized for its warmth, light weight, and sensation of softness against the skin. Rich Romans bought cashmere scarves of exotic and intricate design that had been handwoven in Srinagar, Kashmir (hence the name), and brought to Rome by merchant traders. In India the cashmere, spinning industry was so extensive that by the fifteenth century nearly 60,000 people were directly employed in it. By the ninteenth century, the European aristocracy considered cashmere the most fashionable of fabrics. In England, George "Beau" Brummell and the Prince Regent started a vogue for white cashmere waistcoats. And the years from 1780 to 1880 saw such a mania for cashmere shawls for women that these years are often referred to as the Shawl Period of European costume. In France, Empress Eugénie, wife of Napoleon III, had an extravagant collection of cashmere shawls. Even Queen Victoria, conservative of dress as she was, was enchanted by the style and owned a ring shawl—a shawl of cashmere so fine it could pass through a wedding ring.

These Victorian shawls were imitations of ones made in the ancient Vale of Kashmir. The original designs incorporated symbolic and natural figures in colorful swirling and abstract patterns, which we now call "paisley" because the work was perfected by the craftsmen of the small industrial town of Paisley, on the west coast of Scotland about ten miles from Glasgow. The popularity of cashmere shawls was so great that the fabric was chosen for other woven and knitted garments. In the 1840s and '50s paisley designs were copied for ladies' day dresses of cashmere and for gentlemen's dressing gowns. The first cashmere sweater was knitted in Scotland about a century ago.

Not only were cashmere garments as expensive then as now, but they were in fact much more difficult to clean. Before the recent era of fast-set dyes, cashmere apparel was carefully soaked in tincture of benzoin (benzoic acid) and given a sponging of diluted alcohol and ammonia as a restorative. Today maintenance is much simpler. Multicolored sweaters and other knits should be dry cleaned, to avoid the possibility of colors running into each other. Solid colors, on the other hand, may conveniently be hand-washed with a good quality soap powder (add a drop of bath oil to the rinse to help keep fiber resilient) with no fear of shrinkage. Lay the garment on a towel—never twist—to dry.

Since cashmere is made from relatively short fibers, pilling some-times occurs from friction with objects against the garment. The pills, tiny balls of fiber on the surface, may be removed with the careful use of a safety razor. To prevent pilling from friction with other gar-ments—sweaters in a drawer, for instance—wrap the cashmere article in tissue paper for storage. There are really no other specific require-ments for cashmere that don't apply to other fabrics as well. Tailored cashmere garments, as other tailored garments, should be cleaned and altered only by trusted dry cleaners and tailors. Brushing—after each wearing—should be done with a light, quick hand and a fine brush of natural and soft bristles. Badly crushed nap may be brought back to life by carefully holding the cloth over a steaming kettle—at a safe distance—and then lightly brushing.

COWBOY BOOTS

There are all sorts of reasons to explain why boots became an important part of a man's wardrobe this past decade. If you considered the tremendous proliferation of catalogues selling field-and-stream-type gear, you'd have to come to the conclusion that there are either many more sportsmen around these days or many more who want to give the outward, gentrified appearance of one. And boots are a crucial aspect of those outfits: everything from lightweight trail boots and waterproofed hunting shoes to heavy-duty woodsman's boots of sturdy silicone-treated cowhide. Your choice rather depends on whether you intend to merely kick around a few leaves in some city park or to exert some serious energy on a marathon hike down the Appalachian Trail. Many of these new sports boots, with their multicolored nylon-and-leather panels, D-ring lace-holes, bumper-styled toepieces, and tank-tread lug soles, are in fact very comfortable and durable—even if many of them look as though they'd been designed by someone who had read a great deal about boots and shoes but had never actually seen any.

One aspect of this interest is the resurgence in popularity of the cowboy boot. Last in vogue with young people in the 1940s and early 1950s because of the influence of the cowboy movie, this all-American boot of the Old West resurfaced with the popularity of the country-

and-western recording stars. If singers like Willie Nelson, Hank Williams, Jr., Waylon Jennings, and the rest didn't actually cause the trend of wearing cowboy boots (as well as other western paraphernalia), they added the celebrity quality to it that had been missing since the demise of the western film as a preferred genre.

In the "prole gear" days of the 1960s tan construction boots had been the rage, but by the early 1970s cowboy boots, first plain then fancier, began to gain a quorum of interest. For me the handwriting was on the wall one day when I happened to be sauntering down Madison Avenue in the Brooks Brothers-Paul Stuart-Tripler direction. The men's shops in that vicinity are renowned for their conservative taste and elegant clothing, all pinstripes and broadcloth and foulard. There's a particular English shoe shop into whose window I always fondly gaze, if for nothing more than to admire the snuff buckskin wing tips, which keep escalating in price just beyond my reach. This particular day, there amidst all those staid and proper cap-toed oxfords, wing-tip bals, burnished plain-toed bluchers, and suede tassel slip-ons stood a pair of dazzling cowboy boots! I mean, I was knocked absolutely base over apex. Semi-stunned, I gradually noticed that not a few gentlemen in the pinstriped throng also stopped to gaze into the display window, and drifted away, it seemed to me, deep in thought. Were they wondering what it all meant—this bastion of British conservatism infiltrated by the Wild West—or were they imagining themselves in these resplendent boots, dancing in some dusty cantina in El Paso and throwing back tequila with abandon? I may be wrong, but I was sure I heard someone humming "Don't Fence Me In" as I turned down the avenue.

High-topped boots had been worn by cavalry officers in the U.S. Army even before the Civil War, and the Spanish vaqueros who herded longhorn cattle on the plains north of the Rio Grande had also worn boots, adorned with metal spurs. Particularly after the Civil War men from the east and south began to drift westward in search of adventure, or merely a decent livelihood. A few took jobs tending the huge herds of cattle that roamed the open grazing lands of Texas, the activity that in the decades between the end of the war and the turn of the century would provide the most vibrant, heroic image we have ever produced: the American cowboy.

That colorful period, a mere thirty-odd years, was the time of the long cattle drives. Thousands of head of Texas longhorns were driven up the legendary Chisholm Trail from southern Texas to Wichita and Abilene, and virtually all the myths (and the costume) of the cowboy derived from this unique enterprise. In truth, the life of a long-drive cowboy was a lonely and arduous one, and his clothes were designed from experience to provide protection if not solace. His wide-brimmed hat and calico bandana insulated him from the scorching sun and choking dust, while tough leather gauntlet gloves and chaps (the seat-less over-trousers) took the beating of rope and sagebrush. His boots were a special consideration, arguably the most important and expensive facet of the outfit. By 1880 they had already evolved into what we would consider and recognize as today's cowboy boots: heels were high—about two inches, to prevent slipping in the stirrups—and sharply underslung to dig into the ground as a brace for holding roped cattle; arches were high and tight, and toes were pointed, which made getting into the stirrups easier and staying there less fatiguing. The upper part of the boot was cut straight just below the knee and made of tough leather to protect the leg from horse sweat, cactus needles, snakebite, flailing cow hooves, and a dozen other hazards of the range.

In fact, about the only modern element missing from those boots was a fancy design. By today's standards they were rather plain and simple. Exactly when fancy boots came in, and who was first responsible for introducing them, is difficult to say, but as far as I can tell, the general explanation is the same as for many another development of this kind: as necessity diminished, sport and entertainment began. With the advent of the railroad, the long drives became no longer necessary, and the riders of the Chisholm Trail passed into history and folklore and legend. But the decline of the long-drive cowboy marked the emergence of the drugstore variety. Beginning in the 1880s with Buck Taylor, the first "king of the cowboys," who worked with the Buffalo Bill troupe, and up through the early western films of William S. Hart, Bronco Billy Anderson, and Tom Mix, the "fancy" cowboy was born. He rode a handsome horse, wore ornate clothes, and later played a fancy guitar. In his world the only unadorned element was his moral code: he hated bad men and injustice and knew what to do when he found them.

Tom Mix started the idea of the good guy in the white hat and quickly carried it as far as he could by wearing an entire white outfit—a costume perhaps not conducive to rounding up cattle in open pasture. Not that his boots ever touched open pasture, of course: whether he was fighting desperados or winning the innocent heart of the local schoolmarm, he wore pristine handmade boots of supple leather or exotic skins, with swirls of colorful stitching and inlaid decorations; occasionally these designs were edged with costly silver studs or gems. While Mix can be credited with popularizing this image of the rhinestone cowboy, he was followed quicker than a Dodge City posse by a dozen other fancy-and-fast-shootin' white-hatted good guys who could draw their five-string Gibsons as neatly as their pearl-handled Colts. Roy Rogers and Gene Autry—to mention the two best known—were perhaps responsible for the most picturesque outfits American heroes have ever worn: crimson shirts with lavender yokes and cuffs; drainpipe striped trousers with edged pockets and badge-shaped loops; hand-tooled belts sporting engraved silver buckles; fancy silk bandanas, wide-brimmed hats with turquoise bands, and of course boots of the most intricate designs ever imagined. By comparison, contemporary celluloid space-invaders look like so many intergalactic shrinking violets.

Boots in dove gray and yellow, powder blue and orange, peacock and emerald green, all of the most ingenious design, were not uncommon during this halcyon period of the singing cowboy. Merely to stitch

a monogram was absolute child's play compared to the cherry-colored calfskin inlaid with white longhorn-steer heads; or the sleek black ostrich hide decorated with climbing scarlet roses; or the famous red, white, and blue "spread eagle" boots worn by Roy Rogers. In the late 1940s the Lucchese Boot Company of San Antonio made for display forty-eight pairs of cowboy boots, each pair depicting the particular state-house, flower, bird, and name of a state. This "state of the Union" series is considered the state of the art even today.

In quality and beauty, cowboy boots have rivaled but never sur-passed this high-water mark of the late 1940s, and by the 1950s a trend towards other styles of boots had begun, obliging these stalwart and all-American beauties to share the spotlight. With the advent of the enor-mous Harley-Davison motorcycle, and movie idols James Dean and Marlon Brando, motorcycle boots—with their thick soles, strapped insteps, and bulb toes all in macho-tough black leather—became the ideal accompaniment to tight jeans and multizippered black leather jackets. These boots were often decorated with shiny metal studs and cleats, and they became the first really "cool" footwear, even though they were originally designed for railroad workers and were known as "engineer boots." But we all knew they were cool even before we saw that famous interrogation scene in *Rebel Without a Cause*, when the chief detective snarls to James Dean, "Come on, boy, where's your boots?", characterizing the juvenile delinquent by his footwear.

But the motorcycle boot never made it to the next decade, and by the early 1960s there began an outbreak on college campuses across the country of what may conveniently be thought of as Frye fever: a passion for this high-topped prairie style, usually in natural tan leather, with a moderately high heel, thick sole, and small snub toe. In short, an unadorned, basic western boot for the eclectic generation, addition-ally typified by faded denim, work shirts, and granola. It was a boot that achieved a certain proletarian chic and was gradually accepted by those who couldn't go the whole way with cowboy boots.

By the 1970s boots had taken on a previously undreamed-of diversity of styles, due in part to our newfound passion for active sports and to some new achievements in technology. Everything from the classic, soft "desert boot" in tan suede and crepe sole to high-laced Maine guide boots, gentleman's chukkas in luxurious pigskin, and patent leather dress jodhpurs abounded. L.L. Bean, the backpacky New England retail firm, won a Coty Fashion Award for its rubber-and-leather "Maine Hunting Shoe", which, ironically, had been around for over half a century before it was discovered by the fashion world. Another Down East company, Timberland, entered the boot free-for-all, producing several top-quality work boots. Today this explosion continues unabated. New materials are being used in boot construction to provide maximum protection from wet and cold with less weight. Gore-Tex fabric is being used to make lightweight hiking boots, as is abrasion-resistant nylon, Vibram, and other space-age materials that are both warm and water resistant.

A Short Course in Buying Cowboy Boots

Contrary to the decline in quality of many items we buy, American boots by reputable manufacturers are still made the way they always have been. And unlike many another craft, there are apparently still enough good boot-makers and enough young apprentices around these days to keep business going strong. This also implies a steady demand, in the economic way of things, and despite the waxing and waning of styles over the decades, to say nothing of "urban cowboy" fads, Coty awards, and other fifteen-minute trends, there will apparently always be plenty of people around who enjoy wearing boots, whether because they find them to be the most functional working footwear or just fun to wear. Cowboy boots remain the *real* American footwear, and from the look of things, always will.

If you've decided that a pair of cowboy boots has a place in your wardrobe, there are several points to keep in mind. First, trust the name of the boot-maker. Ready-made boots by the "big five" Texas manufacturers (listed below) are built to meet high standards of quality and styling and are sold in a number of good shops around the country. Second, unless exotic skins are desired, the boots should be made entirely of leather, including both outer and inner soles. Third, most boot salespeople agree that boots should fit fairly snugly at the outset, since they will give a bit in the wearing. Fourth, one must consider the variety of styles to be found in toes, heels, and uppers. Boot toes are either pointed, square, or rounded—everything from the so-called "needle" toes, very pointed and narrow, to the very high and rounded "bulb"-fronted boot. Design here is as much a matter of comfort as fashion. Last year it seemed as though square toes were all the rage among boot-wearers; this year pointed toes seems to dominate the field. More important, however, is comfort: pick the style that best suits your feet and walking habits. Needle-toed boots were simply not designed for strenuous walking.

Heels vary from the simple low and flat "block" style customarily found on town shoes to the classic "stirrup" heel which, because of its two-inch underslung design, can produce a somewhat tottering gait for the wearer and is more at home in the saddle than the city street. The remaining important feature is the height of the boot. Fourteen-inch boots with a V-shaped collar (the ornamental top of the boot) are fashionable at the moment, in the drugstore-cowboy style of the 1930s, but if these are not to your liking, you should know that shorter models are manufactured. Normally the size of one's calf and lower leg determines the width and height of boot required.

All of these variations—and each is important—indicate that the best way to find the right boot is to try on several pairs and get the feel of them before buying. For this reason I am reluctant to recommend buying boots by mail order. It's much better to wait until you're near a shop that stocks a good variety for your inspection. Once you've invested in a good pair of boots, you'll want to take care of them so they'll look good and feel comfortable no matter what age. Several tips on boot care:

1. Keep boots polished. This is the single most important step in maintenance of leather footwear. Before wearing new boots, give them a coat or two of transparent paste wax. Brush and wipe boots after each wearing, apply wax sparingly, and avoid quick-drying liquid polishes because they contain alcohol which will ultimately dry out the leather.

2. Alternate wearing boots at least every other day, since they absorb perspiration and need a chance to dry out. Between wearings insert boot trees to help maintain shape, and use a boot jack to aid in remov-

ing boots. Never store any leather footwear near heat, and air boots overnight before returning them to the closet.

3. Be vigilant about heel and sole repairs. The longer you wait, the more costly the damage, and worn-down heels throw off the balance of the boot, causing the boots to stretch out of shape and tear at stress points.

There are approximately 250,000 sweat glands in a pair of human feet, producing half a pint of moisture a day. For leather footwear to remain supple and in good shape, these three activities—polish, rotate, repair—are essential parts of maintenance. If wet-weather resistance is desired, both waterproofing sprays containing silicone and waterproofing ointments like mink oil will do the job. Both tend to darken leather and are not recommended for lighter-colored leathers and suedes; additionally, silicone tends to clog the pores of leather and will eventually build up a layer if used regularly.

The Big Five Boot Manufacturers

The Justin Boot Company (Box 548, Fort Worth, TX 76101) has been around for almost a century and got a big boost when Tom Mix began ordering his fancy boots from them. They make a wide variety of styles to satisfy everyone from drugstore cowboy to rodeo rider.

Larry Mahan Boots (5814 Gateway East, El Paso, TX 79905) is a newcomer in the field; Mahan is not, per se, a bootmaker with a long tradition but rather a rodeo superstar who knows what a good boot should look and feel like. His boots are among the fanciest around and make what in today's jargon would be called a "fashion statement."

The Lucchese Boot Company (1226 E. Houston St., San Antonio, TX 78205) is considered by many to be the elite of the boot industry. Lucchese boots are known for high-quality leathers and elegance of design. While they make as fancy a boot as can be found anywhere, their specialty is the simple and graceful town boot that is favored with western businesswear.

The Nocona Boot Company (Box 599, Nocona, TX 76255) is a good traditional boot-making firm that manufactures everything from the classic needle-toed and underslung-heeled tough leather riding boot to fancy-stitched beauties in rainbow hues.

Tony Lama (1137 Tony Lama, El Paso, TX 79915) is probably the largest boot-maker of the five, with the most extensive range of both plain and fancy boots for the whole family. The firm has made quality boots for presidents and film stars, not to mention the complete Dallas Cowboys football team.

CUSTOM-MADE BOOTS

Texas Boot-Makers
>Charlie Dunn (222 College Avenue, Austin, TX 78704)
>Dixon Boots (925 Indiana Avenue, Wichita Falls, TX 76301)
>Henry Leopold (P.O. Box 401572, Garland, TX 75040)
>M.L. Leddy & Sons (14 South Chadbourne, San Angelo, TX 76901)
>Dave Little (110 Division, San Antonio, TX 78214)
>Rios Boot Company (P.O. Box 171, Raymondville, TX 78580)
>Paul Wheeler (4115 Willowbend, Houston, TX 77025)

Boot-Makers for Riding Boots
>E. Vogel (19 Howard Street, New York, NY 10013)
>Henry Maxwell & Co. (11 Savile Row, London W1, England)
>John Lobb (9 St. James's Street, London SW1, England)
>H. Kauffman & Sons (139 East 24th Street, New York, NY 10010)
>M. J. Knoud (716 Madison Avenue, New York, NY 10021)

CUSTOM-MADE
SHIRTS

"It's like a gourmet in a restaurant," muses Fred Calcagno. "The food's the important thing, not the ambience. Here it's the quality of the shirt that counts, not how the place looks. My customers want the best shirts they can buy, and that's what I try to give them. Cary Grant never bothers about how the place looks."

Nor, for that matter, have the likes of Aristotle Onassis, Laurance Rockefeller, designer Jay Specter, Yul Brynner, several dozen other film stars, highly visible politicians, or scores of board chairmen and corporate executives. Whether it's royal oxford cloth, Scottish-milled Viyella, or finest Japanese silk, Mr. Calcagno—who is the proprietor and master cutter at Pec & Company in Manhattan—does indeed give them the best shirts their money can buy. There are just two small rooms in this shop-workroom on the fifth floor of a very typical New York office building. The front room, with its blue walls and gray industrial carpeting, contains one full-length mirror and a long row of shelves against one wall, which hold the stock of cloth. The workroom in back has several tables, a few cabinets, and four sewing machines. All in all, the total area is about as large as a fair-sized living room.

Not to worry, though: you have indeed come to the right place. And if you are here for the first time, you may be in for another little shock. Plain cotton broadcloth shirts are at the moment going for about $130, silk at around $200—and Mr. Calcagno will expect you to take a minimum of six shirts for the first order; yet many consider the price quite reasonable, and not just men who have more money than they sensibly know what to do with, either.

It is quite possible to find good off-the-rack shirts. As far as workmanship and cloth go, a Brooks Brothers oxford button-down is a classic, and several other shops around the country sell very nice dress and sports models made here and abroad. There are a few designers who are always concerned for the quality of their products. Further, I know there are several reasons why a man might choose a ready-made shirt—or a ready-made anything, for that matter—over a custom-made one. Reasons that go beyond the price, because some designer shirts cost as much as custom-made ones. Buying a custom-made garment takes rather a long time compared to just whipping something off the shelf, because the work is painstakingly and precisely done by hand, and because fittings drawn out over several weeks or even months are necessary. Then too, one must ferret out a trustworthy craftsman, since the expense and time involved are so great, and since up to now most custom clothiers have not heavily advertised their services; they come by their clients by word of mouth, as their fathers before them did.

Finally, for some people—particularly those, psychologists tell us, lacking great confidence—designer clothing offers cachet to the degree that the garment can become but a foil for the label. The other side of this particular coin is that some men do not trust their own taste in clothes and are embarrassed to even think about selecting fabrics and discussing styling and fit with a shirtmaker or tailor. And these are real objections. It is easier to just pop into a shop and buy a shirt from the shelf on the way back to the office from lunch. Easier yet, if we want to take this line of thought a step farther, to get a wife or mother to do it for us. There are, to my mind, too many men who depend on their wives to do their clothes-shopping—salesmen tell me the number is considerable—and it puts me in mind of a line used by a comedienne I heard recently: "I've just gotten divorced," she said. "My marriage was childless—except for my husband."

A man wearing clothes made to his measure tends to look better and therefore feel better for it. Custom clothing is almost always better made, and since it fits better as well, the strains of wear are considerably fewer, and so the clothing may be expected to last longer. It is a maxim of those who buy quality goods that these are invariably less expensive in the long run.

"I can tell you that John Rockefeller certainly got his money's worth out of the shirts I made for him," chuckles Mr. Calcagno. "Every couple of years he'd bring in his old shirts to be reconditioned: I put on new collars and cuffs and whatever else had to be, patch a hole or something, and he'd get another five years out of them. Then back he'd come again with the shirts for the same treatment. That way he'd get fifteen or twenty years out of a shirt. I wouldn't say he was as close with his money as the original John D. Rockefeller, from what I hear, but he sure knew how to put it to best use."

Exactly. Then, too, the quality and workmanship found in custom-made clothing are appreciably higher than in factory-made garments. When considerations are made for the handwork involved, the real mother-of-pearl buttons (unlike the plastic or composite ones, you know, the kind the laundry finds so easy to pulverize), the first-quality fabrics, and the detailing, one begins to sense that off-the-shelf shirts—no matter whose name is on them—are not comparable. And then there is the most important matter: the matter of *fit*.

Since the shirt is the garment that sits closest the body, the problems of fit can be numerous and delicate: fellows with trim figures often complain of billowing shirt bodies that resemble galleon sails, while broad-shouldered men want more room across the yoke and chest. Sometimes a collar is too high in the nape and too low in the throat, the armhole too loose or the tail too long. Often a man is simply between customary collar sizes and, say, a 15 is too tight and a 15½ too loose. Factory-production can only accomplish so much, and while some of it is very accommodating indeed, shirts are produced from standard patterns for men with average figures. Problem is, as you well know, few men actually have average figures. And as they do with shoes that don't quite fit, some men just resign themselves to muddling through.

Even if your shoulders are the shape of a bottle, your neck like a barrel, or your knuckles scrape the ground when you walk, you are perfectly capable of being fitted. Each of these imperfections can be addressed and corrected by a competent shirtmaker. Good shirtmakers, I've found, combine the more attractive attributes of psychiatrists and sculptors and are geniuses at straightening a curved back, reducing a thickening waist, or lengthening a neck. I don't want to give the impression that these craftsmen function solely as the court of last resort for unusual physiques, or that they are somehow "orthopedic" shirtmakers. Many of Pec & Company's clientele, as with the other great shirtmakers, simply have their own ideas about how they want their shirts to look, fit, and feel and can't be satisfied in the shops.

Any shirtmaker worth his salt will have several hundred bolts of shirting on the premises all the time and will be able to show you swatches of hundreds more from which to select the perfect pattern and shade—everything from English Viyella and French voile to Italian gabardine, Swiss broadcloth, and Japanese silk. It is very much an exercise in individualism, and each customer tends to his own needs and desires. Some men are interested in nothing but the most proper and conservative white business shirt year in and year out, while others

are always interested to experiment and do something new and original: a colored collar on a white shirt, a uniquely designed cuff, or perhaps a conservatively cut dress shirt done in an exotic color.

"Onassis always ordered exactly the same thing," Mr. Calcagno informs me, "a white crepe de Chine dress shirt. As long as I can remember that's all he ever wore. He'd drop by to say hello, or sometimes just phone, and ask for half a dozen shirts. He never gave any other instructions, and I always knew exactly what he wanted. I never made any other kind or color of shirt for him."

Most customers, however, prefer a wider variety of shirtings and enjoy discussing the finer points of styling and detail with the shirtmaker: collar style (long point, English spread, tab, rounded club, button-down, short point, wing), cuff (French, convertible, square or rounded edge, with tab), chest pocket (how many, with flap-and-button closure), monogram (inside the collar band, lower left chest, on the pocket), placket buttons, squared tails, French seamed front, and any special requirements. These are the types of details the shirtmaker concerns himself with and is pleased to discuss and offer advice. He is the expert, and while his taste may not coincide with yours, it is both a pleasure and an education to talk with him.

Once the fabric and styling requirements are settled, the shirtmaker will methodically take about a dozen measurements, exact to within an eighth of an inch, noting the width and curve of the back and chest, waist, and seat, circumference and slope of neck, and length of each arm to the wristbone. From this set of calculations, a paper pattern is struck, registering the necessary configurations of the body. The pattern is kept as a permanent record, which nicely eliminates the necessity for remeasurement each time a new order is placed.

"One fellow I make shirts for," says Mr. Calcagno, "simply hates to shop, so every now and then he just phones up and tells me to send him some shirts like the last ones—only maybe blue. I ask him if his weight has changed any since the last batch I sent, make the adjustments, and mail them on to him. He's one of my best customers, and you know, I haven't laid eyes on him for over ten years now. One day I suppose he may stop by, but he's perfectly happy to have his shirts sent out to him."

The new customer will be asked to return to the shop in two or three weeks for the all-important first fitting, by which time a special try-on model will have been constructed from the paper pattern. This model will at that time be adjusted on the customer until both he and the shirtmaker are satisfied that the fit is everything it should be. This is the most crucial stage because the adjusted model will be the prototype from which the order of shirts, and all subsequent orders, will be made. That is why the shirtmaker will insist that the first order be for not less than from three to half a dozen shirts—it is simply a tremendous amount of work the first time around. After that, the number of shirts ordered is not a consideration. Every good shirtmaker has several customers who order dozens a year and many who order one every other year. It would not be unreasonable to suppose that the average customer orders two or three every year or so.

The shirts will be ready in about six weeks, a long wait perhaps but well worth it: each shirt has been hand-cut and pieced together, with about thirty single-needle stitches per inch, completely hand-sewn buttonholes, the world's best fabric, and real pearl buttons. It looks better, feels better, and will last longer. And one of the nicest, not to mention more economical, points is that when the collar and cuffs finally get a bit frayed, one simply sends the shirt back for new ones and general reconditioning and for a nominal cost has virtually a new shirt again—just like Rockefeller!

There are, finally, two snags in all this that must be mentioned. When I say "custom-made" I mean a shirt cut on a paper pattern that was made solely and exclusively from the customer's measurements. It is *your* pattern and no one else's. There are a number of shirtmaking firms around—including the so-called "custom shirt" section in various men's stores and department stores—that produce what is generally known in the trade as a "semi-custom" shirt: measurements are taken, but an individual pattern is not constructed; rather a standard pattern is altered to reasonably reflect the customer's configurations and get reasonably close to a good fit. This method is certainly superior to simply buying a shirt ready-made, but it should not be confused with a true custom-made one and of course should not cost as much either. If there is any doubt whether the firm you are contemplating doing business with does semi-or full custom-made, ask if an individual pattern is made for each customer. If it is not, you will not be getting a full custom-made shirt.

The other snag is that there are shirtmakers and shirtmakers, and it is expensive to buy three shirts here and six shirts there until one hits upon a good craftsman. With that in mind, herewith are listed the premier custom shirtmakers, in scrupulously fair, alphabetic order.

Battistoni (via Condotti 57–61, Rome 00187)
Beale & Inman (131 New Bond Street, London W1)
Bowring, Arundel & Co. (31 Savile Row, London W1)
Charvet (8 Place Vendôme, Paris 75001)
Coles (33 Savile Row, London W1)
Arthur Gluck (37 West 57th Street, New York, N.Y. 10019)
Harvie & Hudson (77 & 97 Jermyn Street, London SW1)
Harves & Curtis (2 Burlington Gardens, London W1)
Hilditch & Key (73 Jermyn Street, London SW1)
New & Lingwood (53 Jermyn Street, London SW1)
Pec & Company (45 West 57th Street, New York, N.Y. 10019)
Poster (326 East 35th Street, New York, N.Y. 10016)
Seewalt & Bauman (565 Fifth Avenue, New York, N.Y. 10022)
Truzzi (Corso Matteotti 1, Milan 20121)
Turnbull & Asser (71–2 Jermyn Street, London SW1)

THE DOUBLE-
BREASTED SUIT

T here aren't really any rules to this sort of thing that I can
see. It's just a simple matter of good conservative dress." I
was sitting with Douglas Fairbanks, Jr., talking about double-breasted suits. I reckon if anybody wears a double-breasted suit
properly it's Douglas Fairbanks, Jr.; whether in films or fur coat ads,
he always seems to look just perfect, as he did that day: impeccably cut
navy pinstripes, fine broadcloth shirt with English spread collar, dark
blue and yellow rep tie, black tassled slip-ons, and—an absolute *coup
de maître,* I thought—an elegant maroon carnation in his buttonhole.

I had mentioned that I thought there were all sorts of misconcep-
tions about wearing double-breasted suits; you know, such as heavyweight men not looking good in them, or the only correct double-
breasted being a dark gray double-breasted, that sort of thing.

"No, I don't think you can make any rules about it," he reiterated.
"I certainly don't think dark gray is the only shade for a proper suit.
I've got light gray double-breasteds, navy chalk stripes—and I even like
those Prince of Wales checks. The only things that bothers me, really,
is to see an unbuttoned jacket. All that flapping about, with the tie and
shirt hanging out, I find rather sloppy. I've heard men say that they
unbutton their jackets for comfort, but I've always felt that if a jacket's

made properly it should be just as comfortable buttoned, don't you think so?"

Fan that I am, and knowing full well that Mr. Fairbanks has been on the international best-dressed list so many times he was finally elected a permanent member, who was I to dispute—especially since I so entirely agreed?

Did he, I wondered aloud, approve of double-breasted dinner jackets?

"Oh, very much. Yes, in different weights for different climates, with either satin or grosgrain lapels, I should think. Very smart. It was the Prince of Wales and his brother, the Duke of Kent, you know, who started that fashion back in the 1920s. Instead of the stuffed-sausage appearance of wing collar, starched shirt front, and heavy waistcoated single-breasted dinner jackets, they wore soft shirts with turndown collars and double-breasted dinner jackets without waistcoats. It was accepted by the younger crowd immediately, and then by everyone else. With good reason too, because it maintained the elegance of formal dress, but was much more comfortable."

Double-breasted jackets, not to mention waistcoats, have in fact been with us for a long time. The modern suit as we know it developed in England and on the continent in the latter half of the seventeenth century, when doublet, breeches, and hose were gradually replaced by coat, vest, and trousers. By the end of the eighteenth century, double-breasted jackets and vests were already commonplace, as any number of portraits by Raeburn, Reynolds, Gainsborough, and others clearly show. It appears that the jacket always buttoned left flap over right so that the hilt of a sword would not catch on it when drawn.

Over the last quarter of that century in particular, gentlemen's dress was evolving along less formal and more comfortable lines as the landed gentry turned increasingly away from the stiffness, heaviness, and gaudiness of court clothes to the greater simplicity of country dress. The English riding coat became the prototype for correct day wear, the front of the coat cut sharply across at the waist, the square line balanced nicely by a double-breasted fastening, collar, and lapels. By the turn of the nineteenth century, this style of jacket was institutionalized by the great arbiter elegantiae of English society, Beau Brummell, and given royal imprimatur by the Prince Regent. In slightly modified form, it has been with us ever since.

The allure of the double-breasted jacket is that it has always had an unaccountable dash and romantic aura about it. It possesses an undeniable jauntiness, which is the reason dandies have always favored it. Victoria's consort, Prince Albert, gave his interest and his name to a version: a short-waisted, double-breasted frock coat that he was particularly fond of wearing (although it must be admitted that Albert, clothes-horse that he was, was fond of wearing everything from bright tweed knickers to suits of armor). And the Edwardian dandies—Max Beerbohm, Oscar Wilde, and of course Edward VII himself—were addicted to their double-breasted velvet smoking jackets, broadcloth morning suits, worsted barathea frock coats, and even boldly checked double-breasted tweed lounge suits—often worn with matching tweed spats and golf cap.

However, the great age of the double-breasted suit did not arrive until the 1930s, when the sartorially resplendent likes of the then Prince of Wales, Louis Mountbatten, Fred Astaire, Douglas Fairbanks, Cary Grant, and Jimmy Walker took it as their uniform. Whether in sporty brown glenurquhart plaid, chalk-striped oxford-gray flannel, or the dressier navy worsted, the double-breasted suit with its long-roll, low-buttoned peak lapels, full shoulder and chest, and bladed back made every man an elegant boulevardier. The English-cut double-breasted "blade" suit, perhaps better than any other masculine garment, defined the years between the wars.

Actually, the great success of this style, called in the States a "drape" cut jacket, owed much to one man—a Dutch tailor named Scholte. He had come to London just after the turn of the century and apprenticed himself to a tailoring firm—which is still in business today, called Anderson & Sheppard—in Savile Row. He rose in the ranks through diligence and skill, eventually becoming managing director and acquiring a glittering clientele along the way. He also became the official tailor for the officers of the Brigade of Guards, and one day Scholte's genius led him to understand why the Guards looked so masculinely elegant in their dress: the large chest of their greatcoats was accentuated by the tight fastening of their belts! The overriding effect was to give muscles to their appearance. Scholte began to experiment and finally hit upon a way to cut a jacket with a superfluous amount of cloth at the sleeve head (where the sleeve meets the shoulder) while at the same time indenting the waist, so that the back and chest of the jacket had both the fullness of the Guards coat and a suppressed waistline even without a belt. The result was the silhouette of a wide-shouldered man, muscular and with a trim waist: very flattering and perfectly suited to a double-breasted jacket, because the voluminous cloth in the waist and skirt could be reduced and balanced with a full chest and shoulder.

This "English blade suit," as it is properly called, with its broad shoulders, deep chest, and full blade back (which is why it's called a blade suit, because of the fullness over the shoulder blades), is the perfect medium for double-breasted styling because it accentuates the waist and allows for a longer lapel. A straight-cut double-breasted tends to look boxy, the over-flap merely superfluous rather than a point of style. Unfortunately, as often happens, in the perfection of a style are found the seeds of its own destruction. The superficial charms of the blade suit could be achieved easily enough by exaggeration, and soon virtual caricatures began to appear, in which the effect was produced not by subtle cutting but by simply indenting the waist and using shoulder padding vaguely comparable to that worn by defensive tackles on the Green Bay Packers. This became the all-too-familiar bastardized Hollywood version of a classic, worn particularly by cinematic heroes to further project their he-man images.

Coming along during the Depression as it did, the blade suit, according to the February, 1934 edition of *Esquire*, was "the way to dress if you are so sure of yourself under the New Deal that you are unafraid of offering a striking similarity to a socialist cartoonist's conception of a capitalist. Since a good appearance is about all that is left to the capitalist anyway, why not go ahead and enjoy it?" Which is exactly what much of the male population did, capitalist and otherwise, until World War II, when uniforms and fabric quotas took them away from the double-breasted blade suit. The style hung on for a bit through the Truman and Eisenhower administrations, but John Kennedy ushered in a hatless, single-breasted, natural-shouldered era, an era of conspicuous understatement and narrow lapels—known alternately as the Ivy League, Brooks Brothers, or Madison Avenue look.

Now, I don't want to attribute more to this trend than a true scientific spirit ought to allow, and I certainly don't intend to make any socio-political connections here (as, for example, the media does with short skirts and that sort of thing), but I have noticed an increasing number of double-breasteds on the streets and in the shops these past several seasons. Not the 1930s blade model of course, which I suppose these days reminds people of nothing more than an old Alan Ladd film or two, but a slimmer-bodied version, more in keeping actually with today's leaner torsos and athletic life-styles. For example, sauntering along Madison Avenue this past fall, I was absolutely astonished to see a navy worsted double-breasted, of all things, in the window of Brooks Brothers, of all places—in the very temple of the single-breasted, natural-shoulder look! Brooks Brothers has not stocked double-breasted suits since the early 1950s. Quite naturally I rushed in to inquire about this earthshaking situation—these are the kinds of things that make my day. It seems that Brooks was aware that they had been attracting more and more international businessmen, who favor a more shaped silhouette as well as double-breasted styling. Not that Brooks is now bullish on double-breasteds, you understand; they've never accounted for more than three or four percent of suit sales, but if that firm sees a market for double-breasted suits, there must be something to it.

Much of the renewed interest in double-breasteds is, I can't help but feel, because of a renewed interest in formality. Ronald Reagan, even though he wears jeans as Jimmy Carter has, is a more elegant dresser, and whether his administration is the cause or the result of a more conservative, formal tone is irrelevant: it is strong indication and symbol of that tone. Whether it be seen in the increasing number of etiquette books being published or the greater number of tuxedos being sold, there is unquestionably an interest in formality and elegance, propriety and manners; and this, coupled with a more international outlook, has produced more receptivity to the double-breasted suit. In Europe, particularly in Italy and France, approximately 40 percent of all suits sold are double-breasted.

When it comes to wearing a double-breasted suit, there is a myth that I should like to lay to rest, concerning who should and who shouldn't wear the style. There is the false conception that a short, stocky man or an overweight man should not wear a double-breasted jacket; the idea is nonsense. Actually, it's just the opposite, because it is the single-breasted jacket that is always slightly open at the bottom and tends

to reveal a stomach bulge, whereas the double-breasted one, because it is cut straight across the front and overlaps, covers and conceals.

The overlap of material across the front of the double-breasted jacket does, however, have at least potential disadvantages as well. The outer lapel is so obvious as it extends across the chest, so naturaly the focal point of the jacket, that it must be cut well and perfectly balanced. In a poorly made jacket this lapel tends to be stiff, wrinkled, too high or too low, or—we shudder—constructed with a notched rather than a peak lapel. On a well-made jacket the lapel should be soft but wrinkle-free and button easily without tugging or pulling. A good rule of thumb is that the bottom button should not be placed more than an inch below the top of the jacket side pockets. The amount of overlap depends finally on the size of the torso it overlaps, but the average overlap on a size 40R would ideally be about six inches.

The double-breasted jacket should never be worn unbuttoned, since those extra inches of material flapping around are not only unsightly in themselves if allowed to wave around like semaphore flags but will throw off the line of the jacket entirely. This extra material also accounts for double-breasted jackets' being generally cut a bit shorter than single-breasted ones. Long double-breasted jackets can make a man look as if he's been rolled up in a bolt of cloth.

Jacket vents are usually a matter of personal taste or fashion, but the classic double-breasted suit jacket seems to favor either the ventless back or side vents of a moderate depth (the vents should reach no higher than the top of the side pockets); a center vent, while appropriate enough on single-breasted jackets, tends to throw off the symmetry here. Symmetry also calls for a buttonhole in *each* lapel, even though only the left one is ever used for a boutonniere. Finally, double-breasted suits rarely include a vest; in fact, they've really not done so since the 1920s. It seems like both a wretched excess of material as well as a surfeit of buttons (jacket and vest would add up to a dozen buttons strewn across the chest).

But these fine points have nothing to do with the inhibitory myth than men with certain physiques should not wear double-breasted jackets. The word "inhibitory" does, however, bring to mind one other piece of business that must bear some slight consideration. There are some Freudian theories about tightly buttoned clothing, excessive neatness, and concern for posture perhaps indicating a striving for control and denial of sensuality—in short, a repressed personality. There *are*, after all, more buttons on a double-breasted jacket and more fabric with which to encase the body. This much is true.

Now, I don't want the rising tide of enthusiasm for the style to recede just because of an unnecessarily gloomy theory, and as we all know, there is a Freudian explanation for everything, isn't there? And yet, I do remember reading in the New York newspapers—I have the clipping before me at the moment to refresh my memory—of a rather bizarre criminal case in the late 1950s. Someone was going around blowing up things and the police were getting nowhere at catching him, and so they called in a psychiatrist to construct a psychological profile of this "mad bomber," as he was dubbed by the press. After studying letters written by the bomber to the police, the psychiatrist theorized that the criminal was an Eastern European male in his 40s, that he lived with a female relative other than his wife, and that he hated his father but loved his mother. Oh, yes, and when the man was found, the psychiatrist further stated, he would probably be wearing a double-breasted suit—buttoned!

This all sounds very Sherlock Holmes, but nonetheless, and to move quickly to the denouement of this classic little tale of crime and detection, when the police finally tracked down and captured George Metesky, he was indeed wearing a double-breasted suit. Unfortunately, to my knowledge, reporters never pressed the psychiatrist for a complete explanation (although it apparently had something to do with the man's being a paranoiac with meticulous personal habits), so I cannot go into more detail except to mention that just as the doctor had also predicted, the double-breasted jacket was in fact buttoned meticulously.

EVENING WEAR

T he simple fact is that formalism and conservatism are perforce conjoined, so whether the political mood of the country
initiates, capitalizes on, or merely follows in the wake of
the more formal style that has been emerging for the past several years—
in fashion and home decorating it is referred to as The New Elegance
(with capital letters)—is a moot point. What politics and economics
do indicate is that there is a more conservative mood about, and this
is reflected in the style of daily living. Consider all the etiquette books
that have been published this past year or two—several on the best-
seller list and the authors appearing on the Donahue show—with their
emphasis on good, old-fashioned manners. Or the recent statistics that
indicate that marriage is once again fashionable and on the increase
(and seen on another Donahue show). And not only marriage, but
formal weddings as well! Formal weddings, for those of you who grew
up during the benighted 1960s, are ones where the bride wears a long
white dress of lace and satin, and the bride groom wears a tuxedo or
tailcoat.

Even in the art world, Modernism, with Mies van der Rohe's battle
cry that "less is more," seems to be in fast retreat if we consider the
success and showy exuberance of recent museum exhibits that abso-

lutely revel in the splendor and sentiment of the Grand Style (the Second Empire, Belle Epoch, and Landseer exhibits were all judged to be triumps by critics and crowds alike). Historians and laymen have lately taken a decided interest in the Victorian and Edwardian periods—everything from scholarly biographies of eminent persons to PBS series—and many people obviously enjoy a vicarious peek at restrained elegance, taste, and quality, in a world in which everything is now made fast and plastic. The Edwardians, it's often said, knew how to entertain—even if they did always over-eat and occasionally over-dress.

But the really telltale evidence that formalism is asserting itself in daily life is seen in the retail market, all those ads in the papers placed by tuxedo rental firms, whose premises are now bulging with natty cutaways, strollers, and Edwardian evening suits with plush velvet collars. Formal-wear manufacturers are ecstatic, and retailers across the country, it is safe to say, all but salivate when a customer asks for "something in a tuxedo with a kind of Edwardian feeling," especially when heretofore chaps were tending towards the "personal" wedding ceremony, you know, the one in which the minister intoned a favorite poem and the bride and bridegroom wore matching fatigue jackets. Very dampening for the clothing industry those days were. But for the past several seasons sales have been little short of wild, with some retailers reporting sales increases of 50 percent. Well, we don't need all these statistics to make the point: formality and elegance are again in fashion after that almost twenty-year hiatus of *nostalgie de la boue*. Whether it's a special *à deux* evening at home, a theater party, or a Grand Bal à la Versailles, black and white ties are once again appropriate evening garb. The interesting irony of formal attire is that almost without exception, every aspect of the masculine evening costume derives from the sport of horseback riding. Perhaps I should explain.

To begin at the top, the top hat's high crowned elegance didn't appear until the end of the eighteenth century, designed by the English riding gentry as a kind of crash helmet to be worn while in pursuit of the fox—as in fact it is still used to this day, an obvious anachronism since there are more safely designed helmets available. Since the same gentry were perfectly accustomed to wearing their country clothes to town (and even to court, if it came to that, which distinguished them from their various continental cousins), the top hat was soon not an

unusual sight in Bond Street and other fashionable Regency thorough-fares. Beau Brummell and the rest of the London bucks and dandies established this silky topper as *the* hat for swaggering sophistication, and soon all the beau monde at White's Club and Almack's, at Brighton and Bath, gambling at Crockford's or dancing at the Chinese Platform in the Cremorne Pleasure Gardens, had accepted it.

The top hat had gone in less than half a century from sporting attire to normal street dress and was finally consigned to evening dress. As the century moved on, it was replaced first by the bowler, then the homburg and fedora. By World War I the top hat and its collapsible twin the opera hat (also called a "gibus" after the Frenchman who invented it to take up less space in cloakrooms) were relegated to occasions of utmost formality. Utmost formality in this case means an occasion dictating a long coat (actually the academic gown is considered the most formal attire one can wear, but never mind that), either a morning coat or a tailcoat. The name "tailcoat" is something of a confusion here because both a morning coat and a tailcoat have tails. The morning coat, virtually extinct today, is actually a "swallow-tail coat," that is, its tails are formed by a gentle sweep of the bottom of the coat (called a skirt), curving away from the front and falling behind, in appearance rather like a swallow's tail-feathers. There is no definite break at the waist.

The tailcoat, however, is cut sharply at the waist, straight across the front, so the tails proper only fall from the back of the coat—the tail-coat does not even button at the front, as a morning coat does. Both coats, however, derive from the same prototype garment: the English riding coat of the eighteenth century. In the preceding century outer-coats were generally tapered from chest to waist but swept out full in the skirt. Over the years this volume of cloth below the waist of the coat was gradually reduced, particularly in the front of the garment—there was little need for all that cloth draping over the front of the saddle—and eventually completely cut away, leaving little more than the back of the coat divided by a deep vent into two tails. Even these tails were found to be cumbersome in the saddle and some ingenious tailor contrived a method to solve that: he sewed two buttons to the small of the back of the coat and put buttonholes at the end of the tails: voilà! the tails could be folded up and buttoned to the back of the coat when in the saddle. Those two buttons can still be seen on the back of every tailcoat, where as merely vestigial decorations, they serve no real function as they once did.

In evening trousers we likewise see the vestigial traces of their historical use in the strip of satin running down the outside leg seam. Originally this decorative stripe was used to cover a row of buttons that were needed with trousers cut tightly enough to stuff into riding boots of molded sleekness. The only aspect of our evening wear that is not strictly associated with riding is the penguin coloration, although it is historically a distinguishing mark of the fox-hunting aristocracy. White shirt and necktie have always been the true sartorial sign of a gentleman—or at least of someone who could be counted on to afford clean linen. The idea of a black suit for both day and evening wear probably developed as a business uniform as the Industrial Revolution and the growth of cities prompted a more homogeneous society—some say anonymous—in a Victorian world in which the idea of a gentleman triumphed over the outmoded idea of a courtier. Somberness was, in short, preferred to ostentation by those, it has been remarked, who wanted to appear as grave and serious as the banks and factories they owned. As a young man in the early years of the nineteenth century, the brilliant and elegant Disraeli would saunter about town wearing bottle-green velvet trousers, canary-colored waistcoats, and buckled shoes. But after mid-century he dressed in a black broadcloth suit as befitted the leader of the Conservative Party of the House of Commons and the age.

The preeminent formal costume today is the tuxedo (called in Britain a dinner jacket and in France a *smoking* jacket—and all three names point to its origins). It is the product of the Edwardian country house set and was in its inception a considerably more casual outfit than it is now. The dinner jacket is not, as some have thought, merely a tailcoat with the tails missing (so you can forget all those stories about Lord So-and-so standing with his back to the fireplace and suddenly being aware of the smell of burning worsted). It derives rather from a version of the Victorian "lounging jacket," a short coat developed about 1870 as a sporting jacket to replace the ordinary day frock coat. The lounge jacket was worn for riding, bicycling, fishing, rowing, and other outdoor events and is for all intents, purposes, and designs the virtually identical predecessor to the modern sports jacket. We tend to forget that the sports jacket was originally just that: a jacket worn while engaged in sport. Today this function is fulfilled by a variety of other outdoor coats (the parka, field coat, golf blouson, and ranch jacket come to mind).

As it is the rule in masculine attire that styles emanate from either sporting costume or military garments, first being accepted for day wear and finally evening clothes, by 1880 gentlemen had begun toning up their sports jackets to wear in the evening around their country estates. Daytime jackets were made up in bright tweeds and for the evening opulent shades of cut velvet with satin lapels; some were padded and had silk braided belts and cuffs. The tailcoat was still considered the only appropriate coat to wear in the evening if ladies were present, but the "dress lounge," as the dinner jacket first came to be called, was thought to be an informal alternative to wear at one's club, or as a smoking jacket in the country house billiard room when the fellows passed the port and cigars around. After World War I all these Victorian social distinctions passed away, for better or worse, and practically everyone agreed that ladies were strong enough to see a gentleman at dinner in a short coat.

In this country the dinner jacket is called a tuxedo, for which the tobacco tycoon Griswold Lorillard is much responsible. On an exceptionally warm and humid evening in October, 1886, Mr. Lorillard created a spot of bother at the Autumn Ball of the Tuxedo Park Club—he had in fact been instrumental in making Tuxedo Park a fashionable commuting suburb of New York City—by daring to enter the ballroom in a short black worsted smoking jacket rather than the prescribed and customary tailcoat. It is recorded that many of the ladies were shocked, most of the gentlemen offended (or perhaps it was the other way round) by this blatant breech of propriety, and there was considerable jeering and scoffing. And then not a few of the male habitués, as is often the case with fashion, rushed out to order formal smoking jackets like Lorillard's from their own tailors. And so the Tuxedo Park Club members put a new word in the dictionary.

It may not be stretching the point to say that we appear to be on the threshold of a period rivaled only by the 1930s for distinguished wearables. A better period, in fact, because today there's more variety and much more comfort in formal attire. Elegance used to have absolutely no truck with comfort. Before the thirties a gentleman's dress kit consisted of an evening suit (whether a dinner jacket, tails, or both) of eighteen- to twenty-ounce wool serge or barathea; an evening shirt of heavy cotton, board-stiff with starch; a silk top hat or opera hat; a voluminous dress overcoat; and the various accessories and jewelry. It was an outfit that today we should find unbearably cumbersome, weighty, and stiff. It boggles the mind, nay the whole body, to understand how any but the stateliest dances could ever have been negotiated. It was a genre crying out for liberation.

In the late 1920s and early 1930s the then Prince of Wales (later the Duke of Windsor), among other sartorial luminaries, began to discard the more restricting elements of the formal wardrobe, liberating men from the stuffed-sausage look of their fathers and grandfathers. Dinner jackets came to replace tails almost entirely; lighter-weight fabrics— silks, tropical worsteds, and mohairs—came to take the place of the heavier cloths; waistcoats were abandoned; the top hat ceded to the fedora; and the stiff shirt with detached wing collar gave way to one with a soft, turned-down collar and unstarched bosom and cuffs. Double-breasted dinner jackets became very popular (a vest being unnecessary with them), and white was de rigueur for resort wear. By the mid-thirties gentlemen's evening dress had become, in two words, lighter and softer.

These standards held for the next thirty years or so, until the generation of the sixties put on its uniform of jeans and battle jacket, when fashionable attire consisted of having political slogans sewn on one's derriere or having one's ranch-hand denim jacket lined with ranch mink. It was a great age of prole gear, but except for leisure dress it is now past. At least for the moment formality is secure. And there have even been some new variations within the genre, so that today nostalgia, tradition, and the nouveau exist side by side in evening ensembles. And the key to dressing well is to find freedom within the rules. Anyone can be completely different, since it's easy to be outrageous. The trick is to be just that bit different.

When the invitation reads "white tie," full dress is the rule. Full dress comprises a silk-face ("facings" are the lapel coverings) black tailcoat, white pique dress waistcoat and matching bow tie, white pleated dress shirt with wing collar and French cuffs, dress trousers (always black), opera hat, white gloves and scarf and dark overcoat (in cold weather), black hose, black patent pumps (or plain black oxfords), pearl cuff links and studs (or other discreet jewelry), and a white or dark red carnation boutonniere. It used to be the rule that a wristwatch was never worn with tails, only a pocket watch. While that is still the preferred timepiece with full dress, the rule has been relaxed a bit of late, and a dress wristwatch is considered acceptable today by everyone save a few fanatics who would probably also prefer to arrive at the ball by horse-drawn phaeton.

When the invitation reads "black tie," what is traditionally referred to is a tuxedo, and that's about as formal as most of us ever get. A tuxedo is usually accompanied by a white dress shirt (pleated bosom, French cuffs) with turned-down collar, black bow tie and cummerbund, plain black oxfords, and black hose. It is the classic penguin look that has been standard for over a hundred years, but far from being thoroughly prescribed, black tie dressing affords many tasteful choices. For instance, there are several revived interests in this semi-formal area that can be highly recommended. The wing-collar dress shirt is again popular after a hiatus of almost forty years. In the 1930s Wales and his cronies boasted of having dispensed with the wing collar, but today it has become a bit of highly prized nostalgia—apart from its downright spruce appearance—and, combined with a thin, small grosgrain bow, conjures up sophisticated fantasies of Cole Porter evenings at El Morocco. A wing-collar dress shirt is properly made from superfine broadcloth or cotton voile with either small- or full-pleated bosom (large pleats for larger men).

The wing collar is worn with a single- or double-breasted dinner jacket—black for winter, black or white for summer—but a consonant harmony is achieved with a velvet smoking jacket. This semi-formal alternative to the tuxedo is something the Edwardian gentleman really understood. The smoking jackets of the 1880s were rich velvets of bottle green, crimson, or chestnut. Often quilted (to keep one warm in drafty country-house billiard rooms) and frogged, they combined sartorial dignity with comfort. Just as it was then, that sort of true classic must still be hand-built by a tailor. Simpler velvet jackets—with or without satin lapel facings—can be found ready-made in reputable shops. With such attire two basic rules apply: 1. Keep the rest of the outfit simple and 2. a smoking jacket's proper place is in the semi-formal private party spectrum, not the formal public event.

For a full-fig night on the town, an elegant dinner jacket is needed. Anyone who wears a tuxedo more than twice a year is better off having his own: it will fit better, and it's cheaper in the long run if one has bought wisely. In buying an evening suit the best bet is a single-breasted, conservatively cut version in black tropical-weight wool, with either a silk-faced shawl collar or peaked lapels. This will see a gentleman smartly through every black tie affair, winter or summer, at home or abroad. Its propriety is unimpeachable. Next there is the double-breasted dinner jacket, perhaps the most self-assured of evening jackets. In its youth it was cut from stoutly opulent barathea and had heavy ribbed silk facings. It was worn by the likes of Noel Coward, Cary Grant, and Fred Astaire. Today one would want a lighter-weight version in tropical worsted, or for midsummer grandeur, classically cut white gabardine with white satin facings (and as with good white flannel, proper white gabardine has a cream cast to it, rather than being dead white).

For autumn, or for something just that bit different to wear to the annual Christmas bash at the club, there's the wool tartan or paisley dinner jacket. There are literally hundreds of different tartans, from the festively bright red and yellow of the Macmillan clan to the more somberly elegant dark blue and green hues of the Black Watch pattern. It would be nice to wear a tartan with which there is some personal association, but there's certainly nothing wrong with selecting a pattern of one's fancy. It is, however, considered bad form to wear the royal tartans (the Royal Stewart and the Balmoral patterns), as those are reserved for the sole use of the British royal family. Paisley patterns, usually printed on challis (a soft, lightweight woolen cloth), and other small printed motifs—such as sporting designs—make for elegant alternatives to the black dinner jacket, particularly in a country setting. As with the smoking jacket, the rest of the outfit should be kept to the unadorned basics: black dress trousers, white dress shirt, black bow tie, and optional cummerbund.

The cummerbund is not really an essential part of the dress wardrobe today; in fact, it seems to have disappeared during the last two decades (because of the vogue for self-supporting trousers, which also explains the demise of suspenders). But both suspenders and the cummerbund are once again the latest word, and a good thing too, as both increase the opportunity for variety and individualism and thus give an added dimension to evening wear. The cummerbund helps to tuck in the stomach and provides an alternative to the dress waistcoat. Suspenders are often more comfortable than a self-supporting waistband and are better at keeping the trousers from slipping down. Tradition deems that the cummerbund should be black—the exception being for summer wear with a white dinner jacket, in which case a lighter fabric such as madras is acceptable, always with a matching bow tie. It is

always worn with the pleats facing up, from a time long since past when there were no pockets in dress trousers and gentlemen tucked their theater tickets in the folds of their cummerbunds. Classic full-dress suspenders are white silk with white kidskin tabs; black-tie dress customarily calls for black suspenders with black tabs. Some men are sufficiently confident to sport bright red, yellow, or polka dot suspenders with a tuxedo but such unassailable assurance is to snatch a grace beyond the reach of both art and correctness.

A dress shirt is always white, the bosom is always pleated, the collar is always a simple turned-down straight point or a wing collar, the cuffs are always French. (There was a short-lived vogue for a few years for button-down collars, and while this is not considered entirely inappropriate, neither is it to be generally recommended). Dress shirting is either fine broadcloth or voile, although a smooth, lightweight silk is also acceptable.

With a tuxedo one usually wears a black silk bow tie: a small, straight one with a wing-collared shirt and a slightly larger one with a turned-down collar. The butterfly bow, larger still and slightly floppy, may be on the return, but this model should be chosen with extreme caution, because a large, floppy bow tends to make a man of slight build resemble a bad parody of a Left Bank bohemian. There is also a vogue of sorts for colored bows—red, green, even pink and yellow—and polka dots, which strike a Victorian tone, especially if worn with a wing collar. Regardless of the style, I think an untied bow is preferable to a pre-tied one, only because the pre-tied ones usually look too perfectly tied; it is, however, better to look too perfect than too sloppy, so if you can't manage to tie your own, better get the pre-tied one.

Dress at-home evening wear has declined somewhat over the years and is today almost in the lost art category. Too many men who take particular pains to be well-dressed at the office are completely at sea when it comes to at-home entertaining. As formal sit-down dinners are once again fashionable, this becomes something of a timely and special problem. Many an otherwise confident fellow has frustratingly reached, in a last-minute, bone-shaking panic, for his old standby: the navy blazer. Not that there is anything wrong with the blazer approach to dressy at-home attire. With a pair of light-toned flannels or tropicals, and perhaps a discreet ascot, the navy blazer constitutes comfortable and informal party gear. But it certainly isn't the be-all and end-all of outfits for home entertaining. There is the smoking jacket, already mentioned, for one. And because it is your home, after all, wear it in as bright a shade as you fancy: cherry or peacock or burnt yellow. A short dressing gown is another good option, in merino wool, cashmere, silk brocade, or velvet, preferably with satin shawl collar and cuffs and tasseled sash. Fancy smoking jackets and dressing gowns are usually worn with black evening trousers or lightweight gray flannels,

a dress shirt, and either a bow tie or ascot.

Another alternative that has recently come round again is the short-waisted dinner jacket, called a "mess jacket" because it was originally worn in the British officers' mess. It is a remarkably smart-looking jacket, but unfortunately is not for everyone. Resembling a tailcoat cut off at the waist, it requires a svelte silhouette indeed to carry it off properly. If you are trim enough for its waist-emphasizing elegance, the mess jacket is definitely worth considering and looks especially natty done in white duck or linen for summer formality.

At the bottom of the evening outfit is the proper shoe. Gentlemen's footwear has changed relatively little over the past century, and apart from abandoning spats and gaiters, evening footwear has remained the same as it was in, say, 1910. Some men of course will press into service any dark pair of business shoes found in the closet, which is about as appropriate as wearing any old shoes to play tennis or attend a business conference. Evening footwear is characterized by being lightweight, black, and unadorned. Which means that black calf Gucci-type moccasins (minus the hardware) and highly polished plain black oxfords are totally appropriate; wing tips, tan brogues, and cordovan penny loafers are not. Although the elastic-gorged dress boot (sometimes known as a "romeo" boot) of the 1920s, the patent-leather monk strap of the 1930s, and the duck-billed dress oxford of the 1940s are now only sparingly with us, the classic formal footwear holds its ground. The Regency pump has endured with considerable panache in both patent leather and faille silk, as has the Victorian slipper, customarily done in black velvet (but also seen in navy, green, and plum). The plain-toed oxford, in either patent or calf leather, will never go out of style—unlike the patent demi-boot or the polished calf balmoral, the former of which is not popular at the moment, while the latter appears to be.

Now to perhaps the most overlooked accessory to formal attire: the boutonniere. While all sorts of flowers are acceptable for lapel wear during the day, in the evening tradition prescribes only four flowers: the blue cornflower, the coral or red carnation, and the white gardenia. In Victorian times a double loop of thread sewn onto the underside of the left lapel held a tiny vial of water in which the stem was placed to nourish the flower, and although this practice disappeared before the turn of the century, even today a well-made dinner jacket (or any suit or sports jacket, for that matter) will have a single loop on the lapel's underside to hold the stem of the flower in place. Real style dies hard.

A Note On Decorations

Full decorations—medals, orders, and miniatures—may be worn automatically with white tie at any public event calling for that dress. Decorations are worn on the left lapel of the tailcoat, with the highest ranking decoration placed on the upper right-hand side just below the buttonhole; other decorations are placed in descending order to the left and may be slightly overlapped. If a second row is needed, it would begin directly below the first row, following right to left, again in descending rank.

The exceptions are the Medal of Honor and the Medal of Freedom, which are worn around the neck suspended from a ribbon.

With other dress (other than military uniform, that is) only the single decoration most suitable and proper to the particular ceremonial occasion is usually worn, rather than full decorations.

At a private party, the host should determine and decide whether the nature of the occasion makes it appropriate for decorations to be worn and then issue instructions on the invitation cards. Decorations are never worn to private functions unless the invitation reads "white tie and decorations." And a boutonniere is never worn with decorations.

HARRIS TWEED

T here is the mistaken belief (particularly in the States) that the cloth we call "tweed" takes its name from the river Tweed, which rises in southern Scotland and flows a hundred miles northeast to the North Sea, forming a part of the Scottish-English border. In fact, the word tweed, referring to the cloth, owes its origin to the illegible script of a clerk in a woolens house.

For centuries woolen cloth (and all woolens are called cloth, not fabric) has been woven in the highlands and islands of Scotland. The natives were wearing woolen garments when Julius Caesar's legions arrived in Britain in 55 B.C., and there is written evidence of cloth production there since the fourteenth century. This coarse, heavy cloth that the Scots pronounced and wrote as "tweel"—what we now pronounce and write as "twill"—was produced solely for the home market until the early years of the nineteenth century, when London tailors began to advocate its use in sporting attire. They had actually taken the cue from some of their customers, gentry who vacationed in the north to fish and hunt and who noticed that their Scottish field guides kept wonderfully warm in outfits of homespun woolens. And so London tailors and cloth merchants began placing orders with Scottish firms to secure homespun twill for their customers.

In 1840 some bolts of this "tweel" were involved in a rush order from a Hawick woolens firm named Watson's to James Locke, a cloth merchant in London, and the clerk quickly scribbled out the order. In London the illegibly written invoice for "tweel" was misread as "tweed." And thus is has stood.

Scottish cloth first became popular in England after George IV visited the highlands in 1822. He was the first British monarch to have done so since Charles II— the memories of Culloden lasted long on both sides of the border. One commemoration of this visit was a handsome painting of the king in full highland dress, done by the Scottish portraitist Sir David Wilkie; the portrait hangs today in the stately Waterloo Chamber at Windsor Castle.

After George's death England seems to have sunk into masculine sartorial gloom, only to be rescued two decades or so down the road by Queen Victoria's consort, Prince Albert. Albert had a good figure for clothes, at least early in his life, and took quite an interest in them. Both he and Victoria were also both enamored of the highlands after their first visit to Balmoral in 1842. Albert designed a family tartan— the beautiful gray and russet Balmoral tartan, which unfortunately is reserved for the sole use of the royal family—and took to wearing tweed trousers with his frock coats for day wear. His eldest son (Eward VII) confirmed the royal imprimatur on Scottish cloth by having his shooting suits made up in boldly checked tweed from bolts of the cloth he had received as a gift when he had visited the Outer Hebrides. And his son (George V) and grandson (Edward VIII, later Duke of Windsor) avidly followed the tweed tradition for country clothing.

The landed gentry were quite aware of the sensible yet colorful properties of tweed, and its hardy qualities were well appreciated after a day of shooting or riding about in a damp and cold clime, but tweed was also championed in the nineteenth century by the various members of the so-called Aesthetic Movement, those poets and painters who were in revolt against the stuffy qualities of Victorian art. Both the Decadents (Oscar Wilde, Beerbohm, Beardsley, Whistler, among others) and the Pre-Raphaelites (Dante Gabriel Rossetti, Edward Burne-Jones, John Ruskin, and William Morris) attacked the somber and restricting style of dress that had evolved since Victoria had come to the throne. There was an effort to introduce a softer, more natural line and color scheme into the fashions of both men and women. Corsets and frock-coats were equally denounced (Wilde quipped that the thought of a bronze frock-coated statue of oneself added a new horror to death) as rigid, artless, insipid, and unnatural. The advocates of this movement (of which George Bernard Shaw became such an early admirer) were seen to wear soft velvets and homespun tweeds in earthy hues. William Morris always dressed in a voluminous gray tweed cloak, soft felt hat, tweed suit, and handknitted woolen hose.

From these seemingly disparate fonts, Pre-Raphaelite poets and pleasure-loving gentry, tweeds filtered down, and by 1914, that great watershed year, tweeds had in fact become the accepted democratic costume and great social leveler of the age. Everyone wore tweeds. With the war's end came a tremendous relaxation of social convention that served to loosen the bond of attire for both sexes even more. The rise of sports and games among all classes, the erosion of the rules of Victorian class consciousness, and a decrease in poverty that allowed more people vacations and the opportunity for travel—each of these forces had its influence on dress. The tweed jacket and baggy flannels became a uniform for weekends, and some men eventually even took to wearing the outfit to the office on Fridays, for an early getaway. Tweed was established.

The most famous tweed, justifiably so, is Harris tweed. It is called Harris tweed because it is woven on Harris Island. Harris is one—actually half of one—of a cluster of islands off the western coast of Scotland. Men have eked out their existence on these barren rocks in the rough North Atlantic, in the Celtic twilight, for centuries, sepa-rated from mainland Scotland by some forty miles of turbulent water known as The Minch. There are five main islands here—Barra, South Uist, Benbecula, North Uist, and Lewis-Harris—which form the group known as the Outer Hebrides, a total land area of 716,000 acres, few roads, and fewer towns. Stornoway, the largest town, has a population of about 5,000. And even from the steps of Stornoway's city hall one can gaze up to the surrounding hills and see sheep grazing freely.

It is a rugged land, and much of it is barren rock, hard and implac-able Archean gneiss to bruise the heel. Altogether it is not a place particularly favorable to man. And since the eighteenth century many of the islanders have looked towards the sea for the basis of their economy, first for the fish—until just recently, when it began to be fished out, The Minch was perhaps the richest herring pond in the world—and now for the oil. Oil derrick flotels now dot the horizon, and no one here doubts that this newfound wealth will bring changes. Some think the changes will be drastic and are glad for them. Those who are not glad for drastic changes make Harris tweed.

In most townships in the Outer Hebrides more than half of the families own a foot-powered loom for the weaving of tweed cloth. This tweed was first woven in any quantity on the largest island, named "Lewis with Harris," and by the mid-nineteenth century a well-known industry for the exportation of the cloth had developed on the southern half (the Harris side). Thus the cloth came to be known—generically, legally, and universally—as Harris tweed.

Let me pause here a moment to present you with a rather interesting equation. The population of the Outer Hebrides is not growing—is, in fact, decreasing slightly—and since Harris tweed is a handmade product, there is no appreciable increase in the amount of cloth produced. This year production will probably not exceed eight million yards, which has been the annual yardage for over the past decade. The demand, on the other hand, continues to increase at an escalating pace, and so we have the makings of a textbook economic situation.

There has been over the recent years tremendous pressure put on the weavers to join the technological world and produce their cloth with the help of computers, electric-power looms, laser-cutters, and God knows what other "improvements." But those most involved in Harris tweed—the mill employers and employees, the weavers, and other members of the Harris Tweed Association—have their own ideas.

In 1976 the Harris Tweed Association—made up of some 700 weavers, the mill workers and employers, and a ten-man independent board of directors—met to confront the problem directly. The weavers had been asked by manufacturers to give up their small, foot-powered looms and switch to larger, electric-powered ones that would work faster, weave a wider cloth, and therefore greatly increase production. In this instance the weavers turned their collective back on the twentieth century. They refused to adopt mass production techniques, and by a vote of more than 95 percent they said No. It was a clear-cut case of progress-be-damned. They were fully aware that they produce something

more than just yard stuff, that handwoven cloth has a beauty and cachet beyond that.

"If we ever put power on the looms," they say, "we would just be selling cloth."

The Hebridean weaver, it seems to have turned out, is curiously uninspired by the dazzling benefits of modern factory life and production-line existence. He apparently prefers to work in his own home, take his tea break when he wants, go fishing if the weather happens to turn fine for a spell, or visit a neighbor if the spirit moves him. He has no foreman but himself, no time-clock to punch, no prescribed vacation period, no be-in-Cleveland-on-Thursday. Production is perhaps less planned here than elsewhere, because the machine—in this case a Hattersley domestic pedal loom—keeps pace with the person who operates it, not the other way round. The work is also much more individualistic, as the weaver necessarily puts something of himself into the cloth he weaves. The mill does in fact know who weaves each yard of cloth, and each bolt is shipped with the name of the weaver affixed. And the weavers will tell you that those who predicted gloom when the great "backward" decision was made look damned silly today, because Harris tweed is the more popular for it, and the weaver is making twice what he did then.

The making of this cloth is an ancient craft, and the weaving procedure one sees today has changed little over the past two centuries. In early June or July, depending on the weather, the wool is clipped from the hearty black-faced Scottish sheep (all Harris tweed wool must come from Scottish sheep), scoured, baled and marked by a wool merchant, and sent to one of several mills to be made into yarn.

These mill buildings, which can stretch for several blocks, resemble small airplane hangars, with their gray poured-concrete walls and high corrugated roofs. One whole room will be stacked perhaps twenty feet high with these 600-pound bales, bursting with the raw, clean, sweet-smelling wool. First the wool is dyed in large steel pots, a bale at a time. The dyed wool is then dried in huge spin-dryers, blended with other batches of dyed wool, carded (the process of opening and separating the fibers), and teased and oiled (made necessary because much of the natural oil was removed in the original scouring, and the oil must be put back into the fiber so it does not become brittle during the spinning process; later, after the yarn has been woven into cloth, this vegetable oil will be removed).

This processing is done in a mill because it is an arduous, time-consuming job that technology can do more efficiency, freeing people from the hard task, and in fact taking no beauty from the product at all. The processed wool comes off large rollers in a continuous sheet resembling an infinite gossamer blanket. This wool is then spun by machine onto thousands of bobbins at the same time, and then "warped," a vitally important process in which the basic pattern of colors is prepared. Warping is done by hand and is a respected and skilled craft in itself. It is the warper's responsibility to wind the yarn onto a large frame (six by six feet) in a specific pattern that will elicit the desired colors and produce even-tensioned thread of a specific length.

This warp of yarn—together with the weft, or background yarn, and instructions for the pattern to be woven—is then delivered to the weaver, in his own home, where the cloth will actually be woven.

I might mention here, since I've made the point that there have been few procedural changes, that the old method of preparing the yarn for dyeing (the procedure is called "mordanting") by soaking it in tubs of urine is no longer done. Chemical soaks are more expensive and less traditional, but they have been found to do a better job. The various chemical mordants remove the oil from the wool, soften it, and make it more susceptible to the dye, of which there are currently about 5,000 shades. In the trade, the dye is said to "bite" the wool fibers (mordant: from the French *mordre*, to bite).

The homes of the weavers are not quite the same as the ones we conjure up in our minds, having taken our inspiration from ancient picture—books. The old prints tend to show romantic white-washed stone-and-thatch cottages, tastefully landscaped all around with climbing roses and heather, and just that gentle curl of peat smoke rising lazily from the chimney. A perfect Galway Bay-by-way-of-Hollywood sort of thing. There are a few of these anachronisms left, but you would have to search to find them, and they are probably all on the Historic Register.

Modern housing is generally preferred, and while some modern bungalows do have fireplaces accommodating to peat, many are warmed by gas, electricity, or oil. All with modern kitchens and baths. Landscaping is optional. Romantic thatch or not, it is here in the weaver's own home that the true beauty of the craft of tweed-making is seen in its full glory. The yarn is rhythmically transformed into cloth as the shuttle of the loom loudly clacks along the frame, carrying the bobbin back and forth across the strands of yarn. This shuttle moves by foot-power: the weaver pushes one pedal down and the shuttle glides across the frame; a push on the other pedal brings it home. There are eighteen strands of yarn per inch and the pedals must each be pushed once for each strand, each weaver working to his own rhythmn as the shuttle slaps out the beat. It is a wonderful music.

The so-called "tweed weave" pattern of intertwining the yarn that the weaver uses is peculiar in that the yarns are crossed over and under each other two at a time, unlike most "plain weave" cloths, in which the yarns are crossed one at a time. This tweed weave pattern (often called a two-by-two twill pattern as well, since the cloth is technically a twill, and of course etymologically as well) produces a uniquely balanced cloth, dense yet surprisingly pliable—properties that are ideal for tailoring because they drape and hang so well. Harris tweed is also unique in that the "setting" of the pattern of the cloth on the loom (since each weaver owns his own loom) is directly in the hands of the individual weaver.

When the yarn is delivered to him by the processing mill he is also given a sample of the pattern(or pattern instructions), but as with any fine craft, there is interpretation, and it is quite true that there are no two lengths of this cloth that are exactly the same. I mention this by way of caution as well as admiration. It is always advisable, if you are having a suit of Harris tweed made, to have a second pair of trousers done if there is enough cloth in the bolt. It's the only way to get a good match. Over the years any cloth will change color ever so slightly, so it's a good thing to alternate the trousers, so they'll both age evenly with the jacket.

A finished bolt of cloth (simply called a tweed) is ninety yards long, and because the treadle loom is narrow, only twenty-eight inches across (unlike machine-woven cloth, which is twice as wide) and has taken a hundred pounds of raw wool in the making. The weaver can realistically complete no more than three tweeds a week working full-time, and the average is perhaps closer to two. Traditionally, after the weaving was completed the cloth was baptised and blessed with holy water. Occasionally a song—not quite as holy—was sung over the cloth:

> Roll of cloth, roll of cloth,
> Bundle of wool, bundle of wool,
> Tight as a wall,
> Smooth as the egg,
> Thick as the bum
> of the pastor's wife.

Following the same route as he did when he delivered the yarn, the mill driver now collects the tweeds, which are returned to the mill for finishing. In a strict sense, you see, what happens is that the mill acts as producer and sub-contracts the weaving jobs. The weaver, once finished, can simply leave the tweeds in a bundle outside his door for the mill van to collect on its rounds.

Back at the mill the cloth is inspected for loose or broken threads and other imperfections by holding it in front of fluorescent lights. Inspected tweed is then washed in a solution of sodium carbonate to remove any dirt and oil that might still remain in the cloth, and then it is "milled." This process used to be called "waulking," and an arduous job it was: the bolt was unrolled onto a long, flat table and the women— as many as a dozen or so—would pound on it with their fists until it was soft; Scottish folklore is full of waulking songs. At the mill technology provides a better method: the wet cloth is twisted and beaten in a machine especially designed for this purpose. Milling takes the harshness out of the cloth without damaging it and gives it "handle," that is, its fine tactile sense of resilience. In the tweed trade this fine soft springiness is characterized as "loft." A Scotsman's praise for a fine tweed reaches its zenith with the statement that it's "a verra lofty bit o' cloth."

After it's been milled, the tweed is dried and cropped (shaved slightly to smooth the surface and get rid of any hairiness remaining in the cloth). At this point the cloth is met by a formidable representative of the Harris Tweed Association. Harris tweed, you see, like champagne, has been defined by legal judgment. For years manufacturers all over the world were producing tweed that they called "Harris tweed" but that bore little resemblence to the real thing, and the association started to take court action against these counterfeits. As a result of the Scottish court decision in 1964 only tweed that bears the famous Orb Mark of the Harris Tweed Association is entitled to be called Harris tweed. The prime function of the HTA is to protect the integrity and quality of the cloth, so an inspector for the association is always on hand at this stage to satisfy himself that the meticulous standards have been met. Once satisfied, he will stamp the HTA Orb Mark on every three yards of the reverse side of the tweed. This is the assurance that the cloth has complied with the requirements for genuine Harris tweed:

1. That it should be tweed made from pure virgin Scottish wool.

2. That it should be handwoven in the homes of the islanders.

3. That the process of dyeing, spinning, and finishing (as well, of course, as the weaving itself) should be done in the Outer Hebrides.

If you haven't got that, mate, you haven't got the real McKay.

The cloth is an objective correlative for the land and its people: wild and harsh, soft and subtle. The tweed and the weavers have been there for centuries, seen hardships, resisted temptations, clung together, and endured. How long will they both be able to do so, as the contemporary realities of North Sea oil and high technology and quick money come pressuring in, cannot be imagined. Perhaps it will unfortunately come about, as the Scottish poet Douglas Young wrote

> That harmony of folk and land is shattered—
> the yearly rhythm of things, the social graces,
> peat-fire and music, candle-light and kindness.
> Now they are gone it seems they never mattered,
> much, to the world, those proud and violent races.

And yet, perhaps not. They are a tenacious lot. Aye, they are!

HOLLYWOOD

In this century there have been several recognized influences on male attire: the English universities, Madison Avenue, the automobile, various sports, and of course warfare come to mind immediately. But seldom has it been noted what a significant effect films have had on male dress. Undoubtedly female costume has garnered most of the attention, both because of its variety and creativity and because male attire was thought to be less "designed," although Edith Head, Cecil Beaton, Walter Plunkett, and other esteemed film fashion designers produced the costumes for the actors as well as the actresses.

Interestingly enough, it is in great measure because of the movies that we come to the understanding that clothing is in fact costume, an aid to role-playing in all our lives. Just like actors, we dress a certain way to play a certain part in our lives; and if we stick to those clothes diligently enough they become a uniform, an easy means of identification. And identification by outward appearances—a means of form defining content—is the whole point of costume: an evil person should be seen to be evil, not only by his deeds but by his appearance. The "black hat" approach to life (as well as westerns) has a simplistic appeal.

That films now have an impact on what men wear is no longer

denied. For the past several seasons now clothing designers from Yves St. Laurent and Perry Ellis to Ralph Lauren and Giorgio Armani have shown collections for both men and women strongly influenced by films. Armani has acknowledged a debt to 1930s gangster films, and everyone remembers the permeating success of the award-winning *Chariots of Fire* awhile back, which instigated a rage for tweed Norfolk jackets, Oxford bags, Fair Isle pullovers and other nostalgic accoutrements of English university life in the 1920s.

Chariots of Fire was of course not the first film to present this sartorial theme. The English 1920s and 1930s were first exploited realistically a decade ago in the Ken Russell version of D. H. Lawrence's *Women in Love,* and the American period was done even earlier in *Bonnie and Clyde* (1967, the first film for American designer Theadora Van Runcle)—both films achieving more realistic success with costume than previous period films.

But the business of movies influencing what men wear is really an old story. To look to the beginning, the Jazz Age of the 1920s that followed World War I created revolutions on many fronts, few perhaps as socially pervasive as a new American hero—the movie star. Films had become popular literally as soon as they were invented, and the actors almost as quickly became the idols for the generations thereafter brought up more or less on a steady diet of celluloid.

Stars came to represent our ideals. They were richer, better looking, more gifted versions of ourselves. They personified our values and many were distilled into prototype figures: Leslie Howard as the genteel Englishman; Charles Boyer as the continental sophisticate; Gary Cooper the shy American; Valentino the stormy Latin; Cagney the slum-reared gangster with a heart; John Wayne the strong, silent cowboy, an individualist who always went his own way. Each seemed to symbolize a facet of our collective psyche, both a part of ourselves and a way of understanding things apart. Often it became difficult to distinguish between the character and the person, between the role and the actor. The actor became the character, and the costume became the clothes. John Wayne always seemed to have worn the same cowboy getup, the same western jeans, boots, shirt and bandana and hat; in our mind's eye Astaire is always in tails, Cary Grant in a double-breasted lounge suit. When they wore something else, as Grant did in *The Howards of*

Virginia, we found it difficult to accept them. Grant may have appeared in buckskin breeches, but we knew he was suave, mid-Atlantic, and debonair rather than some backwoodsman clever with an axe.

In the 1920s Douglas Fairbanks, Sr., John Gilbert, and Rudolph Valentino gave us an entirely new silhouette. Previously the ideal shape for men had been more barrel-chested and solidly Victorian, but these "new" men were graceful and slim. Fairbanks's acrobatic skills in a score of swashbuckling epics helped establish the mood for the lithe masculine body. Men even took to wearing their galoshes unbuckled, in imitation of the pirate boots favored by him. Valentino too, particularly in such films as *Blood and Sand* and *The Eagle*, presented an almost feline suppleness. Unfortunately, over the brief years of his reign as Hollywood hero, Valentino's approach to attire and grooming became a trifle too fancy for American virility. Perhaps difficult to fathom today—when apparently nine out of ten men have blow dryers—the slave bracelets and cologne he wore were considered clear signs of depravity, and his star was in decline even before his untimely death. But not before thousands of young "sheiks" adopted the close-fitting suits and the patent-leather, sideburned coiffure that was his trademark.

Clark Gable, the Hollywood King of the 1930s, made his sartorial mark in a virtual thunderbolt of influence. In the 1933 classic comedy *It Happened One Night*, with Claudette Colbert, there is a brief four-minute scene in which Gable strips off his jacket, shirt, and tie to reveal . . . a bare torso! Every man between the ages of sixteen and sixty immediately stopped wearing undershirts. Trade manufacturers of this garment felt the harsh financial pang of neglect and languished forgotten for almost two decades, until undershirts were once again popularized by Marlon Brando in *A Streetcar Named Desire* and *The Wild One*.

The 1930s also saw the appearance of the urban gangster look, epitomized by Jimmy Cagney in such films as *The Public Enemy*, *Smart Money*, *Angels with Dirty Faces*, and *The Roaring Twenties*, which set the style for pinstriped suits, snap-brim fedoras, and camel-hair polo coats, not only for other film and real-life gangsters, but for a generation of movie-goers at home and in Europe. Part of Cagney's appeal came from his ability to wear his costume so effectively: there were many rumors down through these years that he really had been a gangster! Nothing could have been further from the truth.

It is the 1940s that should be considered the high-water mark of masculine fashion in Hollywood: Humphrey Bogart and Cary Grant, Ronald Coleman and Leslie Howard, Walter Pidgeon, William Powell, and Gary Cooper provided an impeccability and variety unmatched in any period before or since. The way Bogart wore a trench coat—in *Casablanca, Sirocco,* and *The Barefoot Contessa*—somehow defined the essence of that garment. That most consummate of dressers, Fred Astaire, had paved the way in the previous decade for the polished style of Cary Grant, David Niven, and other Anglo-American types who demonstrated a dominance over formal attire and an unstuffy approach to elegance. The touchstone of these actors was the ease with which they wore even the more restricting of outfits—the evening suit. In fact, their secret is more in an attitude than an outfit, and their appearances have a timeless quality of simplicity, taste, and moderation— amid a whirlpool of excess and flash seen elsewhere at the time. This blend of comfort and correctness became the clarion call of male attire during the difficult war years that preceded the casual revolution that began just afterwards.

The 1950s continued with the Anglo-American sophistication (Grant's accent was so obviously English, yet as a character he was always saying he was from some place like San Francisco), but the new force in film came from the "youth" movies. In *The Wild One* and *Rebel Without a Cause*, Brando and James Dean did as much for the T-shirt as Rita Hayworth had done for nightgowns. T-shirts, jeans, boots (western, engineer, and combat), and leather jackets mark the incursion of prole gear into the world of fashion—an approach to dress that came to dominate the 1960s and reached its cinematic zenith in the quintessential film of the period, *Easy Rider.*

The stylized sophisticated comedies of the 1940s had, by the mid-1950s, forfeited their claim to our attention by degenerating into pallid little sex romps that seem to have distinguished themselves solely in their ability to continuously portray Doris Day as a beleaguered virgin. Masculine film attire, apart from the prole gear getups of the youth films, was equally pallid (one thinks of course of *The Man in the Gray Flannel Suit,* but almost any film starring Rock Hudson, Tab Hunter,

or William Holden will do); and into this vacuum rushed the Europeans: Mastroianni, Belmondo, Alain Delon, and a handful of other French and Italian actors captivated our visual consciousness with their suave and streamlined Pierre Cardin suits in such zeitgeist films as *La Dolce Vita*, *L'Avventura*, and *Breathless*. Perhaps nothing propelled the French designers of the 1960s and the Italian designers of the 1970s into the world's fashion limelight so much as these films (which by 1980 had already become such nostalgic fonts of inspiration that remakes were beginning to appear). As late as 1979 Giorgio Armani, Italy's premier fashion designer, was showing his so-called "gangster look" line, in which his debt to such works as *Breathless*—with the oversized, heavily padded jackets, loose tapered trousers, and blousy shirts—is clear.

In 1961 the Academy of Motion Picture Arts and Sciences awarded an Oscar for costume design to *La Dolce Vita*, a rather direct tribute to the influence of the Europeans. American actors were still much in evidence during the period, but in the second half of the 1960s there was a conscious attempt to return to the "classic" world of a bygone era for inspiration: the interwar period, particularly the 1920s and 1930s. *Bonnie and Clyde* (1967), *Star* (1968), and *They Shoot Horses, Don't They?* (1968) were quickly followed by *Lady Sings the Blues* (1972) and *The Sting* (1973), and then *Chinatown*, *The Great Gatsby*, *The Godfather II*, and *Murder on the Orient Express* all in 1974. Still later *Raging Bull*, *The Postman Always Rings Twice*, and several Raymond Chandler remakes all attempted—some more successfully than others—realistic dress of the pre-World War II period.

The white flannel suits, pastel striped dress shirts, and wide-brimmed fedoras seen in the shops were all products of these Gatsby-type films, and this interest in—and perhaps newfound respect for—the twentieth-century past led to a spate of nostaligc costume films, everything from the Victorian country-house elegance of *The French Lieutenant's Woman* to the turn-of-the-century *Ragtime* from the tweedy Oxford *Chariots of Fire* to the romantically adventurous parody *Raiders of the Lost Ark*, which prompted a vogue for slouch-brimmed hats and distressed-leather flight jackets.

This recherché pre-World War II Anglo-American collegiate look has continued for the past several seasons now in film as well as on the street and designer ateliers, mixed with a pseudo-military-safari type of dressing. I would guess that the tremendous impact of the Australian film industry has had much to do with this. Films such as *Breaker Morant* and *Gallipoli* seem to have prompted a rash of khaki bush jackets, duffel bags, cargo trousers, and Gurkha shorts. A contemporary trend of shoppping is seen in the return of the army-navy store.

But whether it be the sophisticated *Brideshead* look or the macho cowboy hat and tight jeans of *Urban Cowboy*, it is all well within the tradition of influence that the movies have had on what men wear. Roll over, John Gilbert, and tell Valentino the news.

ITALIAN FASHION

T he Italian sense of style is hardly to be argued. Whether it's furniture, sports cars, architecture, kitchen utensils, or clothing, the Italians have made their mark. And it has, interestingly enough, often been said that style is what Italy is all about. Italians nurture it, and cultivate it, wallow in it, and of course export it. It is, to press the point, their stock in trade and it flowers so magnificently in Italy because no other country is so fiercely individualistic. The journalist and social commentator Luigi Bazini, in his book *The Italians*, notes this concern for the individual as a permeating aspect of Italian life:

> Transparent deceptions are constantly employed to give a man the most precious of all Italian sensations, that of being a unique specimen of humanity, a distinct personality deserving special consideration. An Italian considers it a duty to cultivate such illusions in fellow human beings, but, above all, he considers it a duty to himself. Nobody in Italy ever confesses to being "an average man"; everybody persuades himself he is, sometimes for intricate and improbable reasons, one of the gods' favorite sons.

This "illusion" can cut a number of ways, but it does show a concern for individual needs in a world drowning in computer printouts, microwave meals, and cassette therapies. Perhaps the Calabrian writer Corrado Alvaro was right when he wrote in his *Last Journal* that "once Italian humanity is lost, everything is lost."

But this is nothing new. Italy has always had a stylistic edge, and even the most cynical of travelers, Mark Twain, once remarked that the Creator had made Italy from designs by Michelangelo. Today, despite the incredible political and economic turmoil, the artistic flowering of Italy continues, and the influence is felt. Her film-makers, from DeSica and Fellini to Zefferelli and Wertmuller, chart new courses; architects such as Pier Luigi Nervi, with his "bravura" style in concrete, have revolutionized contemporary building; she has surpassed the Scandinavians in modern furniture and rivaled the French in haute couture. And who has produced more beautiful sports cars, printed silks, or contemporary sculpture?

It strikes me that while other nations—those great scientific and technological empires—fulfill their missions on the grand scale, policing the continents, measuring the galaxies, and generally deciding the fate of the universe, Italy is content to provide those minute pleasures, those personal and intimate touches, and to cater to those who seek an elegant pair of shoes or an admirable glass of wine rather than the latest and largest IBM computer or the fastest and deadliest ICBM. Not to say that computers and missiles are not important, nor that we should be so narrow as to concern ourselves solely with what touches us directly. But Italy has become a refuge for those human concerns, those small, daily, direct pleasures that are in rapid and general decline everywhere else, receding unfortunately from England and all but lost here.

This concern for the individual, for the more personal triumphs that craftsmanship bestows, is really part of the larger aesthetic sense. I remember talking with Bruno Piatelli, who is not only one of Italy's best fashion designers but a costume historian as well, about the Italian's sense of physical beauty. He made the connection with craftsmanship.

"The reason the Italian continues his sense of craftsmanship in the world today is precisely because he understands beauty better. And it is really a product of his culture. In a family, for instance, there is a certain atmosphere unique to that family, and a child growing up in that family will necessarily be colored by that atmosphere. That is the way of life. Now during the Middle Ages, because of her extraordinary geographical position and political influence the Italians became the great cloth merchants and traders of Europe. And when you are in commerce you must understand the quality of your product very well and get the best value for it, and so the Italians have had a long tradition of knowing cloth, a tradition which is part of our 'atmosphere.'

"Then too, if one works with his hands—and much of Italian fashion, from weaving the cloth to finishing the suit, is still handwork—he lives in a different way, a more individualistic sort of life in which there is room for both more freedom and more imagination than there is for someone who works at a machine. Machinery does not make works of art. For art, we can still learn from the masters of the past. Look to the great painters, not to the machine, if you want beauty. That is the culture of Italy."

And culturally, it has been said with substantial justification, we are all Italy's children. The list of great minds who have responded to Italy is a chain too long to rattle here. Her influence is the subject of thousands of books and hundreds of university courses, and the hobby of Italians everywhere.

Historically Italy has been the great bridge, delicately balanced between Northern Europe and the Middle East, sensitive to the pressures of France, Germany, and England, as well as Greece, Turkey, India, and beyond. As early as the thirteenth century one could have seen in that thriving port of Venice cargo ships from every trading nation in the known world. It was this unique geographical position, this strange amalgam of influences, that produced Italy.

The Renaissance belongs to Italy. By the end of the thirteenth century, when London was still a walled medieval town of dark, narrow alleys, Venice had already reached its height of prosperity: a city of sumptuous palaces, gold-encrusted churches, spacious sculpture-filled piazzas. Silk, that regal fabric so much in demand in aristocratic households of Northern Europe after the fifteenth century, had been made at Palermo since 1148. By the beginning of the 1400s Italy had begun to develop industrial production, international trade networks, a modern banking system—all of which were reflected in the growing mercantile wealth of Genoa, Venice, Florence, Milan, and Bologna.

Italy was built of marble, Northern Europe of brick. By 1500 the Renaissance in Italy had reached its climax. Its influence in the arts and sciences, in commerce, exploration, politics, philosophy, and a host of other endeavors has been so pervasive it is still being studied. One of those endeavors, a lesser pleasure as it were, was fashion.

After the fall of the Roman Empire in the West, accomplished piecemeal over decades by those northern harassers and invaders that none of us seems to be able to keep straight (I remember in my history text the Visigoths were the green arrow), Roman dress began to be influenced by the ethnic characteristics of their enemies. It is conjectured, for example, that trousers moved, geographically speaking, from north to south, originating possibly in Britain. The fashions of the Gothic north were, however, not completely accepted in Italy. They were not so conducive to the warmer climate; they were thought barbaric; and they were not as luxurious as the Byzantine fashions of the East. In short, during the four centuries of her renaissance, there was a melange. Italian fashion in this period of enormous wealth and activity is characterized by intricately decorated, delicate, and sumptuous fabric that only became more heavily ornamented towards the end of the period. *The Wedding of Boccaccio Adimari* painted at Florence about 1470, shows a degree of fashion sophistication that makes the dress of Gothic Europe decidedly drab. Looking at other paintings from that watershed century, one feels instinctively that the North represents the past, the old-fashioned, the outdated, and the aged. It is Italy that is the future, the vigorous and new, the young. It is, in a modern analogy, the difference between the 1920s Bright Young Things and their Victorian parents. By the time the Renaissance reached bloom in France under Francis I (1515–1547), it was centuries old in Italy, and by the time it came to fruition in England during the reign of Charles I (1600–1649) it had passed into the dignity of age in the South. Rich velvets and heavy satins caused bodily movements to slow, to become more formal and stylized, and the wearer took on a stately demeanor no longer young.

By this time history had lost its preoccupation with the Mediterranean. First Spain, then Holland, France, and finally England rose to prominence as the great herring pond of the Atlantic promised a highway to the New World.

At this historic juncture all of the ingredients that make Italian fashion what it is today are already present: a richness of cloth, a concern for dignity, a tradition of beauty. These points translate into an acute concern for appearances, something which other commentators have noticed in the Italian character. Barzini feels that a reliance on symbols and spectacles is a fundamental trait of the national character. Almost as an aside he adds:

> It is, incidentally, one of the reasons why the Italians have always excelled in all activities in which the appearance is predominant: architecture, decoration, landscape gardening, the figurative arts, pageantry, fireworks, ceremonies, opera, and now industrial design, stage jewelry, fashions, and the cinema. Italian medieval armour was the most beautiful in Europe: it was highly decorated, elegantly shaped, well-designed, but too light and thin to be used in combat. The Italians themselves preferred the German armour, which was ugly but practical. It was safer.

I am convinced that appearances are so important in Italy because the Italian is a public man. The Englishman says his home is his castle and has to join private clubs to get away from it and into a rather contrived gregariousness. But the Italian lives in the world of the café and the piazza. He spends much of his time in public places. "In Italy," Stendhal noted, "only a total lack of decency could keep one from joining the daily corso." And even the dour New Englander Nathaniel Hawthorne, who was often critical of things Italian, reacted favorably to this aspect of the national personality. "I never heard from human lips," he wrote, "anything like this bustle and babble, this thousand-fold talk which you hear around you in the crowd of a public square; so entirely different it is from the dullness of a crowd in England, where, as a rule, everybody is silent, and hardly a dozen monosyllables will come from the lips of a thousand people." And Hawthorne was not the sort to wear his heart on his sleeve about people.

This concept of the street as *salone del popolo*, the people's parlor, makes every *via* a stage, every piazza a place to see and be seen, every café repast a social occasion. Climate, of course, has made a difference. The Mediterranean has given the Italian sunshine and warmth and vibrant colors, which in turn have given him a strong sense of the visual, of the physical environment, of bright colors played against each other. This awareness of color, of the vividness of the physical environment, has also produced a love of the land, an affection for the physical beauties of nature.

It is quite true that just as they get the politicians they deserve, men get the tailors they deserve. Italian men have a well-trained eye for beauty, for color, for line and detail. They are, as we all should be, fastidious and demanding, and this produces the supreme tailors to meet the challenge as well as very high quality ready-wear clothes. The best bespoke tailoring exists, with one or two exceptions, in England, the United States, and Italy. I hate to be dogmatic about it, but there you are. In England, it is the Savile Row area of London; in New York, those several blocks in the upper fifties off Fifth Avenue. In Italy, however, there are two equally prominent sartorial encampments, one in the north at Milan, and one in the south at Rome. It would perhaps be a bit tidier, certainly simpler, to have everything in the same place, but when one is dealing with art allowances must be made. And in fact geography does not here account for any stylistic differences. In both places there are conservative and avant garde tailors; the quality of workmanship is equally high; similar cloth is used.

The north has taken the more influential fashion edge in the past decade or so because the ready-made industry has been there. The clothing factories and the fabric mills are centered around Milan, and the majority of the designers are now there. The firms of Basile, Barba's, Canali, and Redaelli and the designers Gianni Versace, Enrico Coveri, Gianfranco Ferre, Ermenegildo Zegna, and Nino Cerruti are all there. One name stands apart in its creativity and influence—Giorgio Armani. Armani has done as much as anyone to put Italian menswear on the map.

About a dozen years ago, in the pre-Armani days of fashion, the Italian silhouette was much different from what it is today. It was much leaner, more highly constructed and built up. Jackets were very close-fitting, with a shallow chest, very narrow sleeves, a concave shoulder with an extremely high pad, and narrow hips. Trousers were usually cut with a slightly lower rise (the distance between waistband and bottom of crotch), a tight seat, and legs that often flaired slightly below the knee. The suit, as such, had a very stiff, formal, uniformed look—

grand, elegant, and just a bit haughty. It was, in a sense, an approach to dress that originated with Pierre Cardin in the early 1960s. Cardin had reacted against the nondescript styles of the 1950s—bastardizations of the classic natural-shoulder Brooks Brothers look—by building up the silhouette, while at the same time narrowing it. It was an approach the Italians perfected in the 1970s. And it was to this heightened silhouette that Armani reacted.

He was born in the quaint northern Italian town of Piancenza and as a young man hoped to become a simple country doctor. He became disenchanted with studying medicine, however, and after trying several other jobs was hired as an assistant menswear buyer for a large department store chain. Not only he but others quickly discovered he had an intuitive understanding of the subtle relationships among color, texture, and shape. He was asked to help design a line of clothes by a leading menswear manufacturer and in 1974 created his first collection under his own label. What Pierre Cardin did for the 1960s, Giorgio Armani has done for the past decade.

Armani may be said to have revolutionized businessmen's daytime wear by making elegance more casual and easy. He is responsible for making the sports jacket the center of the wardrobe to the extent that the fashion press has said he re-invented it. Not true, of course, but it does point up the central notion in Armani's aesthetic philosophy of dress: to soften business wear and give it a comfortable, lived-in look. He is the first to have understood how to move men in the direction of casualness in their wardrobes.

To achieve this, Armani took the emphasis away from the business uniform, the suit, and made the sports jacket acceptable daytime wear. He re-cut it and infused it with new colors and textures to make it softer. The classic Armani jacket is less constructed, less built up, more like a cardigan sweater than a suit coat. It has, in fact, a purposely broken-in aura: shoulders are wide, à la 1940, but sloped downward; the collar and lapels are slung low, with the lapel gorge lowered by a full two inches; sleeves are cut looser; the chest pocket is several inches lower than one would normally expect, as is the button stance; and the chest area is slightly oversized, so that it gently creases. All in all, it is a successful attempt to design a jacket that appears broken in even when new, that feels worn and comfortable even at the outset. Both jackets and trousers in the Armani collection have this slightly "pulled down" look that clothes normally take on only after years of wear, and it is a part of Armani's belief that clothes should be old friends, that they are more comfortable to live with that way.

This silhouette is part of the vogue for old clothes that has taken hold this past decade, clothes that are soft and faded, slightly wrinkled, and a tad too large. It was undoubtedly a reaction to the shoddy and the synthetic on the one hand, and the highly constructed and constricting on the other, the highly pressed and shiny look that swept in on a wave of polyester fabric. Armani was the first to thoroughly understand this reaction in the design field, and who better to understand it than the Italians? This silhouette is bound to change—as all fashion must—but that is what has catapulted Armani to the forefront of Italian and world fashion.

KHAKI

There is a rumor—I'm starting it now—that things are getting better. My yardstick is the observation that the mania for designer jeans is now mercifully behind us. There are undoubtedly numerous tides in the affairs of men, and some folks waded into that one until the waters closed over their heads. Not that I mind people spending $50 or even $100 on a pair of jeans (as they say is done in the Soviet Union, so great is the demand for American-style clothing) if it makes them happy. It's just that so few look good in them. Not to mention what that spray-can fit must do to their circulatory systems.

Actually, more than circulatory systems. Some scientists argue that tight clothing can make a man sterile. It's a matter of heat, they say. Back in the 1960s a group of Swedish scientists opined that very tight trousers could cause, as they put it, "an unnatural heat . . . likely to have a cumulatively serious effect upon the male organs." The serious effect they were concerned with and about was genetic harm in the form of spontaneous mutation. I'm not just making this up, you know. Even the American physicist Dr. Edward Teller got in on the subject by suggesting that too-warm clothing could cause genetic damage, and a British Medical Association magazine connected certain cases of sterility with a fondness for too-hot baths. It's enough to make a man take up the kilt.

Unnecessary, of course, to go to that extreme, since there is—and always has been—a better alternative: khaki trousers. On college campuses in the 1950s they were often called "chinos" (because much of the cotton drill cloth came from China), and they were sometimes "polished," that is, given a dull-finished sheen. Occasionally there was a strap-and-buckle in the back. They were neat and respectable and uncomplicated. There was no snobbery or status associated with them. They were standard equipment.

Khakis were, in short, clothes that worked. They were tough, resilient, and durable. They had literally come through the war. Khaki trousers became particularly evident in this country in the fall of 1945, with the college man returning to classes after military service. Cotton drill general-issue trousers were comfortable, inexpensive, adaptable. Most GIs had several pair, and there were always the army-and-navy stores for those in more need of books than fancy clothes. Neutral coloration made khakis ideal mates to brighter tweed jackets and sweaters, and they were easily cared for by young men with more important things on their minds than perfectly pressed trousers. They could be thrown in the wash and hung up anywhere to dry—even out a dorm window—and a few wrinkles only added to their *sprezzatura*.

In truth, khaki had been around long before the college men of the 1940s made it popular. About a hundred years before, and its roots were in utility and war then too. This is one of those places, as it happens, where history is fairly precise. The use of khaki is incorporated with the use of the uniform in modern warfare. Traditionally thought to be a costume calculated to instill respect and awe—and of course to strike fear in the hearts of the enemy—the uniform as we think of it is a product of the eighteenth century, when various kinds of troops were first distinguished by their dress as well as their weapons: cavalry, infantry, artillery, navy. Even at this time officers had considerable leeway and privilege to wear pretty much whatever they wanted. And what they wanted was usually very grand. At Waterloo, Napoleon's generals swaggered about in gold-threaded uniforms of their own designs, while on the victorious British side it was only Wellington's personal feelings about what constituted gentlemanly conduct that forbade his officers from carrying their blue and green silk parasols into battle. As late as the Crimean campaign (1853–1856), British uniforms were brilliantly erratic: tunics of scarlet, emerald green, and royal blue, slashed with dazzling white cross-belts and studded with gilt buttons. The Guards regiments marched proudly in their bearskin hats, the Hussars and Horse Artillery displayed fur pelisses (long cloaks thrown over their shoulders) laced with gold, while others wore white and scarlet plumage, cherry-striped black trousers, and yards and yards of gold braid.

It was all very individual, colorful, and grandiose. The British had indeed lost what they considered an inconsequential war to quite improperly and unsportingly dressed backwoods colonists almost a hundred years previously. The straight and unwavering lines of redcoats had made wonderful targets for the ill-clad American troops, but that lesson was late in the learning. By the mid-nineteenth century, though, it began to dawn on the British Army that there might be something to be said for concealment. The idea took root in India. In 1846 Sir Harry Lumsden was in command of a native troop of guides at Peshawar. Their sparkling white cotton drill uniforms, Sir Harry noticed with depressing regularity, made them terribly obvious targets for unsporting snipers in the dusty countryside; not to mention all the time spent to keep the uniforms clean in all that heat and grime. The ironic lesson was that those who actually disobeyed orders by avoiding the regulation spit and polish lived considerably longer than those who played by the rules of gentlemanly confrontation. The lesson was not lost on Sir Harry. Some say the sturdy cotton was originally dyed with tea, others argue for river mud, but the resulting camouflage kept Lumsden's guides alive longer.

The first European troops to follow this lead and adopt khaki—from the Persian word "khak," meaning dirt or dust—were the 74th Foot, who when fighting during the Kaffir War in South Africa (1851–1853) wore khaki tunics with their tartan trousers. From that point on, khaki has had a continuous history of employment in war uniforms. It was worn by the loyal regiments during the Indian Mutiny of 1857; in the Afghan Campaign of 1878; and the Sudan Wars of 1883–1898. The British Health Exhibition catalogue for 1884—the same year a patented dyestuff produced a colorfast khaki—stated that khaki cloth had officially been adopted by the War Office as the material for troops on active service. There would be no more pomp on the battlefield, only circumstance.

American soldiers first wore khaki in 1898, during the Spanish-American War. It became general issue for troops by 1914, when the Great War rendered brilliance forever obsolete; when mechanized and impersonal weaponry reduced dazzle and posturing to anachronisms and formal gestures. In the war of 1914–1918 entrenched soldiers saw little use for gold braid and scarlet tunic and fur pelisse. Passchendaele, Neuve Chapelle, Verdun, and the Marne were hell-holes of mud and disease. The Battle of the Somme was the largest, as well as the most impersonal, battle ever fought: 1500 guns fired a quarter-million shells, killing 20,000 men on the first day of fighting. And the fighting went on at the Somme for months. There were no uniforms of glory to be seen on either side.

And when it was over, the Irish poet Winifred Letts was only one of many who wrote of the sacrifice (in this case made by the university students):

> God rest you, happy gentlemen,
> Who laid your good lives down,
> Who took the khaki and the gun,
> Instead of cap and gown.
> God bring you to a fairer place
> Than even Oxford town. *

Over the past several seasons khaki has been drafted into the service of fashion. Designers such as Ralph Lauren and Perry Ellis have made considerable use of the fabric in their summer collections, and a designer named Robert Lighton started a company a half-dozen years ago called British Khaki to produce a range of clothing and accessories authentically made of khaki cloth from an Indian mill that was in operation a hundred years ago and has maintained the original dyeing process used in the days of the British raj. Lauren also tapped into this "adventure-bound gentleman" anachronism when he did a collection of khaki clothes reminiscent of what might have been worn on a Victorian safari in colonial Africa, or the mufti wardrobe of one of Rudyard Kipling's officers of the Calcutta Light Horse. Authentic detailing went so far as to use button flies on the trousers, which is about as anachronistic as you can get.

Additionally, the resurgence of the so-called preppy look and an increased interest in the L. L. Bean type of rugged outdoor gear both in and out of the fashion world have helped to boost the popularity of khaki. All of which speaks to a nostalgic gentrification of the wardrobe. The field-and-stream gear, the ersatz military clothes, and all the other rugged sportswear outfits are a strange blend of fantasy and function, comparable only to the contemporary attempts to recreate colonial country decor in redeveloped inner city historical areas. Just as these rooms are sprinkled with objects now obsolete that were once functional—stained-cherry baskets, duck decoys, a rusty scythe perhaps—so these "call of the wild" jackets and trousers are replete with cartridge

---

* From "The Spires of Oxford" by W. M. Letts. Reprinted by permission of E. P. Dutton.

loops, game pockets, D-rings, epaulets, and holster hooks—in fact all the necessary survival paraphernalia for a rugged weekend in the wilds of East Hampton.

Well, this too shall pass, but the basic khaki trouser will retain our interest because it does function so well—which is the mark of the real classic.

LOAFERS

I've often thought that what I would like to do sometime is write an article about all those little touchstones that mark changes in our lives and yet go completely unnoticed, all those unsung but pregnant little moments that signal or symbolize a shift in the old *modus operandi*. There is one such touchstone in a wonderful scene from the film *That Touch of Mink,* when Cary Grant— playing the familiar international corporate head—saunters into his Madison Avenue wood-paneled office of an average morning. He's wearing his familiar dark, impeccably cut business suit, white shirt, conservative tie, and black straight-tip oxfords. He is the very glass of business fashion and mold of form.

It's important that you get this picture in your mind, because what he does next, coming as it did back in the early 1960s, was an absolute clarion call of liberation comparable in the minds of young executives everywhere to the Boston Tea Party. Grant next removes his suit jacket and town shoes and dons a discreet but obviously very comfortable lightweight cardigan and pair of tassel loafers! Right there in the office!

I realize that today this all has a rather quaint ring to it, but I mention it as an example of those less-than-earthshaking events that mark the road we have traveled. The point is, of course, that until that time this was not the sort of attire a serious-minded man with a correct sense of his own dignity and place in society would want to make his appearance in. Not outside the privacy of his own castle, that is. Casual clothing was still not exactly the thing to wear in the business arena. One of the most prevalent, and certainly picayune, criticisms made of the advisers John F. Kennedy brought to Washington with him was that so many of them were in the habit of wearing sports jackets— which became a symbol of a renegade, intellectual approach they were thought to have taken. Some found it invigorating, others merely brash.

Actually, the sports jackets, the cardigans, and the loafers are telling symbols of both outmoded Edwardian standards of propriety and the rising tide of comfort that after World War II finally reached into board rooms and presidential offices. Even the first-class compartments of planes, which twenty years ago would have been uniformly filled with gentlemen in business suits and ladies in traveling suits and dresses, are awash with unisex jogging outfits. Times have changed.

At the turn of the last century gentlemen were still wearing heavily padded suits, starched collars, top hats and high-buttoned shoes. How terribly uncomfortable, we would think, and yet our Edwardian ancestors did not really expect comfort from their clothing in the degree that we do. Propriety and dignity were all that was available. Gentlemen were supposed to be solid, stolid, and serious—if they were to be taken seriously. It was not thought they should be buddies to their sons, and dressing younger than one's years was a clear sign of dementia. Even the ladies, if one can use Kipling's poem "My Rival" as evidence, thought forty-nine the perfect age for womanhood. Dignity was in fact antithetical to comfort—and it is comfort that differentiates twentieth-century clothing from its predecessors. Because of paved streets, convenient transportation, climate-controlled buildings, a growing awareness of the value and benefits of hygiene, and various technical developments in the production of clothing, our wardrobes are considerably different from our grandparents'.

Today high-buttoned gaiters and crinolines are a thing of the past, and for footwear the past began to end in the first decade of this century. In fact, almost every form of contemporary footwear for men seen today was established in the first ten years of this century. By 1915, for example, the legendary Brooks Brothers catalogue contained practically all the shoe models the store now regularly stocks: patent-leather oxfords for formal occasions, black calfskin wing-tip town shoes, white buckskin, and canvas tennis shoes with rubber soles, as well as black and brown toe-cap oxfords, along with a variety of the more old-fashioned laceup gaiter types that had been in style for the previous several decades. To see these newer low-cut shoes side by side in the Brooks catalogue with the then more traditional higher-cut shoes is to realize immediately that back in 1915 the tide was unquestionably turning—had already turned in reality—and that men were allowing themselves more comfort in their dress. Heavy suits and boots, stiff collars, and high hats were all on the way out. Lightweight tweeds and flannels, button-down shirts and soft golf caps, shetland sweaters and white bucks, had arrived.

The only noticeably absent shoe from that 1915 catalogue is the loafer (a.k.a. moccasin, slip-on, and casual), which is the logical extension of this trend for comfortable and casual dress that marks the current century. The loafer didn't become popular until the 1930s when, as everyone knows, it arrived here from Norway.

Oh, you didn't know that? Well, yes, truth is that the loafer (even though the word "moccasin," of Indian origin, is equally used to name this shoe) is really a model of a Norwegian peasant shoe: a laceless leather shoe of soft construction, in which the vamp (top front part) is sewn to the sides in a single piece, and with a strap over the instep. First worn by Norwegian fishermen, who made it for themselves during their off-season winter months, this casual shoe became popular with Englishmen and Americans traveling in Scandinavia after World War I. Loafers became particular favorites of young men, who by the 1940s made them the predominant footwear on campus. Along with khakis and crewnecks, they became part of the *de rigueur* undergrad outfit and were known first as "weejuns" (which is of course a corruption of "Norwegian"), and later, as the fad of keeping pennies in the instep slot caught on, as "penny loafers." There was virtually not a middle-class young man or woman in the United States who did not own a pair of oxblood-colored penny loafers in the 1950s. At Brooks this type of shoe has always been called a slip-on, but the English custom shoemakers (firms such as Maxwell, Lobb, Poulson-Skone, and the rest) are rather traditionalist about it and still refer to it as a

"Norwegian slipper," a generic term for a laceless shoe of moccasin-style construction.

Also in the first decade or so of the post-war period there was an increased emphasis on summer and resort clothing—higher wages allowed more people resort vacations—and the new slip-on lightweight loafers became an important item in the warm-weather wardrobe, a trend that soon included sandals, rope-soled espadrilles, tennis sneakers, boating mocs, plaited and perforated leather town shoes, white bucks with red rubber soles, spectator-styled black-and-white oxfords, and cloth-and-leather casuals. In some cases, where shantung or sail-cloth was used, there was an attempt to match up the fabric of the shoe with the trouser or jacket. The era of the casual shoe, which so dominates our own day, had arrived.

None of these informal innovations, however, came close to challenging the penny loafer as the favorite campus casual. It's perhaps an obvious point to make that even today when the college grad enters the business world he must to an extent change his wardrobe, retiring the penny loafers, tweed jacket, and khakis in favor of three-piece suit and town shoes. The former uniform he relinquishes reluctantly, inasmuch as it has not only accompanied him through so many formidible and exhilarating experiences but also accords him so much maintenance-free comfort. What is perhaps not quite as obvious, though, is that for the comfort-loving American young man there has always been the attempt to bridge the gap between business- and pleasure-wear, the movement in the direction of comfort constantly encroaching on the business end of the spectrum. In the mid-1950s there was a development of the Gucci slip-on. There is no question but that this now legendary shoe deserves its reputation for having revolutionized casual footwear, which is the reason a Gucci slip-on is included in the costume collection of New York's Metropolitan Museum.

The Florentine leather firm of Gucci began as a saddlery in the first decade of this century and quickly achieved a considerable reputation for high-quality craftsmanship, detail, and design. The family-owned firm then turned to luggage, handbags, and other small leather accessories, acquiring more cachet along the way, and inevitably began making high-quality and stylish shoes. The famous Gucci slip-on was actually designed, coincidentally enough, in the late 1930s—just about the time "weejuns" were first being seen on campus. Although the original version was constructed of a heavier saddle leather, the design was what it faithfully remains today: a successful effort to retain the comfort of the moccasin while adding the fashion and elegance of a dressy shoe. In short, it was the shoe that first bridged the gap between casual and business footwear. This dressy slip-on was refined with fine, lightweight calfskin, a pared-down shape, and a metal snaffle bit, and as such it became avenue-elegant and gained acceptance in corporate board rooms and country clubs alike.

At the same time that the Gucci shoe gained its first whiff of status, the tassel loafer was being noticed. This casual slip-on was originally the design of the English custom shoemakers, and it was much favored by men who found it a wonderful compromise between the traditional town oxford and the too-casual penny loafer. Also made of expensive

leathers and skins, the tassel loafer maintained a small cult following throughout the 1960s, when in the wake of the Gucci success it began to be embraced by more and more men as an alternative to dressier shoes of more traditional styling. Cary Grant's tasseled soles of discretion were merely a step ahead of general trend. Even the penny loafer has now gone that same exact route, from peasant footwear and campus casual of moderate price to upscaled city shoe. Every good men's shop now stocks expensive penny loafers, hand-lasted and with hand-sewn vamps in fine calfskin (with or without kiltie fringe, snaffle bit, striped canvas inserts, or even pennies). In fact, statistics show that the best-selling *dress* shoe now is the quality loafer, not the dress oxford, by as much as four to one.

While the classic cordovan penny loafers still seem a bit too casual for the board room, a pair of black box calfskin tassel slip-ons is no longer the anathema it once was. There is another advantage to these dressier casuals. A businessman needs a compact wardrobe when traveling, and shoes are notoriously heavy to pack. A lightweight loafer can serve triple duty, worn with a suit, sports jacket, or even jeans if it comes to that. This type of loafer has been known to be pressed into service as beach shoe and bedroom slipper, and it seems to slip on and off easier during those tedious long-distance flights when anything to increase comfort becomes a tender mercy indeed.

The history of the loafer, it seems to me, takes issue both with the opinion that decent standards of dress are melting like butter and the world is going to hell in a hand-basket and with the theory, on the other hand, that we are entering a new age of formalism. What it does simply indicate is that our material lives are potentially more comfortable than were our grandparents', and that proprieties are perhaps a bit more flexible and subtle than our Edwardian ancestors'.

MADRAS

"I suppose many people do not understand how very much hand-loomed fabric India produces. But the fact is, it is really so extensive and important an area of production to the national economy that the Indian government considers this craft a priority." So explains Mr. Mohan Shah, whose firm, the Minerva Overseas Corporation, imports much, if not most, of the Indian hand-woven cotton and silk fabric sold in this country.

It is of course something that we may not realize, perhaps not even think much about—living in a high-tech society as we do, in which cybernetics, robotics, and micro-chips garner the lion's share of attention—that there are societies in which thousands, and in this case millions, are employed in craft work. We do, upon reflection, have at least vague inklings that there are probably a thousand or so weavers of tweed in the Scottish islands, and perhaps as many as several hundred cottage weavers shuttling away in New England. But the Indian hand-woven fabric industry tends to make the old imagination boggle a bit. Ready?

"The figures for cloth production have been fairly stable over the past several years," notes Mr. Shah. "India produces about six billion yards of fabric annually, slightly more than half of which is hand-loomed. I would estimate that there are perhaps five million individual hand-powered looms in India today for the weaving of cotton alone. It is without question the world's largest cottage industry, as well as the very backbone of the Indian economy." It also explains why a spinning wheel is emblematically at the center of the Indian flag.

The bulk of this hand-loom production is the cotton fabric we know as "madras." Traditional Indian madras is 100 percent handwoven, fine yarn-dyed cotton in either solid colors, random stripes, or plaids of various patterns. The term madras, according to the Federal Trade Commission, may not be used in labeling or advertising unless it is Indian cloth of this description. Originally the cotton yarn was colored with natural vegetable dyes that were not stable (chemically stable dyes that stay set in the yarn are said to be "fast"), and when the fabric was washed the colors would "bleed" into each other and thus produce new effects after each laundering. The appearance of a madras shirt new was not an exactly reliable indication of what it would look like after two or three launderings. Far from being a liability, however, this effect was highly prized and considered a unique and novel clothing experience, and in fact the beauty of "bleeding madras" was seen to lie in the weathered appearance that accrued from this blending property of the cloth. In the halcyon 1950s, no summer attire branded one more an arriviste than a bright madras shirt and spotless white buckskin shoes. They both wanted a bit of breaking in, of seasoning—and so did the man who wore them.

Today most madras cloth is fast-dyed, colors no longer run and blend after washing, and bleeding madras is virtually as much a thing of the past as crinolines and perukes. The other properties of great beauty and comfort, though, remain intact. It is one of the best warm-weather clothing fabrics ever devised. This particular cotton fabric is called madras because it is traditionally produced in the southeast part of India, the economic center of which is the port city of Madras (accent on the second syllable). This part of the subcontinent is ideal for grow-ing cotton: there is an average temperature range of 75° to 100° F. and an average rainfall of about fifty inches or so. The city itself is the fourth largest in India (after Calcutta, Bombay, and New Delhi), with a population of some three and a half million spread over an area of fifty square miles extending back from the Bay of Bengal towards the Deccan Plateau.

Funnily enough, none of the cloth we call madras is actually woven in the city of that name, nor, to extend the semantic irony a bit further, is it even called "madras" there. The cloth is referred to simply as "sixty-forty" cloth, meaning that the lengthwise warp of the fabric comprises sixty threads and the crosswise weft forty—which has been found to be a perfect combination to produce the desired lightness of weight and still maintain optimum strength of the woven cotton. The weaving itself is done mainly by farmers living in the outlying villages surrounding Madras. Practically every village home has a hand loom for cotton weaving, to provide a supplemental income for farming families during the long crop-growing season when there is little work to be done in the fields. Then every family member will take his or her turn at the loom, and practically everyone from head of household to youngest child is adept at spinning and weaving.

The particular type of loom used in this intricate and meticulous labor is known as a "pit loom," because it is actually set in a five by five by two-foot pit in the ground, unlike other hand looms that are raised on a frame to the height of the weaver's waist. The design for the pit loom developed because of the scarcity of wood in the area. Instead of building a high and elaborate frame to elevate the loom so that it reaches the weaver, the weaver in essence lowers himself to the loom: he sits on the edge of the pit, with his legs and feet resting on the bottom, no need even for a chair; it is ingenious and simple, as many ancient crafts are.

The history of cotton production in India is an ancient one indeed, and it could be argued that the making of cotton fabric for clothing is one of India's great gifts to civilization. A dyed fragment of cotton cloth found at Mohenjo-daro—the southern capital of the Indus culture of antiquity—confirms the suspicion that cotton cloth had been spun, woven, and dyed in India for at least 4,000 years. And the production of hand loomed cotton has been inexorably interwoven into the history of India ever since. It is economic life-blood, political symbol, and craft of great skill.

Even the introduction of European-managed cotton factories in British India after 1850 had relatively little effect on the destiny of handwoven cotton. What did almost destroy the extensive cotton cottage industry was the mercantile nature of the British import-export laws. During the second half of the nineteenth century Britain came to visualize her

Indian domain as both a vast source of raw cotton fiber for her burgeoning Lancashire weaving and finishing mills and as a huge consumer outlet for the finished goods of those mills. It was a theory of political economy that had prevailed in England since the reign of Henry VIII and centered on establishing colonies to guarantee a favorable balance of trade—for the mother country, of course. And so, from shortly after mid-century until the end of World War I, the British government instituted a number of customs acts to make it difficult for India both to keep out British cotton goods and to protect her native cloth production as well. The result, put simply, was that British imports, munificent though they might have been for British manufacturing, all but destroyed the rich variety and tradition of the Indian handicrafts and cottage industries. To make matters worse, the British government was little inclined to create new industries for the unemployed peasants who had lost their livelihoods because of these laws. And from this sort of situation ill feelings oft accrue. Specifically, the stage was set for the rise of Mr. Gandhi and an independent India.

In both 1904 and 1908 there were successful boycotts of British cotton goods. Indians were urged by their leaders to wear "svadeshi" cloth (the term for homemade goods), and homespun became a potent symbol of national pride and political unity. The svadeshi movement led directly to the revitalization of the dying cottage industries of handspinning and weaving and ultimately to economic and political independence. Although there seems to be little unanimity among his followers and critics as to what his real economic policies might have been had he lived longer, Gandhi apparently felt that India was not ready for rapid industrialization, and that it was better to improve life in the agricultural villages than to move large numbers of the rural population to the few industrial centers. His brilliant solution was to use handicrafts both as a means of employment and as an instrument of revolution. He particularly entreated his supporters to symbolize their resistance to the Raj by devoting daily time to spinning and weaving—as he himself did!

With independence in 1947, the Indian leaders, having achieved their main political objective, were faced with the harsh economic realities of going it alone. The Election Manifesto of the ruling Congress Party therefore concentrated on a planned approach to economic development, stating two primary goals: increased agricultural productivity and encouragement of cottage industries (handicrafts such as art metalwork, ivory carving, ceramics, brass and wood carving, leather footwear and clothing, and most important, hand-loomed cloth). Cotton textiles quickly became the rallying point and leading industry, with over five billion yards produced annually after 1956. More than half of that yardage is handwoven, and most is madras.

One of the most fascinating aspects of hand-loomed fabric is that production methods throughout the world are basically the same, whether it be Scottish tweed or Indian madras. The dyed yarn and basic pattern of the cloth to be woven are provided and distributed by the local cloth mill to the individual weavers, who are as often as not farmers. These farmers then weave the cloth in their homes on looms that they own and then return the woven fabric to the mill for finishing and distribution to clothing manufacturers. The mill pays the weaver for his labor according to the yardage turned in. It is a simple and universal system that allows for individuality and flexibility, particularly at the point where creativity is most important—the actual weaving of the cloth. It is a system that integrates craft and industry and gets the best of both.

The cloth itself is soft and light, but stronger than gauze or other loosely woven cottons, so it is perfectly suited for warm weather. Not only is it the least expensive handwoven cloth (wholesaling here for between two and three dollars a yard), but like any handmade article, each piece has its own individual appearance. Handweaving is an art, not an exact science, and the patterning is still somewhat at the discretion of the artisan who works the loom, and he or she will necessarily impart his or her own feelings into the work and the fabric, which is part of the beauty of the finished garment in which the fabric is used. When it comes to the actual weaving, often the pattern of the cloth is more or less exclusively established by a particular village. Either the weavers themselves in a village will have a particular pattern they are accustomed to weaving by tradition, or the yarn distributor will ask one village to weave a certain pattern or two and ask another village to weave a different pattern. There develops something of a proprietary feeling about these patterns by the villagers, and they become quite skillful and creative about their unique work. This specialization also insures a great variety of patterns and colors for the cloth, which is reminiscent of the traditional knitting techniques, for example, that developed among the families of the Aran Isles, off the southwest coast of Ireland, where every family has its own pattern for knitting those hefty scoured-wool sweaters worn by the fishermen who ply the cold waters out from Galway Bay.

The finished cloth is used for almost every lightweight article of clothing that men and women wear in warm weather, from skirts and trousers to jackets, handkerchiefs, belts, neckties, walk shorts, watchbands, and even athletic supporters. Madras bow ties and cummerbunds, not seen since the mid-1950s, are being resurrected at the moment, and can summer dinner jackets of madras be far behind? Brooks Brothers introduced madras clothing to this country at the end of the last century, but it wasn't until the 1930s that it really became popular. Vacationers to the Caribbean had first spotted the fabric being worn by West Indian natives, and before long shorts and swim trunks, sports jackets and golf trousers were all the rage round the links and club pool. By the 1950s there was not a campus in the country that didn't sport a full complement of plaid Bermuda shorts on male and female students alike—worn either with tennis shoes or with knee-high hose and dress shoes, English style. The denim mania of the sixties and seventies dampened enthusiasm for madras in some quarters, but it remains, along with polo shirts and penny loafers, very much a part of the Eastern Establishment summer uniform.

The Ivy League shops, whether actually on campus or not, have always been the place to find madras clothes: J. Press, Chipp, Paul Stuart, and Brooks in New York; the Andover Shop in Cambridge; Britches in Georgetown; Langrock in Princeton; Julian's in Chapel Hill; Eddie Jacobs in Baltimore: those sorts of places. And as those stores attest, the campus summer uniform has not changed much in the past thirty years. Plaid madras sports jackets worn with oxford button-downs and khaki trousers are still de rigueur for parties and dances, and madras trousers or walk shorts worn with polo shirts and penny loafers or topsiders without socks are still standard day wear.

The only real difference of course is the price. In the late 1940s you could buy a pair of madras walk shorts for $5, while today you can expect to pay closer to $50, but then that's true of everything, isn't it?

Finally there is the matter of the proper look of madras. The cloth, whether it's the old "bleeding" variety or the newer color-fast stuff, should not be bright and clear. Rather, just as good tweed, it should have a soft, muted, weathered look. And just as with good tweed, it takes some breaking in to achieve this effect. There are a number of quick ways, it's often said, to do this: taking showers wearing your clothes, or filling the pockets with small stones and hanging the garment in the rain for a week or two, that sort of thing. I also know that we are living in a world of fast food and speed reading, and that instantaneous gratification has become a way of life, but some things—perhaps the best things—can't be rushed, and I think cloth is one of them. The only advice I can give on how to achieve a worn effect is to wear the garment; wear it around the house when you are alone if you must, and launder it frequently. Eventually it will break in and settle down, and you can take it out in company.

MAIL ORDER
CLOTHES

T he postman and the public can certainly attest to the fact that catalogue fever is sweeping the country. A flip through the latest L.L.Bean, Orvis, or Paul Stuart catalogue conjures up wish lists to indulge the wildest fantasy. Items not usually stocked in the local haberdashery, such as authentic Irish fisherman sweaters and World War II bomber jackets, fine Sea Island cotton underwear, sturdy English country walking shoes, goose-down vests, and pith helmets abound, as do millions of imaginative accessories to please the mountain man, the Marlboro man, or the businessman.

Sitting in homey comfort, leisurely thumbing through a catalogue, writing a check, and sealing an envelope has become for many men the preferred way to shop. Farmers initially pondered over the wonders of Montgomery Ward and Sears Roebuck as they shopped by mail for tools and the latest in farm gadgetry. Today, catalogues offer quality, good value, and fashion—usually at a good price. Prices, in fact, are generally competitive, but shopping across state lines by mail saves you the sales tax, which on a nylon wristwatch band may not amount to much, but on a Burberry raincoat and a couple of suits can save you a bundle.

Catalogues perform an incredible service for the person who is either too busy to shop or who dislikes shopping. Parking and package-lug-ging are avoided, and the goods are "edited" for you. Some catalogues specialize, for example, in active sportswear (some even specialize in sportswear for a particular sport), or in a certain style of clothing, or even in a particular price range (one catalogue has handsome cotton sweaters for $20, another has cashmere ones for $725).

The cascade of catalogues arriving daily presses some people into becoming collectors—original old catalogues command high prices at ephemera shows, and even facsimile editions have become popular reading—and the fine print can be full of insightful instructions and folklore. For instance, did you know that the U.S. Army has deter-mined that for a material to be waterproof it must have a water entry pressure of twenty-five pounds per square inch (Orvis); or that the word "chaps" is short for "chaparreras," Spanish for leg armor (Kauffman); or that Captain Cook thought the Seychelles the original Garden of Eden (Banana Republic)? This is knowledge not systematized enough perhaps to gain you a Chair of Humanities at Cambridge, but damned fascinating nonetheless.

Many men's shops send out flyers, brochures, and catalogues of one type and other, and some have extensive mailing lists—on which you may request to be included. Paul Stuart in New York does a superb catalogue, as does Louis of Boston, Britches of Georgetowne, and other more regional suppliers of menswear. But in choosing which cata-logues to include here, the guiding principle must be a concern for the firms that are accustomed to a national or international business.

Each of the firms listed below is so. Each guarantees every item sold, and with the general exception of merchandise that has been monogrammed, will exchange, substitute, credit, or refund money according to the stipulations in the catalogue. Learn to look for the guarantee (usually found on the order form page), along with other specific and pertinent information about shipping procedures, gift cer-tificates, measuring charts, gift wrapping, sales tax, and such. The Lands' End Direct Merchants Catalogue is an absolute exemplar of clear, concise prose on this point of guarantees: "If you are not com-pletely satisfied with any item you buy from us, return it and we will refund your full purchase price." It seems to me you can't say it better or fairer than that.

Other catalogues have similar statements and will customarily do everything reasonable to please. Orvis, for example, actually prints photos of their telephone operators in the catalogue, so you may see to whom you'll be speaking should you phone in your order or make an inquiry. In the edition I have before me at the moment, customers are requested to phone Greg Comar, a nice-looking chap, "if you're wondering what type of gear to take on a fishing trip," which does indeed lend the personal touch in this age of computers casually conversing with answering machines.

These phone operators are there to help and are incredibly knowledgeable—unlike many a clerk in many a department store—particularly when dealing with matters of clothing, in which sizing can be a realistic fear and problem. Often measuring charts are included in the catalogue, or other instructions given concerning fit: the Shepler catalogue informs us that when buying the original "501" model, button-fly Levi's, "For a good fit, we recommend to add 1" for waist sizes 29–32; 2" for 33–38; 3" for 40 on up. For inseam 29–34, add 3"; 36 inseam up, add 4"." When washed, the jeans can be expected to shrink by that much, and the good folks at Shepler's want us to understand that and order accordingly. Such advisory statements as "full cut," "runs large," "slight shrinkage," "tapered," and other admonitions relating to size should be heeded. If these statements appear confusing or vague, phone or write for further, specific information.

DOMESTIC CATALOGUES

Avirex (627 Broadway, New York, NY 10012)
Avirex began its manufacturing operations as a U.S. military contractor for flight apparel and equipment in the 1930s, and with this history of technical expertise they have built the most solid reputation for producing in precise and authentic detail the complete range of jackets and other paraphernalia used by World War II aviators. There are the classic leather pilot and bomber jackets, an officer's deck coat with a jaunty belt and mouton collar, several versions of sheepskin flight jackets, capeskin gloves, leather helmets, hundreds of insignias and badges, and even the de rigueur six-foot white silk aviator's scarf! Additionally,

there is an ever-changing selection of THE REAL THING: authentic vintage bomber jackets and other accoutrements from "The Collector's Corner," for aces and aficionados who fantasize about catching the Red Baron.

Banana Republic (P.O. Box 77133, San Francisco, CA 94107)
This firm was established half a dozen years ago to offer an extensive selection of safari-type and tropical-military clothing and has received rave reviews from those who prefer functional, intelligently designed, well-made casual clothes. And it is not merely co-opted fashion stuff, either, but has an authenticity to it: the Australian bush hat is in fact made in Australia, and the British Army drill trousers are the real 100 per cent cotton khaki version worn by British troops in Africa and India (when they were there, that is). The company's line of Kenya safari clothes are made from 100 per cent Egyptian cotton—strong, cool, and lightweight shirts, trousers, jackets, and shorts. There is even a genuine Bombay pith helmet ("For extra protection on particularly scorching days, we suggest dunking the hat occasionally in cool water") and French Foreign Legion canvas boots, for those who want the total look.

Brooks Brothers (346 Madison Avenue, New York, NY 10017)
I would ordinarily not include a men's store in the list here, but Brooks is enough of an exception to warrant attention and consideration. It is not only our oldest men's store, but it has done a catalogue for almost all of the twentieth century and has thousands of customers who have shopped from it for countless years. Of special significance always are the firm's own-make oxford cloth shirts (the best you can buy) and wool suits; a superb selection of fine English town shoes (including suede tassel slip-ons, calf wing tips, and cap-toe oxfords); the largest selection of silk neckwear; and world-famous Lock hats and caps.

Cabela's (812 Thirteenth Avenue, Sidney, NEB 69160)
Authentic hunting clothes, from camouflage bib overalls and decoy bags to Sorel fleece-lined mukluks, Everest socks, and red wool union suits.

Cable Car Clothiers / Robert Kirk Ltd. (150 Post Street, San Francisco, CA 94108)

Cable Car Clothiers specializes in fine English imports: Church leather town shoes, Burberry raincoats, Byford hose and sweaters, Gloverall duffel coats, Harris tweed sports jackets, Clarks desert boots, British "braces", and for the very properly turned-out gentleman, English bowlers.

Caswell-Massey Co, Ltd. (Mail Order Division: 111 Eighth Avenue, New York, NY 10011)
Caswell-Massey is the oldest perfumery in the U.S.A. (it was established in 1752) and supplies the largest selection of toiletries and grooming aids to be found anywhere. Particularly to be noted are the colognes, several of which were first blended for important figures of the American Revolution ("No 6" was first concocted for George Washington, who liked it so much he recommended it to the Marquis de Lafayette). There are nine scents in all, and most can be had in bath oil, toilet water, talc, and bath soap, as well as cologne. There is a complete stock of hand and pedal implements (scissors, rasps, orangewood sticks, files, tweezers, and nippers of every size) and shaving supplies (badger brushes, wooden and porcelain shaving bowls, straight or safety razors, strops, and moustache scissors). The firm is also the supplier of the renowned Knize fragrances, originally created in Vienna for the Austrian Imperial Court.

Cutter Bill's (5818 LBJ Freeway, Dallas, TX 75205)
Top-of-the-line, high fashion western gear: exotic skin cowboy boots, chamois leather fringed jackets, full beaver ten-gallon hats, very elegant silver-and-turquoise jewelry, and other ranch wear for those who mosey on down the trail in their Mercedes 450 SLs.

Dunham's of Maine (P.O. Box 707, Waterville, ME 04901)
Dunham's has been around since 1887, selling quality dress and casual clothes for men and women. There is no active sportswear, but a select line of suits, sports jackets and trousers, and leisure clothing of traditional cut and styling. It is one of the few catalogues offering well-made suits (full linings, bone buttons, fine fabrics). The firm also stocks Alden shoes (leather inside and out), lambswool hose in solids and Argyle patterns, cashmere pullovers, English flannel trousers, and handsewn Italian silk neckwear.

Eastern Mountain Sports (Vose Farm Road, Peterborough, NH 03458)
Backpacking gear, flannel and wool shirts, ponchos, anoraks, expedition footwear, and other hiking supplies and clothing.

Eddie Bauer (Fifth & Union Streets, P.O. Box 3700, Seattle, WA 98124)
Mr. Bauer started his company back in the early 1920s to provide appropriate clothing for field and stream sports. His heavyweight duck cloth coats and trousers have been favorites of hunters for over half a century now, and his goosedown parkas, thermal underwear, sports gloves, and hunting caps provide as good protection as you can get.

E. Vogel (19 Howard Street, New York NY 10013)
This is one of the only places that will make custom, English-styled riding boots from mail orders. The firm uses only the best leathers (samples included in catalogue) and offers a variety of traditional styles, including polo boots.

French Creek Sheep & Wool Co. (Elverson, PA 19520)
Situated in the beautiful Chester County, made memorable in Wyeth paintings, the French Creek Co. began about a decade ago making a small supply of quality shearling outercoats and soon found themselves swamped with orders. The firm now makes over thirty different styles in a dozen differently finished skins: calf-length town coats in featherweight Tuscana lamb, blazers in glazed Nappa, sable ponchos, dapple-toned pea coats, blousons, ranch jackets, trench coats, and vests among them. There is also a range of quality handwoven sweaters.

Gokey's (84 Wabasha Street, St. Paul, MN 55107)
This is one of several outfitters specializing in outdoor clothing, even though the firm now carries everything from tweed sports jackets to cashmere dress hose. Foremost of the rugged gear is the firm's collection of "Sauvage" hiking boots and shoes, made of tough nine-ounce bullhide; and the "English Sportsman Series" of soft luggage, made of eighteen-ounce canvas with heavy leather trim and brass hardware.

Hudson's (97 Third Avenue, New York NY 10003)
Army-navy clothing, jeans, parkas and field coats, chambray work shirts, khakis, and other camping accoutrements.

Jos. A. Bank (109 Market Place, Baltimore, MD 21202)
It's perfectly possible to buy a mountain parka, ragg mittens, or rugby shirt from Bank, but the decided emphasis is on city clothes. The firm has the largest selection of business suits and sports jackets of any catalogue: over fifty suits are listed (from gray flannel double-breasted to olive-hued Donegal tweed and tan poplin), and thirty different sports jackets (cashmere blazers, tweeds, camel-hair, corduroy, hopsack, seersucker, madras, and every other traditional fabric). This is also one of the very few catalogues that list quality dress topcoats (including a British warm, wool Chesterfield, and classic cashmere). And of course a full complement of dress shirts, odd trousers, and ties.

Kauffman & Sons (139–141 East 24th Street, New York NY 10010)
Founded over a century ago, Kauffman has everything for horse and rider, from the most proper custom-made shadbelly show coat and hand-lasted English box calf boots to yellow rubber saddle slickers, Kentucky jodhpurs, western fancy shirts, and canary hunt waistcoats. For English or western riding, casual hacking about, dressage, or polo, Kauffman has it cap-a-pie.

Kreeger & Sons (16 West 46th Street, New York NY 10036)
Ideal clothes for hiking and camping, including ragg sweaters, corduroy knickers, waterproof parkas, and trail boots.

Landau (114 Nassau Street, Box 671, Princeton, NJ 08540)
The place to get those dense and incredibly warm Icelandic sweaters, in Nordic patterns of white, brown, and black.

Lands' End Direct Merchants (Lands' End Lane, Dodgeville, WI 53595)
Unlike some catalogues in which the clothing shares space with hardware, furniture, food, or pet supplies, this one is virtually all clothes— although there is the occasional fish-cleaning knife or pair of binoculars—and some soft luggage. The luggage collection is, in fact, the largest offered by any catalogue: about thirty different styles and sizes (duffel bags, canvas attaches, toilet kits, racquet sports bags, garment bags, carry-ons, and shoulder bags). Sweaters are an excellent value in either wool or cotton, and the firm stocks a plentiful supply of poplin slacks and shorts.

L.L. Bean (Freeport, ME 04033)
L.L. Bean is the grandfather of the mail order catalogue business in this size range, and if not the oldest (that was Montgomery Ward), it is certainly the most influential today. Items here are generally of the field-and-stream variety, but there is also an ample selection of town clothes (but no suits), biking gear and jogging suits, and skiing togs. See "Sports Clothes."

Miller's (123 East 24th Street, New York NY 10010)
For riding clothes, both English and western, and accessories.

Norm Thompson (P.O. Box 3999, Portland, OR 97208)
There are casual clothes (including tweed sports jackets and shetland pullovers) and hunting clothes, but what is perhaps most noteworthy is the incredible variety of outdoor headgear: everything from a solar-powered pith helmet and straw planter's hat to thermal balaclavas and Irish tweed bog hats.

North Beach Leather (P.O. Box 99682, San Francisco, CA 94109)
Highly fashioned leather coats, jackets, vests, and trousers in dozens of styles, colors, and finishes.

Orvis (Manchester, VT 05254)
Orvis carries good country clothes (warm cotton-wool checked shirts, corduroy trousers, Harris tweed Norfolk jackets, and other classics of the genre), Gore-Tex rainwear in a variety of models, Viyella tartan robes, sheepskin slippers, moleskin field jackets, loden cloth blousons, Irish tweed fishing hats, and other distinguished accessories.

W.C. Russell Moccasin Co. (285 S.W. Franklin, Berlin, WI 54923)
Founded in 1898, this small firm produces about thirty-five different styles of handmade moccasins and boots (from a nine-inch double vamp bird-shooting boot to a three-eyelet dress moccasin), with a choice of several fine leathers and sole constructions.

Shepler's (P.O. Box 7702, Wichita, KAN 67277)
Shepler's is the world's largest western clothing store and stocks everything that pertains to that outlook on life, from oil-tanned leather Indian moccasins to bull whips, boot jacks, and silver belt buckles. There are literally thousands of pairs of jeans always in stock, a complete line of

Stetson hats, and the largest selection of western boots (Shepler's sells more handmade Lucchese boots—which start at about $300 the pair—than any other store in the world). Most of the merchandise is real saddle-built stuff: flannel-lined range jackets, sturdy chambray work shirts, deer-hide ranch gloves, rough-out leather chaps, shearling vests, and all the other accoutrements to make one feel very much at home on the range.

FOREIGN CATALOGUES

Cambrian Fly Fishers (The Old Vicarage, Trevor, Llangollen, North Wales LL20 7YR)
This firm specializes in English-style country sports clothing for hunting and fishing: Derby tweed shooting jackets and breeks, heavy ribbed wool sweaters, cleated rubber estate boots, cotton / wool shirts, and tweed hats and caps.

J.C. Cording & Co. (19 Piccadilly, London W1V OPE)
Retailers of top quality classic raincoats, riding macintoshes, shooting clothes, and country footwear. The firm was established in 1839 and is the supplier of Grenfell cloth garments (the weatherproof cloth used on the Everest expeditions), British warm topcoats, tweed Inverness capes (very Sherlock Holmes), and the superb Husky and Barbour coats.

Herbert Johnson (13 Old Burlington Street, London W1X 1LA)
This is one of the world's best hatters, and every hat made by the firm—from tweed golf caps and soigné felt fedoras to boaters, top hats, and polo helmets—is absolutely top quality.

Leather School (Piazza Santa Croce 16, Florence, Italy)
Originally founded by the monks to train young men in a craft, the School does a complete range of fine, hand-tooled leather goods: wallets, passport cases, photograph frames, attachés, eyeglass cases, key holders, and desk sets.

Loden Frey (Maffeistrasse 7-9, Munich 2, Germany)
The famous Austrian loden coat has become over the past several years something of an institution in outerwear. This is the place to buy the

original dark green overcoat, as well as a number of other styles in navy, camel, and misty gray.

Robertson's (13–15 High Street, Hawick, Scotland)
Hawick is the center of the Scottish sweater industry, and Robertson's has the best selection of classic knitwear, from Shetland crewnecks to cashmere cardigans, in a mind-boggling array of colors.

Royal British Legion (Cambrian Factory, Llanwrtyd Wells, Powys, Wales LD5 4SD)
The best buys on fine Welsh tweed in soft heathery hues, sold by the yard, to be made up by your tailor. Alternately, the firm will do made-to-measure suits and sports jackets from your measures and cloth selection.

St. Andrews Golf Centre (St. Mary's Place, St. Andrews, Scotland KY169UY)
Golf shoes of superb English make, tweed caps and plus twos, cashmere Argyle pullovers, tartan trousers, and everything else for the back nine—including quality clubs, balls, and bags by Ben Sayers, Swilken, Dunlop, and others.

Shannon Airport (Shannon Mail Order, Shannon Free Airport, Ireland)
In the past years the Shannon catalogue has turned more and more to Belleek china, Waterford crystal, and Royal Doulton figurines, but they still stock those marvelous off-white Aran sweaters for men and women, as well as Irish tweed hats and caps, lambskin slippers, wool driving blankets, and a small selection of other quality items for men.

Trickers (67 Jermyn Street, London SW1)
Traditional English shoes for town or country, benchmade in fine leathers: wing-tip brogues, plain oxfords, their famous tan Derby walking shoe, and velvet slippers are all to be recommended.

A NOTE ON CUSTOMS DUTY

When you buy something that must be shipped to you from outside your own state, you save the state or country's sales tax where the purchase was made. That is good. On the other hand, you may have to pay customs duty on items purchased outside the U.S.A. This is a fee imposed by our government and collected by the postman who delivers the parcel. To have some idea of what amount of duty you can be expected to pay, telephone your nearest customs department, or write for a customs duty brochure for the latest information to:

Office of Information and Publications
Bureau of Customs
Treasury Department
Washington, D.C. 20026

MAINTENANCE

A while back I received in the mail a book to review called *Crinolines and Crimping Irons: Victorian Clothes, How They Were Cleaned and Cared For*, by Christina Walkley and Vanda Foster, and looking through it I was struck by how far we have come from the days when one would pop into his local department store for an ounce of Dragon's Blood, a gram or two of Gregory Powder, or a vial of Black Draught Acid. And who even knows to what use these exotic-sounding concoctions were put anymore?

Improved hygiene, chemical solvents, colorfast dyes, synthetic fibers, and machinery have all in great measure freed us from much of the real drudgery of cleaning. One thing hasn't changed, though: Victorian magazines—just as ours today—were replete with a hoard of household hints and recipes, proffering ingredients as diverse as hydrochloric acid, gin (they said it was good for removing stains from silk), stewed rhubarb, and fig leaves to solve the annoying and stubborn cleaning problems of the day.

All of which put me in mind that maintenance is still a concern today, with all our miracle fibers and professional dry cleaning establishments. More of a concern, really, than it has been for several years, if you've noticed the price of clothes lately. As prices continue to escalate, taking care of one's wardrobe—you heard it here first—will be even more necessary in the coming years. And with this in mind, I thought to offer some advice on the subject. Nothing terribly technical, mind you, these are all rather in the realm of tried and tested tips. Common sense plus experience, you might say.

The underlying philosophy of this discussion is that you have good clothes and want to keep them and wear them for many years. If you are the sort who throws everything out at season's end and buys new, any advice is waste of breath. This is a conservation movement. I should also say at the outset that I am opposed to over-cleaning. Generally, spots, stains, and wrinkles don't do as much harm and damage as over-processing. Unless the situation is extreme, there is little reason to have tailored clothing or even sweaters cleaned every time they are worn. Because, one suspects, of media advertising Americans have an absolute mania for cleanliness that passeth all understanding. Cleaning and pressing break fibers and dry them out; they become shiny, flat, and weak. Localized treatment for spots is best, and don't mind a few wrinkles. Good flannels and tweeds, for example, actually look better after they are well broken in.

GENERAL PRINCIPLES

1. Read the fiber content labels on your clothing. They are affixed there by law and will tell you exactly what kind of fabric you are dealing with. It's as important to know what type of fabric is stained as it is to know what caused the stain. Labels will also relate cleaning information (such as "Dry Clean Only"), which is particularly important when dealing with synthetics and blended fibers (where the manufacturer's guidelines should be followed).

2. Brushing and airing are still the best ways to keep clothes clean and fresh. Brush your clothes after wearing them to remove dust (an abrasive that damages cloth), and hang them somewhere to ventilate (in order to get rid of stale tobacco smoke, other odors, and moisture). Then hang them in a clean closet. Never throw them on a chair, where wrinkles and odors will set. Anyone who drops his clothes on

the floor to lie there or for someone else to pick up is beneath our contempt and concern.

The only extensive exception to this rule is knitwear, which should never be hung up (it causes stretching), but rather folded and kept in a drawer. Luxury knits, such as cashmere, may be wrapped in tissue paper to prevent wrinkles and pilling.

3. Always remove stains and spots as quickly as possible. Try the least harmful method first, and test solvents on an unimportant piece of the garment (such as the inside of a cuff or seam). Have a reliable, easy-to-use book handy for information on specific stains and their removal (Best Bet: Home and Garden Bulletin #62, prepared by the U.S. Department of Agriculture and available from the Superintendent of Documents, Government Publications, Washington, D.C.).

4. As an alternative to pressing, which is harmful to fabric, many wrinkles can be steamed out by hanging the garment in front of a boiling tea kettle for a few minutes, or in the bathroom when you are taking a shower. In general, iron and press clothes as little as possible, since it causes wear, makes the fabric shiny, and breaks the fibers, particularly at the creases. Never iron directly on woolens or silks. Use a slightly damp and very clean cotton or linen cloth (such as a handkerchief or tea towel), always start with low heat—you can always increase it, but a too-hot iron will cause real and permanent damage—and never bear down hard.

5. Learn to sew on buttons properly: it's cheaper, quicker, and less harrowing than leaving it to someone else. With all the shoddy workmanship around these days, buttons are bound to come off, and there are few things more infuriating or potentially embarrassing than missing buttons. The rules are: use good thread; make sure the proper side of the button is up; use an X cross-over pattern with a four-hole button; wind some thread between the button and the cloth to make a shank; knot off. New buttons, by the way, can spruce up an old jacket dramatically. Tender Buttons (143 East 62d Street, New York City) is a most incredible button bank and has everything from genuine horn and leather to brass, gold, cloisonné, enameled, and even antique and military.

6. Alterations are worthwhile. A good tailor or seamstress can turn a shirt collar and rework cuffs to give your shirt extra life—and usually the collars and cuffs fray long before the body of the shirt is worn out. Shirtmakers, although they prefer to work on shirts they've made (a good reason for having them made), can make new collars and cuffs for your shirts if the material can be matched or if white contrasting material can be substituted.

Don't throw away a coat because the lining is worn. At today's prices a good coat that cost $200 in 1960 costs perhaps three times that today, so having it relined—even if the job costs $50 to $100—is something to consider.

Other safe alterations:
    taking in or letting out trouser waist
    widening or tapering legs
    removing cuffs
    suppressing jacket waist (maximum two inches)
    easing a seat
    tightening a sleeve

Difficult alterations (easy ways to ruin a garment):
    narrowing a lapel or collar
    lengthening a jacket

easing the chest
re-cutting the trousers
taking in anything more than two inches
letting out anything more than two inches

Trust alterations only to a competent tailor or seamstress. A competent tailor is one who works in quarter-inches, and any tailor who tells you he can take in or let out a jacket waist more than two inches and still have it sit properly is not a competent tailor.

Tips: 20 of the Best

1. Creases in trousers can be sharpened by rubbing the wrong side with a piece of dry soap.

2. If a zipper is not working properly rub it with pencil lead, soap, or candle wax.

3. Use clear polishes on handbags, briefcases, and luggage because colored polishes will stain clothing that comes into contact with the leather.

4. The most highly recommended waterproof for leather is still silicone spray, but there are drawbacks: it darkens the leather, and since it not only keeps moisture out but air as well, it will dull and crack leather. Use it sparingly.

5. Stains on suede can often be removed by gently rubbing with a gum eraser or emery board. Try this before going to a spray remover.

6. To help keep colors fast add one teaspoon of Epsom salts to each gallon of wash and rinse water.

7. To raise the plush on velvet add a little ammonia to a pan of boiling water and hold the garment, pile down, over the steam. Then hold the fabric over, but not touching, a hot iron.

8. Never wash woolens in hot water; don't rub, twist or wring them, either; don't soak them; and never use strong detergents. Use lukewarm

water only and pure soap flakes (or Woolite, or very mild detergent), hand-wash (unless stated otherwise on the label), rinse and squeeze gently, shape, and lay on a clean towel to dry. This procedure will maintain shape and size.

9. Stay away from antiperspirants containing aluminum salts (read the contents), which are acidic in nature and may damage the fabric and leave a whitish salt stain very difficult to remove.

10. Avoid garments that are made by "fusing," a process by which cloth is glued together rather than sewn. When the glue starts to dry out or when the garment has been cleaned and pressed a few times, the cloth will begin to separate. This cannot be rectified.

11. Buy good clothes brushes and use them. The best are of natural bristles; synthetic bristles, being harder and with less "give," tend to scratch and pull the fibers. Buy three brushes: one very soft (for cotton, velvet, linen, and other more delicate fabrics); one firm (for woolens and tweeds); and one stiff (for suede). And keep the brushes clean as well.

12. A small, low wattage light bulb kept burning in a closet will often provide enough heat to prevent mildew, and at small expense.

13. Smooth leather clothing may be safely cleaned by a simple washing with soap and water (lukewarm). This is recently possible because all leather processed since 1960 has been tanned with a chemical agent called glutaraldehyde that insures that the leather will remain pliable and will not crack, stiffen, or lose color.

14. Pilling of sweaters can be minimized by turning them inside out to wash. Pills may be removed by carefully shaving them off with a safety razor. This operation should be done slowly.

15. Moths are known to attack woolens, cottons, and furs. Hot sunlight kills moths, as does dry cleaning (moths prefer soiled garments) and mothproofing (with a stainless insecticide that is not harmful to humans). Clean the garments, put them in mothproof containers, and sprinkle with moth crystals. Potpourri and herbs are claimed by some to be just as effective as moth crystals and balls, and they certainly have a more pleasant odor.

16. Old wives' tales notwithstanding, a wet umbrella should be left open until it is dry, to prevent streaking, mildew, rust, and wrinkles.

17. Neckties should be hung up, to unwrinkle and refresh them. Always unknot the tie immediately after wearing. Tiecrafters Inc. (116 East 27th Street, New York City) will revamp old ties: dry cleaning, relining, pressing, and narrowing. It makes them like new again, and the prices are reasonable.

18. Cedarwood shoe trees should be placed in shoes when the shoes are not being worn. Shoe trees absorb moisture and odor and put the shoes back into shape. Never, by the way, dry shoes over heat (which will shrink and crack them); dry them naturally.

19. There's little use fooling around trying to clean suede or shearling coats (apart from the odd spot). It's best to send them to an expert cleaner when they are dirty and soiled. Less than specialized methods here may well ruin a costly garment.

20. Candle wax can be removed from fabric by placing a sheet or two of tissue paper over the wax and gently ironing—the heat will melt the wax and the paper will blot it up and absorb it.

PACKING

_____
_____
_____

Not packing properly can ruin both a business trip and holiday, and whether one is planning an overnight trip or a month's excursion there are several rules and procedures to follow that can make packing less burdensome, complicated, and threatening. The first point to make is that one should plan ahead: know what you are going to need on the trip and be sure it's clean and well-maintained *before* packing. Few things are more frustrating and infuriating than arriving at your destination to discover shirts or jackets with missing buttons, unmatched socks, or broken cuff links. Inspect your clothes well in advance, and if a particular garment hasn't been worn for more than a season or so better try it on to make sure it fits properly—most of us have weight fluctuations from season to season.

See that the clothing is clean. Dealing with laundries away from home can be very risky, and even though it may be heavier to lug a few extra shirts, the added weight is preferable to trusting unfamiliar laundries, a list of whose combined atrocities would turn Attila the Hun pea-green with envy. I once got a batch of shirts back from a laundry in London so stiff with starch I thought they'd been dipped in cement. So have your laundry done at home where you know and trust the quality of the service. For travel purposes at least, it's helpful to have shirts professionally cleaned, folded, and sealed in plastic wrap—keeps them cleaner and easier to pack. Decide how many changes you'll need and for what occasions—and pack an extra change or two as insurance against emergencies.

The second general point is that fabrics are like wines: some travel well and some don't. Avoid clothing made of fabrics that need constant care and attention, such as thin silks or linens, which tend to wrinkle at a gaze. Blended fabrics containing a small amount of synthetic fiber—35 percent or less—are usually lighter and more wrinkle-resistant than 100 percent natural-fiber fabrics. Polyester-cotton shirts and underwear, for instance, can even be acceptably self-laundered should the need arise. They need little or no pressing and dry faster.

Third, always coordinate the travel wardrobe carefully. Clothing on a trip must do double and triple duty, and complete changes of outfits for every occasion are a luxury denied most of us these days. Stick to basic color schemes and keep the essentials to a minimum. If business attire is required, a gray suit and navy blazer are always appropriate. The appearance of both may be conveniently varied with different shirts and ties; the suit may be broken up and the trousers worn with the blazer or another jacket; and the blazer can easily be dressed up or down by one's haberdashery to fit the occasion. A pair of black calf slip-ons—in a plain style, without all the hardware and gewgaws—works well with suits, sports jackets, even polo shirts and slacks; and since shoes are among the heaviest items in the wardrobe, these soft lightweights are an excellent travel shoe. Light blue business shirts (in either straight or button-down collar) show less dirt than white ones, can be worn with almost any color of jacket or trouser, and are generally flattering to the appearance. A basic slip-on V-neck sweater, dark gray socks, discreetly patterned neckwear, appropriate underwear, and a travel raincoat complete a basic business travel wardrobe.

As the wardrobe should be kept basic and light, so should the grooming kit. Grooming supplies such as bottles of cologne and tubes of toothpaste can add up to several pounds, and the solution is to use lightweight containers and take only what is necessary. Most drugstores sell travel sizes of toothpaste, deodorant, shave preparations, and the like as well as those gigantic family-size tubes and jars. One plastic throwaway razor (sold in every pharmacy) provides dozens of shaves, and they're inexpensive and lightweight. Alternatively, fill small plastic bottles and jars with the amount of toiletries you'll need, which is even less expensive than buying the travel-size variety, whose packaging costs are a larger percentage of the price.

But while the idea is to lighten the load as much as possible, it's prudent to provide for emergencies. A small sewing kit (including two or three needles, plastic thimble, four small spools of basic colored thread, and perhaps a tape measure) comes in handy; even buttons that were checked and found snug and secure at home have a maddening habit of popping off twenty minutes before the big sales meeting is scheduled to begin. An extra pair of eyeglasses and a more than sufficient amount of any necessary medications do not constitute a wretched excess of weight—and always carry the prescriptions for medicines and eyeglasses as well, since in addition to other considerations, they help to alleviate the suspicions of rummaging customs inspectors who understandably prefer that all drugs be properly accounted for.

The next consideration is the type of suitcase in which to pack the necessities of the trip. In the past quarter-century the basic nature of suitcases has changed for two reasons: first, more and more people have been traveling by plane; and second, more plane passengers are now preferring to carry their own luggage rather than entrust it to porters and wait at the end of the plane ride for it to spill onto the revolving carousel at the baggage claim area. Consequently, heavy wooden-framed and leather-covered suitcases are on the wane and air-weight, soft-construction carry-ons are preferred. The primary criticism of the newer soft luggage is that it is not as strong as molded suitcases are, which is quite true. But if you carry your own bags and avoid the various abuses of baggage-handling systems, and if you pack properly, your clothes *can* be as secure and well-maintained in soft luggage as in hard. The trick is to select the right luggage and to pack properly.

First consideration when selecting carry-on luggage: size. Airlines restrict the size of bags that are allowed to be carried on the plane and are well within their rights to refuse to let you board with carry-on bags that exceed those limits. While there are some slight differences in the dimensions each airline allows (this information is customarily printed somewhere on the flight ticket), they are all comparable: a carry-on underseater may be as large as 20 inches (length) by 12 inches (depth) by 8 inches (height) without incurring the wrath of the authorities; garment bags are all approximately the same size (about 45 inches long, 25 inches wide, and 5 inches deep when open).

If the trip is a short one, for just a day or two, a garment bag with pockets to hold extra shirts and other accessories will probably suffice. For a trip of a week or more probably the underseater *and* garment bag will be necessary. Buying good quality, well-constructed, and well-designed luggage at the outset is the best value from all points of view. Good soft luggage is well made: no chintzy zippers, badly sewn seams, flimsy fabrics, or other signs of cheap materials and shoddy workmanship. Points to look for: handles that are large and padded, and double-sewn or riveted to the bag; a detachable shoulder strap with a wide, padded area for additional shoulder support and comfort, and soldered D-ring hardware; zippers that are double-stitched, with large pull-tabs and solid brass locks (which are not to prevent theft—since the whole bag can be easily taken—but to prevent accidental opening). Any other hardware should be kept to a minimum, and all buckles and straps, snaps, and other fastenings should be placed where they won't snag your clothes as you carry the bag. Metal or plastic skids on the bottom of an underseat bag keep it from directly touching a wet pavement should you have to set it down there.

While leather has been the traditional covering for hard suitcases, soft luggage is found in an ever-increasing list of materials: polyurethanes, vinyls, nylons, and treated cottons are the primary ones of the moment, while space-age technology is developing new ones yearly. All are easy to keep clean and are amazingly lightweight compared to leather. Polyurethane is a bit more pliable than the vinyls, some of which have a tendency to crack under extreme temperatures. In many respects nylon luggage is a good choice: it comes in a variety of weights (from four-ounce twill to eight-ounce pack cloth and eleven-ounce Cordura, a very abrasion-resistant fabric made by Du Pont) and colors (from fashionable primary shades to pastels and high-tech black and gunmetal) and is usually treated with urethane or some other waterproof coating. Cotton canvas luggage, first popular as field-and-stream bags with rubber liners, also is found in lots of colors and is usually treated with a waterproof interior backing of vinyl or some other type of plastic. If the seams are sewn correctly and welted, all of these types of bags should provide as much protection from dirt and moisture for your belongings as hard cases do.

Catalogues such as L. L. Bean, Lands' End, and Orvis and practically every department store sell dozens of brands and styles of soft luggage. Apart from concerns of construction and size, choice depends on design and price. Most bags come in a choice of colors that fall into three categories: 1. the khaki and olive greens of traditional game bags, usually trimmed in saddle leather; 2. bright colors such as red, yellow, royal blue, and orange; and 3. the sleek high-tech looks of gunmetal gray and black. The other basic element of design is found in the compartmentalized exterior and interior pockets, flaps, and closures. Outside pockets should be easily accessible, and if they are needed to hold something more valuable than a magazine, should be closed with either a zipper or strap-and-buckle arrangement. Interior compartments should preferably have a sensible mix of large and small areas of adjustable partitions that can be rearranged to suit your packing needs; and an interior zippered waterproof pocket is very handy for storing not-quite-dry items.

The effective way to pack luggage, whether it be an underseat soft bag or a molded two-suiter, is to pack tightly, because then *you* can determine where the creases will fall. Clothing gets wrinkled more and worse when it is packed loosely and gets jumbled and tossed about in the bag. The rule is to make sure that everything in the bag is securely in place and stays there! While luggage comes in a great variety of shapes and sizes, let's say, for the sake of simplicity, that we are dealing with a basic box-shaped compartment and want to fill it with a full complement of clothing for a business trip of several days. First fold the trousers in half slightly below the knee and lay them in the bottom of the bag against the near side. Against the far side will go the shoes (after they have been stuffed with rolled socks), soles down and in shoe bags. Next go in shirts (in professional laundry bags) and folded pajamas. Now fill in the spaces with tightly rolled or folded underwear, handkerchiefs, and anything else that can be conveniently squeezed into those little areas to prevent the load from shifting and tumbling about. The bag should now be about half full and the top layer as flat as you can make it. Then lay in the ties, folded in half and either secured in a tie bag or wrapped in tissue. Next the sweater, folded as little as necessary, and travel robe.

Finally, the jackets will go on top. There are probably more systems

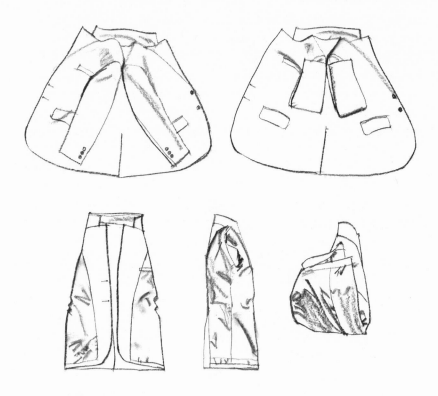

for folding jackets in a suitcase than there are pastry shops in Paris, and after trying most of them (the folding systems, not the pastry shops), here's the one that I think works best. First check that all pockets are empty, that any pocket flaps are laid flat, and that the jacket is brushed clean; lay the jacket lining-side down and completely open on a flat surface, like the bed; next fold the shoulders in towards the center of the jacket until they just touch, and fold the sleeves in half; then turn the outeredges of the jacket in to the center until they touch; finally, fold the jacket in half lengthwise. At this stage you will have a long, thin bundle to set in the bag. If it's a bit too long, fold it crossways at the waist. Two jackets folded this way may conveniently be placed side by side on top of the bag, and when shaken out should be relatively wrinkle-free.

You may be thinking that I have neglected to pack your toilet kit, but actually I've found from experience that it's best not to put the kit in the suitcase. I'm not primarily concerned that a bottle will shatter, saturating the contents of the bag with after shave or anything like that, because (we hope) the toilet kit will be leakproof. What is of greater concern is that should the suitcase become temporarily lost or permanently stolen, you can still shave and generally freshen up for an appointed business meeting if you've carried the toilet kit with you separately. This advice also pertains to any business papers, cassette tapes, and other documentation, as well as medicines, eyeglasses, passports, money or checks, and jewelry or other valuables.

Identification should be placed on both the inside and outside of the bag. Some travelers use business addresses on these tags, to foil thieves from ransacking their homes after stealing their luggage. And finally, remove any old airline destination tags that may still be left on luggage from previous trips—this may help curb airline luggage's natural desire to say bye-bye at the terminal and fly off to spend a week by itself somewhere.

THE POLO COAT

"**W**ell, you know," I said offhandedly to the Maharajah of Jodhpur, "all male costume in the West derives either from warfare or sport."

Not the sort of conversation I have every day, you understand, but I had had the good fortune to be introduced to the maharajah at a party, and a charming gentleman he is too. We got into a breezy discussion of one thing and another, and the subject of clothes somehow came up. I asked him if it were true, as I had read, that one of his ancestors had in fact designed the polo trousers known as jodhpurs. He confirms that it was his great-grandfather.

"And of course," he reminded me, "not a few masculine articles of attire have come from the sport of polo."

Whether as played first in India, or later in England and the United States, polo has provided our everyday wardrobes with a list of items unparalleled in variety and dash: the button-down collared shirt (designed to prevent the collar points from flapping into the face, and still called a polo collar by Brooks Brothers, who introduced it to this country from England in 1900); the polo sweater (alternatively now called a roll-collar in Britain and a turtleneck here); jodhpurs; chukka boots (a boot that extends slightly above the ankle and fastens with laces through two eyelets; the name derives from "chukker," a period of play in the game); the polo belt (a wide, usually leather or coarse-woven wool surcingle, and a very popular fashion item with women at the moment); and the polo shirt (a knitted pullover with attached knit collar and placket front, in either cotton or lightweight wool; the famous Lacoste alligator shirt is the most prevalent example). All of which have been freely adopted even by those of us who don't know a polo mallet from a sledgehammer.

And then there is the most distinguished offspring of the brood: the double-breasted, patch-pocketed, half-belted camel-hair polo coat, the aristocrat of topcoats. There have been few outercoats in this century that have had more acceptance than the polo coat. The chesterfield with its sophisticated velvet collar, the jaunty trench coat, the British warm, the truncated car coats of the 1950s, and the toggle-fronted duffel coats have all had their advocates and their day. But the classic polo coat has always been considered the best-looking topcoat a man can wear. Perhaps the associations one makes in part account for its allure: Saturday afternoon football games in crisp autumn air, tailgate picnics, early spring boat races. In part it is another fine example of the peculiarly American penchant for clothes that combine elegance with comfort, that casual dressiness that has always typified our college campuses. And in part it is the polo coat's ability to perfectly adapt to any mood, to dress up or down and be equally at home with flannel town suit or casual sweater and slacks. Some men are even able to carry off a polo coat with evening dress, but this sense of style is a nameless grace that no method can teach.

Actually, the origin of this most American of coats is, funnily enough, not American at all. About the *fin* of the last *siècle* English polo players began to devise a casual robe-like coat to throw over their shoulders between periods of play (chukkers) in a match, to keep themselves warm while they waited for play to resume. At first any old coat was pressed into service, but then gentlemen began to develop ideas about how this coat should function, and their ideas were translated into what came to be called "wait coats" by English tailors. In the 1920s, when polo began to be popular in this country, and international matches held on Long Island, the English wait coats did not go unnoticed.

There was a long definite swagger and cavalier deshabille about them, combining as they did the comfort of a robe, the warmth of a topcoat, and the aura of an expensive and elegant sport. They were mighty appealing to undergraduates on summer leave, and as fall terms arrived "polo" coats were soon seen on Princeton's Nassau Street, in New Haven, and in Cambridge. By 1930, the polo coat outnumbered the raccoon at the Yale-Princeton football game, which was as sure a sartorial barometer as could be found!

In the past decade or two, however, there has been not only a tremendous proliferation in outerwear—particularly of the parka variety, which more and more men seem to be wearing even with business attire—but a steady decline of quality, which in tandem make it very difficult to find a true polo coat. I don't mean some bilious polyester-and-wool belted horror that passes itself off as a polo coat, I mean The Real Thing. And the requirements of the genre are explicit and strict: an authentic polo coat is double-breasted, full-length, and full-cut camel-hair cloth; it has patch pockets, set-in sleeves, cuffs, and a half-belt. You could always have one done for you by a tailor whose skill is worthy of the cloth and cut. One thinks of Anderson & Sheppard, Poole, or Huntsman in London, or Fioravanti in New York perhaps; for ready-made Chipp or Brooks in New York, Louis in Boston, Wilkes Bashford in San Francisco, those stores. Regardless of the source, the price will not be cheap. Top quality 100 percent camel-hair cloth probably costs considerably more than a real camel these days: anywhere from $150 to $200 a yard, with a minimum of four yards needed to make a coat. Hand-tailored, with real horn buttons and top quality lining, and you begin to see where this kind of thing can lead. It can lead to over $2,000 easily for custom-made, and close to half that off-the-rack.

While we are on this matter of camel-hair, by the way, you will want to know that the cloth cannot be woven from the hair of just any old camel. The beast we are here concerned with is the rather special Bactrian camel, which is actually a cross-breed of the dromedary (or Arabian) and the Asian (he of the two humps). The coat of the former possesses great heat resistance, and the coat of the latter great cold resistance, and ideally enough, of the coat of the cross-bred Bactrian combines both qualities (and the animal has two, not just one and a half humps). Not just a special camel, but special hair on that special camel. Hair on a camel (or any animal, for that matter, including humans) is not of uniform quality with respect to strength, thickness, color, and coarseness. There are basically three grades of camel hair, distinguished by fineness: the best is obtained from the thick, soft undercoat, and it is this that is used for quality cloth in quality clothing. The other grades—each from the outer coat—are used for less expensive fabrics and yarns: carpet yarns, pack blankets, interlinings, that sort of thing.

The reason that first-grade camel hair produces one of the true luxury cloths is that it perfectly combines warmth, lightness, and beauty. Any other cloth of natural fiber would have to be several times as heavy to produce the equivalent warmth of camel hair. Its other quality—one it shares with cashmere and vicuña—is its incredible softness, which in fact presents something of a problem. Pure top-quality camel hair is so soft that, like all delicate cloths, it wears rather badly and is not all that durable. Polo coats of 100 percent first-quality camel-hair cloth tend to wear out at the collar and cuffs, and lapels and buttonholes, rather quickly. This upsetting feature has led cloth and clothing manufacturers to experiment with blended cloths to overcome the delicacy of camel hair. A blend of roughly 50 percent camel hair and 50 per cent good lambswool achieves a perfect fabric for the polo coat: it combines maximum warmth with minimum weight and is durable enough to last for years of wear. Blending the camel hair with wool to make it a bit tougher also ameliorates the other problem of luxury fabrics: garments made from delicate and soft cloths tend to bag and lose their shape. In a coat, shoulders sag, the front may lose its line, lapels can droop, and wrinkles become a problem; if a person sits in the coat a great deal, the seat will wear away or become shiny. And since the polo coat in particular has set-in sleeves (rather than raglan ones, in which droop is not such a problem), shape retention is rather more difficult to achieve than in other topcoats.

So ironically here, reducing the amount of first-quality cloth improves the quality of the garment—not to mention reducing the price.

POLYESTER

T here has been a battle waged of late by the producers of polyester to portray their product as luxury fabric. Their advertising message is that it is as comfortable as cotton and as elegant as silk, yet is better than both, in their words, "because its good looks aren't interrupted by wrinkles." While polyester has been with us a very short time, it is now perhaps the most prominent of the large group of synthetic fibers (also called man-made, as opposed to, for instance, cotton which is made by plants or wool which is sheep-made) used in the manufacture of clothing. Synthetic fibers are produced from chemicals.

The first chemical fiber was invented in 1884 from cellulose by a Frenchman named Hilarie de Chardonnet. Rayon, the generic term for regenerated cellulose fibers (which are derived from trees, woody plants, and cotton), however, was not produced in quantity until the invention of the viscose process, patented in England in 1892. The product was known as "artificial silk" and was first produced in the United States in 1910 by the American Viscose Company. Its considerable success led to the hope of creating an entirely synthetic fiber—that is, a fiber chemically created rather than found, even in a raw state, in nature—and this was finally accomplished in 1938 when nylon, the first truly man-made fiber, was invented and processed by Du Pont. Today there are about two dozen general categories of synthetics, the names of some bearing more of a resemblence to drugs than fabrics (such as Nytril, Novoloid, Vinylon, and Milium).

One such fiber, of woven Aramid with the trademark "Kevlar," is used in the manufacture of antiballistic clothing by a New York-based company called Emgo U.S.A. The firm advertises their line of sports vests, suburban jackets, and après-ski coats as "protective outerwear for today's active life-styles," and their media information sheet leaves little to be imagined about their definition of "active": "Once every fifty seconds in the U.S. someone is being robbed or mugged, and 60 per cent of these crimes last year were armed assaults. As one answer to the escalating crime rate and rise of terrorism, Emgo U.S.A. has introduced a unique collection of bulletproof fashions . . . Clothing has always protected people against the natural elements. We've just taken it one step further—now it can guard against the unnatural elements as well." The sports jackets, which have been tested against high velocity rifles, 38 Specials, and 357 Magnums, are available in six fashion colors and with coordinating accessories. Obviously in a life-style that active one has more to worry about than a few wrinkles.

Most synthetic fiber in this country used for clothing is polyester, which takes its name from being composed of polymers (molecular structures) made from petrochemicals. These polymers are processed into filaments of polyester, textured—usually to resemble some material we would be familiar with—and made into yarn. Finally the yarn is manufactured into either 100 per cent polyester fabric (the main trade names are Dacron, Fortrel, Trevira, and Zefran) or blended with natural or other man-made fibers to produce percentage-blended cloth. Fiber content labels on clothing reveal by law the nature and percentages of these blends.

The primary reason for using polyester fabric for clothing is its low cost. The production cost of polyester fiber is about three-fourths of the cost of cotton fiber production, for example. Interestingly enough, synthetics generally have something of an image problem, even though they account for over 60 per cent of the total textile fiber business in this country. In fact, last year's statistics indicate that while the combined production of cotton and wool did not exceed 3,200 million pounds, there were 9,600 million pounds of polyester fiber produced! Despite these enviable statistics—envied of course by the cotton and wool producers—polyester has never really been thought of as a luxury fabric; we associate it more with the much-joked-about leisure jacket than the custom-tailored suit. Better tailors in fact rather shudder at the thought of working with polyester cloth, or even polyester thread if it comes to that.

Originally touted as a release for housewives (and perhaps bachelors) from a sizable portion of domestic drudgery by providing relatively maintenance-free clothing—meaning that the clothes could be machine-washed and dried, and then worn without the necessity of ironing—polyester's advantages were more than spurned: they were made to look lower-class. Better clothing manufacturers began to boast that their garments were made from 100 per cent natural fabrics, and haute fashion indeed started to flaunt those very aspects of dress that synthetics were noted for eliminating: wrinkles. Designers have seemed to emphasize their disdain for synthetics and their collections have, in many cases, taken on an increasingly corrugated look, outward messages in graphic terms that the wearers are rich enough to afford the more expensive natural-fibered clothes, and probably don't do their own laundry either. For those wealthy-but-unschooled folk who don't actually know whether they are looking at, say, linen or polyester, designer labels often include the message "Guaranteed to Wrinkle," which translates as "This little garment will undoubtedly put a crimp in your Mastercard, but here technology and science must take a back seat to gentrification."

The mind does tend to slip its moorings a bit when reverse snobbery like that turns the world upside down, and it is only the poorest among us who are wrinkle-free, but this recent development does indicate that fashion is indeed responsive to significant social and economic laws. Analyzing the psychological and economic bases of social institutions in his *Theory of the Leisure Class* (1899), American social scientist Thorstein Veblen argued that conspicuous consumption and conspicuous waste were the very mainsprings of fashion; and were he alive today, Veblen might well have thought this wrinkle-mania an ironically amusing example of his theory.

Whether or not one agrees with Veblen, it is difficult to call polyester a "luxury" fabric without destroying the social implications of that word completely. It is truer to say that polyester is the workhorse of the garment industry, and that it has changed the patterns of clothes-buying since the 1950s. Today, as with other "throw-away" aspects of contemporary life, more people have larger wardrobes than ever before. Instead of buying one good cotton shirt for, say, $30 or $40, some people prefer to buy two, three, or even four synthetic shirts. And when they grow tired of them, they are thrown away and replaced by others. Some people are happy to do this, just as they are happy to eat their meals at fast food restaurants.

While 100 per cent polyester garments are generally not considered appropriate for business wear, blended-fabric clothes do have their place. Since they are relatively wrinkle-free, synthetic-natural fiber shirts and tailored garments are quite good for travel, especially in warm weather when lighter-weight clothes are worn. Because natural fibers still have greater porosity, allowing the body to breathe easier, the blended fabric should contain only the amount of synthetic fiber necessary to inhibit wrinkles. What is the ideal blend? In polyester-cotton fabrics the amount of synthetic can be as little as 5 per cent or as much as 85 per cent, depending on the manufacturer—and these percentages should be clearly indicated on the garments themselves (either stamped on the fabric or printed on the label)—but there is much disagreement about what constitutes the proper blend, and personal taste plays its part. If avoiding wrinkles is the goal, then the more polyester the better; but particularly as the amount of polyester rises above 40 per cent, fabrics tend to take on a shiny look and a slippery hand. Polyester simply does not look or feel like cotton, and whether in shirts, pajamas, robes, underwear, or what have you, the amount of synthetic should be kept to less than half. More than that and, it seems to me, the avoidance of a few wrinkles is outweighed by a loss of porosity and a slick look.

Basically the same rule applies to tailored garments (trousers and jackets), when a small amount of polyester can be of value for warm-weather wear. For example, linen trousers and jackets are so susceptible to wrinkles that they begin to crease as you put them on. In the past, the only way to deal with this problem was to make the linen as heavy as possible, which rather negated its value as the summer fabric it was intended to be. Today a small amount—perhaps 35 per cent or a bit less—of polyester can be blended with lightweight linen to produce an admirable summer suiting that resists wrinkles and yet retains the look and feel of natural linen. It is, to my mind, superior to natural linen.

Tropical-weight worsted, the other stalwart summer suiting, will also not suffer drastically by the addition of a like amount of synthetic, as in fact most lightweight worsted suiting has been blended with polyester for the past two decades. The important point to remember, in this battle between the natural and the man-made, is that trade-offs must be made: you can have fewer wrinkles, but you will sacrifice some aesthetic qualities of the natural fiber and can lose some comfort. The solution—in those situations where the blended fabrics have their place— is to minimize the losses. Polyester seems virtually indestructible, not merely wrinkle-proof, but this unassailability has its price.

This indestructibility has in fact been brought into poetic light by John Updike. "Terylene" is a British trade name for polyester.

My tie is made of terylene;
　　Eternally I wear it,
For time can never wither, stale,
　　Shred, shrink, fray, fade, or tear it.
The storms of January fail
　　To loosen it with bluster;
The rains of April fail to stain
　　Its polyester lustre;
July's hot sun beats down in vain;
　　October's frosts fall futilely;
December's snow can blow and blow—
　　My tie remains acutely
Immutable! When I'm below,
　　Dissolving in that halcyon
Retort, my carbohydrates shed
　　From off my frame of calcium—
When I am, in lay language, dead,
　　Across my crumbling sternum
Shall lie a spanking fresh cravat
　　Unsullied *ad aeternum*,

A grave and solemn prospect that
Makes light of our allotted
Three score and ten, for terylene
Shall never be unknotted.*

* "In Praise of $(C_{10}H_9O_5)x$" by John Updike. Reprinted from *Telephone Poles and Other Poems* by permission of Alfred A. Knopf, Inc.

ROYAL DANDIES

T oday of course it is the royal women who are written about and pictured as the very glass of fashion and mold of form. The books of photos of Princess Diana alone must reach from here to there, while the gentlemen—the Princes Philip, Charles, and Andrew and the other male members of the royal family—are merely thought to be as appropriately dressed as any British business-man in London. They are paradigms of propriety, sedate and respect-able; flamboyance and exaggeration—in a word, fashion—are seen as rather beneath consideration. The attitude of the British monarchy today is that kings and their subjects alike are ideally gentlemen and should therefore dress with a sense of quiet refinement and dignity. Correctness and understatement are the virtues of dress for royal males today.

This was not always so. Henry VIII, if we may believe the evidence of Holbein and other portrait painters of the period, outshone his var-ious queens for gorgeousness and drama of costume. And while male attire generally began to quiet down from the early seventeenth cen-tury onwards, several British monarchs have had something of the dandy about themselves. Both Charles I and II were solicitous and very par-ticular in their attire, although not as obsessively exacting as Victoria's son Edward VII, who it appears was forever going around admonishing his male acquaintances for their sartorial shortcomings. Not exactly a Dale Carnegie, he. It was perfectly all right for him to wear a pink tie with a green suit if he wanted, or glaring plaid knickers with matching spats, but God help the man whose trousers were not properly creased when in Edward's presence.

But by far the most interesting British monarchs in dress were George IV and the uncrowned Edward VIII, who, had a lifelong devotion to the subject of their wardrobes. In his elegant biography of Beau Brummell, Captain William Jesse points out that while full credit must be accorded that great fashion plate for improving the taste of his age, it was in fact George IV himself who was "the Maecenas of tailors; and perhaps no King of England ever devoted so much time to the details of his own dress." Devoted so much time, and we would have to add, so much money.

Primarily what strikes one about George IV is that he was thoroughly self-indulgent, given not to duty but to pleasure. One of his latest biographers, J. B. Priestley, belatedly warned, "A constitutional monarch is not expected to rival an imperial Charles V, a Cromwell, a Louis XIV, a Napoleon. He governs his kingdom in name." This modern truth George never seems to have grasped. The brutal and coarse caricatures of him by Rowlandson, Cruikshank, and others elicit our sympathy for him, but his compulsive indulgences obviously knew no bounds, and vain extravagance proved his ruin. Perhaps his love of sartorial finery is the most telling example of his self-indulgent life.

It is usually thought that it was Beau Brummell himself who introduced the king to considerations of dress, but this misrepresents the unique part Brummell played in George's life. Beau Brummell was a mere sixteen when he was first introduced to the then Prince of Wales, who was a mature thirty-two and whose perspective, life-style, and habits had long been set. Further, it's clear that George had an inordinate interest in clothes long before he met Brummell. As an adolescent he was already interested in building a wardrobe that would show him in the best light to female eyes, and he frequently not only sought the advice of women about his dress, but enlisted their help in choosing cloths and patterns from his tailors.

And build a wardrobe he did! There are numerous newspaper descriptions of his youthful appearance at functions that gave him ample opportunity to dazzle. In 1788, at the queen's birthday ball, the *Ladies' Magazine* in typical style-column reportage noted,

> The Prince of Wales was arrayed in a superb dress; the coat was a pale ruby ground, covered with a rich work of white and silver; the star of St. George was formed of brilliantes; the loop was also of diamonds; the waistcoat was of white and silver, highly rich and beautiful. The hat in which His Highness appeared in the evening at the ball, had a beautiful brilliancy.

At a ball celebrating George the III's birthday, the *St. James's Chronicle* opined that George was the zenith of fashion.

> He wore a bottle-green and claret-coloured striped silk coat and breeches, and silver tissue waistcoat, very richly embroidered in silver and stones, and coloured silks in various devices and bouquets of flowers. The coat and waistcoat embroidered down the seams and spangled all over the body. The coat cuffs the same as the waistcoat. The breeches were likewise covered with spangles. Diamond buttons to the coat, waistcoat, and breeches, which with his brilliant diamond epaulette, and sword, made the whole dress form a most magnificent appearance.

There is even some indication that it was not Brummell who brought the high, starched neckcloth into fashion—though it became his signature and the focal point of his wardrobe—but George himself. He had been prone since childhood to swollen glands in his throat, and always conscious of his appearance, took to wearing extremely high neckcloths to mask this ailment.

The most conclusive evidence of his interest in dress, though, is the state of his finances. Throughout his life he was incapable of curbing a proclivity for spending—at one point he agreed to marry simply to relieve himself of his debts (it didn't help!)—and the amount he spent on clothing was enormous by any standard. On his twenty-seventh birthday (in 1789, the year, ironically, of the great revolution against the French monarchy) he found that, among his other debts, he owed his tailors almost £34,000. We should keep in mind that a middle-class shopkeeper at this time would have considered himself to be doing nicely on £50 a year.

George's yearly expenditures for clothing and jewelry easily exceeded

£2,000, as his wardrobe bills reveal. He is known to have ordered sixty waistcoats in the space of a month; in one six-month period he bought ten dozen pairs of white gloves, and cambric handkerchiefs, black silk hose, doeskin trousers, and flannel underwaistcoats were ordered in batches of three and four dozen at a time. From white beaver morning gowns and black astrakhan caps to Scottish tartan suits and Welsh flannel-lined jackets, the lists go on and on—everything custom-made and of the finest quality.

Had the Prince of Wales not already been a devotee of dress, he might well have never taken notice of the young Beau. Because of his infallible taste and ready wit, Brummell quickly became a member of the prince's brilliant inner circle (which included the dramatist Richard Brinsley Sheridan and Charles James Fox), and the friendship deepened. Often George would visit Beau to watch him at his toilette and stay so late that he sent his carriage home (understandable enough since Brummell spent nine hours of his waking day changing clothes).

The two of them spent many an evening together discussing the fashions of the town, and impressed more and more by Beau, George allowed himself to be advised by the younger man, who had become the arbiter elegantarium along Bond Street and in the clubs of St. James's. On at least one occasion the prince was reduced to tears when told that Brummell did not like the cut of his coat (actually, Tom Moore, the poet who was present, says the prince "blubbered").

Brummell's fame and influence grew, but so did his conceit, and that apparently became his undoing. Perhaps he became so confident that he began to think of his relationship with the prince as merely one gentleman to another, rather than as subject to sovereign. At any rate, the apocryphal story is that one evening, amidst the talk of tailors and haberdashery, Brummell took the liberty of criticizing the prince's mistress to his face, and was quickly made to realize that he had overstepped the bounds of royal favor. Socially, George cut him dead.

As it happened—and to this part of the story there were witnesses—the prince might well have eventually forgiven Beau had they not accidentally met several weeks later. Brummell and a companion, the gambler and man-about-town Lord Alvanley, were strolling down Bond Street one afternoon when they came unexpectedly face to face with the prince and a companion strolling in the opposite direction. According

to the account given by Jesse, the prince waited for Beau's apology, and not receiving any, spoke only to Alvanley and ignored Brummell. Then, just as the prince turned to continue his saunter, Brummell casually but loudly asked, "Alvanley, who's your fat friend?"

It was a nasty jest, and painful because it was true; George was running towards corpulence, although he was too vain to admit it and too weak to check himself. Brummell, for his part, had been a lucky and gifted man, but now his fortune changed: he was cut off from the prince and soon lost most of his small fortune gambling, so that he ran to France to escape his creditors. Poverty-stricken, he died in the Bon Sauveur nunnery in Caen. George became regent in 1811 and finally king in 1820; he never looked back, but found new fashion advisers, new tailors, and new styles as he went exasperatingly ever further into debt. His obesity began to seriously undermine his health, and the tailors could no longer disguise his huge stomach with even the stoutest corset. When he died, one might say of overindulgence, in 1830, the extent to which he had, as Jesse remarks, "indulged his passion for dress can be seen in the proceeds of the sale of his wardrobe, which amounted to the enormous sum of £15,000." It is estimated that this collection of royal garments had originally set George back at least £100,000.

In the end perhaps it was Caroline of Brunswick, the wife he so thoroughly hated, who understood George best. In a letter written about ten years after their marriage, she noted,

> [I] ought to have been the man and he the woman to wear the petticoats . . . He understands how a shoe should be made or a coat cut, or a dinner dressed and would make an excellent tailor, or shoemaker, or hairdresser but nothing else.

Looking at the family portraits at Windsor one day (including several of George IV), the Duke of Windsor commented that "they show, I am gratified to observe, that the Kings of England and their relatives were, on the whole, well enough dressed." It isn't surprising that this is what he noticed, for he had a life-long interest in clothes and has been a considerable influence on men's attire in the twentieth century. Before his abdication and fall from grace, he was considered a golden boy and "the British Empire's best salesman." Praised in song and endlessly photographed, he was of perennial interest to the public. A future king of a great empire, he was young, handsome, and well mannered; superficial perhaps, yet idealistic, casual yet gracious, a born aristocrat yet willing to hobnob. Except for a few members of the greater and lesser nobility who found him a trifle vulgar (he thought many of them dull and tedious), he was thought engaging and charming. On his early visits to the United States (1919, 1924, and 1927) the newspapers were full of him, reporting everything they could about the man. His style, that marvelous blend of propriety and nonchalance, and his clothes attracted more attention than anything. His large and ever-changing wardrobe was daily described cap-a-pie, and he had only to wear something once (a Fair Isle sweater, chalk-striped double-breasted suit, glen plaid jacket, Guard's regimental tie, Argyle hose) to make it immediately the rage. There were men, it was said, who had standing orders with their tailors to copy every suit he was seen in. After the prince was photographed in a glen check suit, the pattern became instantly popular and is known even today as a Prince of Wales plaid.

He did have incredible style, and he is at least partially responsible for bringing a new dimension into men's clothing: comfort. As a young man he had fretted against the rigid social conventions of his Victorian ancestors that still held sway in turn-of-the-century Britain. He himself saw the wearing of bright tweeds and patterned sweaters, rather than the somber black broadcloth suits and bowler hats, as a gesture aspiring not merely to comfort, but in a more symbolic sense, to freedom. He seems to have waged a war of his own with starch, and won freedom from the red neck for all of us in the bargain. This liberation from stiff collars and cuffs was of historic importance to him, as he notes in a book he wrote about clothing, *Windsor Revisited;*

> [In the early 1920s] I had taken to wearing a soft shirt, with a single-breasted dinner jacket, and if my shirt was stiff, my cuffs were now often soft. I was still faithful to the stiff collar, but it was usually of the comfortable turned-down variety . . . Meanwhile, however, we began to find that with the double-breasted dinner jacket, a soft collar looked just as neat as a stiff one, and by the thirties we were all beginning to "dress soft," thus combining, as no previous generation had done, sartorial dignity with comfort and ease.

This was the beginning of the movement toward functional simplicity and comfort in dress. The only jewelry he wore were cuff links, his ring, and shirt studs for evening shirts (ironically, he never wore the crown either). Along the way he also discarded the vest for both day and evening wear, which he was quick to see as unnecessary with a double-breasted jacket. As an interesting footnote of sorts, it should be understood that the Duke of Windsor (as he should be known for his last title) was so concerned with function in dress that he designed a special type of short trouser with legs that rolled up and buttoned above the knee to offer coolness. These he wore on a trip to East Africa, much to his satisfaction.

The second quality associated with the duke and his dress is fastidiousness. Whether it was the cut of his hair or his trousers, he was an incredible stickler for fit and detail. He insisted on exactly four buttons on his jacket sleeves, and his specially made neckties—again, designed by him—with an extra thickness of lining to produce a larger than customary knot led to a style still referred to as a "Windsor" knot. Most incredible of his dress requirements was what his wife called "pants across the sea." While his Savile Row tailor cut what he considered was the perfect jacket, the duke was never satisfied with the trousers. On a visit to New York, after he had been appointed governor of the Bahamas, he happened to find a tailor who cut his trousers so well that from then on he had the suit jackets made in London and the trousers made in New York.

He not only popularized Fair Isle sweaters and socks, suede shoes, the spread-collared shirt, the Windsor knot, regimental ties, the double-breasted suit, and brightly checked tweeds, he could be considered something of an authority on the history of modern costume for men. He was able to trace the history of many styles and could discuss in great detail the evolution of trousers, cravats, waistcoats, the Eton jacket, walking sticks, frock coats, uniforms, and practically every other item of dress worn today and yesterday. In his book he is illuminating on the questions of why the bottom button of the vest is left undone, who introduced the trouser crease, why the cutaway was replaced by the frock coat, and other points of legitimate historical concern.

If the early accounts of his life, the breathless reportage and editorials, were effusive and uncritical, the several biographies written in the past dozen years or so since his death have balanced our view. His weaknesses and pettiness, shortsightedness and recalcitrance, have been painted boldly. But what strikes us still, when we look at those old photos in which he appears amidst a group of somber or frolicking acquaintances, is that he has the modern face, the youthful body, while many of the others seem so clearly old-fashioned and of another age. He had captured and directed the modern style. He was the brightest of the Bright Young Things, slim and easy going, given to jazz and slang, night clubs and open convertibles. He set a tone and mood for his time that is still with us today.

SAVILE ROW

T he Prince of Wales' tailor was heard to say recently that while His Royal Highness is in fact rather particular about his clothing, the only firm stipulation he makes is that nothing should be "too way out." Which is precisely what we would expect from a future monarch of Great Britain: that he will not only be a sovereign, but a gentleman as well.

He is, of course, in the name of protocol, occasionally required to don the odd Eskimo parka, Scottish kilt, Caribbean festival shirt, Indian turban, or Canadian cowboy hat in his role of official royal spokesman, but his everyday clothes—if that adjective can be said to apply easily to a person so much in the public eye—are indeed paradigms of propriety: pinstriped suits of impeccable and conservative cut, spread-collar shirts and regimental neckwear, and black oxfords for town garb; pullovers, corduroys, tweed jackets, checked caps, and the traditional green Barbour jacket for country occasions. Definitely nothing trendy, or even highly fashionable for that matter, you understand, merely the tried-and-true aura of easy elegance, a tradition of propriety, if you will, which tends to indicate that Savile Row is perhaps more a state of mind than a thoroughfare. It is, in fact, not really much at all as a thoroughfare—but it is the greatest tailoring street in the world. Period.

Tailoring as we know it, like almost everything else as we know it, began with the Renaissance. Well, actually, cutting and tailoring—the two basic aspects of the craft of constructing clothing from pattern—began to develop gradually between the twelfth and fourteenth centuries, depending on where you were at the time, and moved along rather rapidly after that. The *Oxford English Dictionary*'s first reference to the word "tailor" gives the specific date of 1297, and the Geneva Bible, with its famously amusing translation of Genesis 3:7—"They sewed figge tree leaves together, and made themselves breeches"— wasn't published until 1560, by which time the ideas of tailoring had obviously taken firm hold.

The reason we must look to the Renaissance for the birth of tailoring is to be found in the influence of what has come to be known as humanism: a broad as well as a deep concern for the human, for life in this world as opposed to life in the next. The difference between the other-worldly concerns of the Middle Ages and the worldly concerns of the Renaissance can easily be discerned in the dress of the two periods. Contrast the Gothic miniatures, for example, with fifteenth-century portraits (portraiture itself is a product of the Renaissance), Giotto's *Lamentation* (*ca.* 1305) with Jan Van Eyck's *Giovanni Arnolfini and His Bride* (*ca.* 1434). More often than not, human figures in medieval paintings look as though they are wearing long sheets of aluminum foil, coverings which give little indication of the body beneath. Renaissance portraits seem to exalt in corporeality—and this is our basis for fashion: from this point in time onwards, fashion tends to accentuate various parts of the human body, in an attempt to idealize it. Idealization of anything provides, of course, constantly changing views. Consider Holbein's celebrated portrait of Henry VIII, with the incredibly enormous shoulders and codpiece, as an antithesis to any of Van Dyck's portraits of Charles I.

It was not until the guild systems of the late Middle Ages that there was even any differentiation between clerical and secular dress. During the Middle Ages clothing was regarded as a means of concealing the body. With the rise of humanism, however, came the accentuation, even the glorification, of the human form. The loose robe, the standard uniform of the medieval period, was shortened and tightened, and eventually cut and pieced together in attempts to approach the idealized contours of the human body. These attempts called for expert skill and division of labor; in short, the cutter and tailor joined the other craftsmen as important members of the community. The British tailors' guild dates from 1300.

Until this time all but the most aristocratic made their own clothes, from simple woven cloth stitched together and draped on the body. The weaver produced the cloth, the distinguishing feature of clothing, but more and more after 1300 the tailor took on equal importance with the weaver, and gradually he came to overshadow him. This development parallels the rise of the city in Europe. Master tailors in the growing towns were responsible now for the clothing of society, and from the fourteenth century the art and science of tailoring became a highly specialized, complex, and jealously guarded craft. First Italy, next Spain, then France became the center for fashion in concert with the power, wealth, and influence of those empires. France reached its fashionable peak for tailoring during the long reign of Louis XIV, when foppish young men from all over Europe flocked to Paris for their wardrobes. Almost every comic play written between 1660 and 1715 includes a Paris-dressed fop, perfumed and beribboned in the latest French mode. But when Louis died in that year, wearing the doublet and hose he and his courtiers still favored, there had already begun a shift in influence.

Across the channel, the English nobility had all but abandoned the highly decorative French costume in favor of coat, waistcoat, and breeches—a style of dress which, with slight modification, men have worn ever since. The English had just come through a bitter but democratizing civil war which, among other things, called into question the brocades and velvets, the silks and pastel satins and powdered wigs and other ostentations of court dress. Over two centuries later Oscar Wilde would quip that the Puritans and Cavaliers were more interesting for their costumes than their moral convictions. During the eighteenth century this fashion revolution was completed. Because of their love of country life, the climate, the interest in field sport, and growing industrialization, the English moved away from highly decorative and delicate court costume and took up a more practical form of dress. The costume of both the landed gentry and city businessman became progressively less gorgeous and far more somber. By mid-nine-

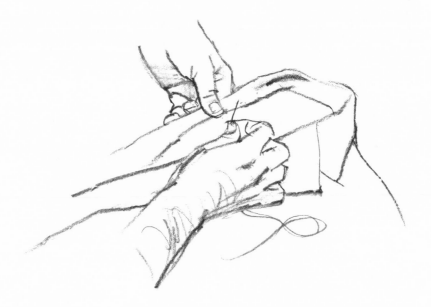

teenth century, sobriety (in dress at any rate) had penetrated even to the court itself, and rulers were seen to dress in manner almost identical with their subjects. And it is here that the genius of the London tailor blossomed.

London tailors came to dominate men's fashions in the nineteenth century for basically two reasons. First, the English had evolved a style for masculine clothing that was a blending of landed gentry sporting attire and bourgeois business wear produced in the wake of the Industrial Revolution. Even coming at the very beginning of the period, a figure such as Beau Brummell becomes a prototype and blatant symbol of the style. Second, the clothes up through the seventeenth century had not been constructed so much with a concern for fit as they had with concerns for decorative styling and color. But when the shift away from delicate fabrics, pastel hues, and ornamentation began to occur, fit became the criterion of dress for men. And in fit the English tailor had the decided edge. He trained in woolens (and had, as he still does, the best woolen cloth in the world), and over the years of experimentation and practice he developed techniques for "molding" clothing quite close to the body without duplicating exactly the form of the wearer. Brummell would not allow his clothes to show a single wrinkle, and with his constant emphasis on a perfect fit helped to elevate the tailor into a true artist. Some dandies of the Regency period even had their coats weighted down with strips of lead sewn into the hems to assure a perfectly smooth line.

In a sense, the appearance of Brummell and the other Regency dandies marked the end of an era as well as the beginning of one. They were proof by their very appearances that the ancien régime of privilege by birth, of ostentation and aristocracy, was being pushed aside. Geoffrey Squire summarizes this shift when he says, in Dress and Society: 1560–1970:

> When men gave up doublet and hose in favor of coat, waistcoat and breeches they had taken an irreversible step towards the modern world, in which technology, science and industry take precedence over instinct, intuition and craftsmanship.

And it was at this historical juncture, those early years of the nineteenth century, that the appearance of the aristocracy and bourgeoisie met. Brummell was—at least in his dress—a gentleman, characterized by unobtrusiveness and respectability. For the gentleman (itself a nineteenth-century term), ostentation and gorgeousness were frowned upon, sobriety and simplicity favored. Pastel silks and velvets were replaced with more somber shades of wool, cut and tailored to perfection in London.

London tailoring is often thought to be synonymous with Savile Row, although the terms are somewhat misleading. All London tailors are not "Savile Row" tailors, and in fact all "Savile Row" tailors are not Savile Row tailors. Let me try to explain that. First, and here is the rub, not every tailor in London is capable of producing the quality of work associated with the image conjured up by the term "Savile Row." The Greater London telephone directory lists over seven hundred tailoring firms, dozens of which are every bit as incompetent as can be found anywhere. In fact, the most repulsive suit I think I ever saw was in the shop window of a tailor in Charing Cross Road. A horribly cheap purplish affair that still gives me the occasional nightmare.

Almost without exception, the top-quality tailors of London are to be found exclusively in the West End of the city. Not even just the

West End, but in one square mile of the West End, with the street Savile Row more or less running through the middle. Bordered on the east and west by Regent and Bond Streets, and on the north and south by Conduit Street and Burlington Gardens (which is a street), this is the Golden Mile of Tailoring. As far as Savile Row itself is concerned, it is a mere three blocks long, a few dozen buildings on either side of a narrow but straight city street. The "Savile Row" area, however, actually extends two blocks farther south across Piccadilly into Jermyn Street—called "Shirt Street" because so many of the world's best shirt-makers are there—and two blocks farther west to Albemarle and Dover streets. Within this general area, within even the three short blocks of the Row itself, are found, quite simply and without qualification, the best collection of fine tailors in the world.

The Savile Row area is not particularly old by London standards. The present scheme of streets, squares, and original architecture dates only from the eighteenth century. On its northern border lies fashionable Hanover Square, and two blocks west Berkeley Square, where the nightingales are wont to sing. Most of the land between Hanover Square and Piccadilly was owned in the early years of that century by Lord Burlington, who first developed the area, leased the lots, and supervised the building of town houses in what is now Burlington Street, Cork Street, and the Row itself. The famous arcade that stands on one side of Burlington House, the fashionable Burlington Arcade, was not actually built until 1815—the year of Wellington's victory over Napoleon at Waterloo.

In the early years of the nineteenth century, Savile Row was the haunt of physicians and surgeons. The building now housing the famous tailoring firm of Huntsman & Sons was the home and surgery of Richard Bright, the physician who first described and categorized the various forms of kidney inflammation named after him. By mid-century, however, the doctors were being driven out of the Row—by tailors. The first tailor to set up shop in the Row was Henry Poole. His father had been a tailor before him, had in fact been situated at various locations in London before opening a shop at No. 4 Old Burlington Street in 1823, just around the corner from Savile Row, one street over. In 1846 Henry's father died, leaving him the business, and being a forward-looking fellow, he immediately set about enlarging the premises.

He made the main entrance out of the back door of the building, into Savile Row, and thus became the first tailor in the street that would gain fame as the world center of tailoring.

Poole's reputation prospered, and other tailors began to set up shop close to him. The year 1860 is perhaps the most important in this history in that it served to solidify Poole's influence as a preeminent tailor and guarantee the importance of the Row. One night in the fall of that year, the Prince of Wales (later Edward VII) attended the theater to see a performance of *Ruy Blas*. The costumes, as it happened, had been made by Henry Poole. The prince admired the play and the acting, but admired the clothes more, and soon Poole's was supplying most of HRH's wardrobe. Other esteemed and celebrated clients followed, and soon the firm was making the clothes for most of the British and European gentry. "We are Poole's," became their slogan, "the rest are merely puddles." Good tailors seem to pull others along in their slipstream, and by 1875 the Row was a favored haunt of aristocratic young blades, some of whom spent the better part of each day sauntering from one shop to another.

Perhaps a bit sadly, the architecture of Savile Row has changed considerably since its Victorian heyday of quiet dignity. Some of it was bombed during World War II, and much is quite modern. Then, too, there are any number of establishments here that have nothing to do with tailoring: a record company, a bookshop, the Forestry Commission and a lovely Art Deco police station, a parking lot, and several office buildings. The handsomest house in the street is occupied by the English couturier Hardy Amies (at No. 14). There are still to be seen several wrought iron gates and fences fronting the remaining Georgian houses, but a recent article in the *Times* (London) sums up the current attitude:

> Savile Row today is a pale shadow of its Victorian glory, when the royalty of Europe headed glittering lists of patrons and when the "gilded and sporting youths of the aristocracy" would flock from the daily fashion parade in Rotten Row to their tailors, as if to a club, there to sip the claret and hock reverentially provided. But it retains much of the dedication, dignity, and discreet pride that for the foreign customer still makes it the Mecca of good taste.

BY APPOINTMENT
SHIRTMAKERS AND HOSIERS
TO THE LATE KING GEORGE V

Things had been, I am afraid, slightly glum-making on the Row since World War II: the improvement in the quality of ready-made clothing and changing life-styles meant fewer and fewer men going to tailors, and rapidly rising rents drove many firms off the Row, if not out of business altogether. But for the past several years the Row has been undergoing a renaissance. Ten years ago there were only half a dozen of the old firms left here—the others had been pushed into less prestigious thoroughfares by high rents, or had simply gone out of business. Henry Poole's had moved into neighboring Cork Street. Apparently, though, businesses that took their places have not flourished, and landlords were happy to have the tailors back when the opportunity arose. Additionally, there is a growing, perhaps a renewed, respect for the workmanship and quality the Row produces—certainly any number of the new breed of celebrity menswear designers have stated their indebtedness both in the press and in the clothes they create. Today there are about twenty first-rate firms in the Row. Kilgour, French & Stanbury is now here; so is Tommy Nutter; Helman; Malcolm Plews; Anthony Hewitt; and Norman; Anderson & Sheppard; Norton & Sons, Huntsman; Sullivan & Woolley; Nutters; Welsh & Jefferies; and Gieves & Hawkes are all here. And best of all, Henry Poole, who started it all in 1846, is back in the Row. The tradition has reasserted itself: Savile Row Lives!

SEERSUCKER

T he only thing that's changed about the seersucker suit over the past fifty years has been the price. In the 1930s the two-piece, single breasted, 100 per cent cotton classic sold for around $15. After the Second World War, Brooks Brothers raised its price from that figure to a whopping $18.50, and the price has been rising ever since. Today Brooks gets around $200 for their traditional blue-white or gray-white striped patch-pocketed model—which I reckon is still not an unreasonable amount to pay for a classic, along with the assurance that it hasn't been meddled with or cheapened. Not to mention that you could go over it with a divining rod and not find any polyester. Which, as it happens, is one reason why the price of a 100 per cent cotton seersucker suit will continue to rise.

Back in the 1960s cotton farmers took something of a beating when the synthetics fabric industry managed to convince a large number of people that a wrinkle-free appearance was the prime sartorial criterion. The designer ilk, led by the resourceful Italians, countered by flaunting a corrugated look. The space beneath the name on the label carried the ironically chic phrase "Guaranteed to Wrinkle," cotton became a terribly upscale fiber, and it became possible to theorize that all human life was divided between those who found the shiny, slippery, wrinkle-free stuff a boon to their appearances and those who would rather look like unmade beds. In that quarter, "natural" was a word to die for. Unfortunately for the cotton industry, however, synthetic fabrics continued to grow in popularity. From roughly 1960 to 1970 cotton's share of the fiber market was reduced by half, from 60 to 30 per cent. Many farmers who had made their living growing cotton converted to soybeans and grain. Lately the natural-fiber industries (silk, wool, cotton, linen) have been vigorously fighting to turn folks away from the synthetics. The Wool Bureau, for example, recently made known that it will increase its advertising spending by some $8.5 million a year for the next five years, in the face of increased promotional efforts by its competition, manufacturers of synthetic fibers. The reality is that while natural fibers accounted for 70 per cent of all textile fiber business in 1960, today—even after the much hyped "cachet" resurgence started by the designers—it accounts for just under 40 per cent.

Well, I don't want to bog us down in statistics, when the point is merely that cotton is the prototype opposite of the man-made fibers. The first record of cotton cloth is from the Indus Valley culture of India, around 2000 B.C., although cotton textiles have also been found in pre-Inca graves in Peru and in the tombs of ancient Egypt. Europeans first discovered the fabric through their trade with the East. Crusaders brought home gossamer cottons as part of the spoils of war and eventually began the trade expeditions to India and China, where some of the world's best cotton is still to be found. Columbus saw cotton in the Bahamas and erroneously believed he had discovered the long-sought sea-route to India. Magellan found extensive cotton cultivation in Brazil. Methodical cotton textile manufacture in the West began in the seventeenth century, and mercantilism made it a thriving industry, particularly in Britain where subsequent inventions such as Hargreaves's spinning jenny (1764) and Arkwright's power loom (1785) helped lay the foundations for the great Industrial Revolution of the nineteenth century.

In the New World cotton was one of the first staple crops considered acceptable for export by Virginia settlers, and later, after 1793 when the New Englander Eli Whitney invented the cotton gin—that famous machine that tremendously reduced the man-hours of labor involved in separating the cotton seeds from the boll—the whole economy of the South was profoundly changed. "King Cotton" established socio-logical patterns of both rural South and industrial North that existed for generations and eventually led to a terrible and bloody civil war in which the homesick soldiers of Dixie often took strength and consola-tion from singing of how they wished they were in the land of cotton, where old times were not forgotten.

Indications are that the particular cotton fabric we have come to identify with our summer suiting was first woven in India, the name seersucker being a Hindi corruption of a Persian phrase, "shir shak-kar," which translates as "milk and sugar." Conceivably this etymology is meant to explain the alternating rough and smooth textures of the stripes, the distinctive feature of the cloth that is achieved by what is called slack-tension weaving. In slack-tension production alternating fibers are held under normal tension, while intervening ones are kept slack; the resulting fabric has a pattern of puckered and flat stripes that is permanant and intrinsic. Garments made of seersucker fabric are persistently puckered, and ironing becomes rather superfluous. This makes it not only seersucker's distinguishing characteristic but its great-est virtue as well. One doesn't worry about wrinkles because the stuff is permanently wrinkled, which, when it comes to the problem of what to wear in hot and humid climes, presents a solution near to genius.

We could say that unwrinkled clothing represents some sort of aes-thetic ideal, to be sure. Still, seersucker's appeal would tend to contra-dict, and make us fall back on sociology. Wrinkled clothing (as understood by, say, Thorstein Veblen and his followers) can of course bespeak a slovenly person, just as unwrinkled and clean clothes were thought by the Victorians to be next to godliness. But unwrinkled clothing can also be interpreted as a symbolic message that the wearer is wealthy to the point of not having to crease his clothes by manual labor, and you could say that all of those products and all of the adver-tising geared toward promoting wrinkle-free figures cater to some sort of bourgeois ideal and represent an auxiliary part of the "white-collar" syndrome. Veblen's theory of conspicuous consumption (as laid out in his *Theory of the Leisure Class*, first published in 1899) can nicely be applied here. The problem is that with the invention and popularity of inexpensive synthetics, a wrinkle-free appearance is no longer an aris-tocratic ideal.

Science has, in short, made it necessary to change the rules of fashion, even though the underlying principle remains the same. Particularly in a consumer-oriented society, that which is most expensive is most highly prized; and even in a democracy, if something is easily achievable by everyone, it loses its cachet. Until the 1920s seersucker was still considered work-clothes–type fabric, worn by manual laborers in the South. But when university men began to take it up it gained status rapidly, first on campus, then at the country club. And today, as it becomes even more expensive (the summer seersucker-type suits that are blends of cotton and polyester sell for about half the price of an all-cotton one), seersucker—the all-natural, guaranteed-to-look-about-as-wrinkled-as-you-can-be—is recognized as a monarch of summer suiting.

SPORTING CLOTHES

I t was back on a bleak November day in 1977 that Abercrombie & Fitch, the most famous sporting goods store in
the world, closed its door at 45th and Madison. Today "the
adventure goes on," as their catalogue says, in a number of much
smaller Abercrombies around the country. These chain-branches of A
& F are, in themselves, fine stores indeed. They stock a small, select
variety of sports clothing (safari suits, waterproof fishing ponchos,
yachting caps and parkas, and the like) and excellent equipment (Scottish fly bags, Fenwick rods, Jaques croquet sets, fine golf clubs, exquis-
ite game knives). But they are *not* the old Abercrombie.

The days appear to be at least temporarily gone when one could find
all the best sports gear under one roof, as it was in the glorious heyday
of A & F; when you could buy a handmade, split-cane fly rod on the
fourth floor, a pair of Scottish wool hiking socks on the second, and
be outfitted for a safari on the sixth. Rex Gage, the chief instructor and
master shot at London's famous gunsmith Holland & Holland, used
to fly over to New York twice a year to personally take measurements
for custom-made shotguns at the store. What Brooks Brothers is to
business wear, Abercrombie & Fitch was to sporting gear, and many a
sportsman made annual pilgrimages to that hallowed ground to be put

in full sporting fig and came away feeling that once again reason and quality had triumphed.

Then fell the swift hammer: a notice in the *New York Times* that A & F was having a tremendous sale, everything must go, the store was closing. There were lines around the block all of that fateful week, as folks made a last-minute dash to grab what they could of the loot and the legend. Both *Time* and *Newsweek* devoted a page to the event. It was the passing of an era.

Not within memory has a store been so sorely missed, and since then many people have been rather traumatically fogged in about where

to find first-class sporting clothes: a proper fishing bag, quality hiking boots, a correct hacking jacket, or well-made golf shoes. Many have taken to aimlessly strolling through suburban shopping malls, loitering in department stores, rummaging through piles of army-navy surplus, sighing their way about these chains of ersatz "sporting goods stores" that seem to deal exclusively in running shoes and polyester sweat shirts, and frantically thumbing the various field-and-stream catalogues in search of THE REAL THING. Such behavior is not at all conducive to relaxation and a sense of security.

But the truth of the matter is that while one must now look under several roofs, excellent quality sporting clothes can still be found. With sporting clothes, style inevitably derives from function, the prime attribute and distinguishing characteristic of the genre. While a necktie is included in a business outfit for fashion or social reasons, a stock tie is an integral part of a riding habit for quite other reasons: it serves as a bandage and sling for both man and beast caught in an accident. It is important that sporting attire function well: that it be comfortable, durable, and designed to serve the requirements of the game.

In the next section, I've listed first the general emporiums, then the firms which more or less specialize in clothing and equipment for a specific sport. It is rather difficult to quote any prices that will hold firm for any length of time, and the better procedure is to write for current prices and catalogues.

THE EMPORIUMS

Au Petit Matelot (27 Avenue de la Grande-Armee, Paris 75016)
Founded 200 years ago, the firm is really more of an institution than merely a shop. It was originally concerned with the outfitting of French sailors, and one of its best sellers is still the navy pea coat, which the firm is said to have invented. It is obviously the first choice for the classiest sailing duds around—Breton canvas trousers, striped cotton jerseys, blazers and the like—but there is also a fine selection of general sportswear, including down-filled vests, corduroy hiking breeches and shooting jackets, waterproof parkas with endless numbers of pock-

ets for fishing gear, and authentic Austrian loden hunting coats, not to mention the classic yachting cap, which boasts all the traditional features from embroidered visor to gold anchor insignia.

Brigatti (Corso Venezia 15, Milan 20121)

This Italian firm stocks sybaritic clothing for the sportsman who believes that function should not be devoid of style. Whether it be for golf or tennis, fishing or hunting, Brigatti designs are made of the finest materials and meticulous detailing. Fishing jackets are made only of the best long-staple poplin; warm-up suits—unlike the dull gray sweat suits we are all too accustomed to—are found here in a variety of attractive shades and made of the most functional stretch-cotton to be had; tweed hunting jackets are of impeccable cut, with reinforced shoulder gun patches of matched pigskin. Very fine outfitters indeed for those who dress to win by intimidation as well as skill.

L. L. Bean (Freeport, ME 04033)

The legendary U.S. outdoors outfitters now mail several million copies of their famous catalogues every year, and while many another wilderness outfitter has come along in their slipstream, they are the granddaddy of the form. The Bean catalogue has the best dollar value anywhere for chamois shirts, canvas duck field coats, camouflage parkas, insulated waders, whipcord shooting pants, wool balaclavas, buffalo plaid guide shirts, English moleskin trousers, deerskin mittens, and literally hundreds of other types of camping, fishing, and hunting gear. The rubber hunting shoe, now so much a standard part of any outdoor wardrobe, was invented by Mr. Bean himself back in 1912, and his version, which now comes in a dozen different styles, is still the best. Everything in the catalogue is fully and unconditionally guaranteed.

Morrie Mages Sports (620 N. LaSalle Street, Chicago, IL 60610)

This is one of the largest sporting goods stores in the world, and its eight-storey building is an absolute mountain of equipment and clothing: everything from ski pants and baseball hats to dumbbells, bicycles, and hockey sticks. It is in fact the sort of place where sheer numbers overwhelm, from the dozens of brands of parkas and thousands of roller skates to hundreds of football jerseys, thousands of basketball shorts, and a zillion different hats and caps and other sporting head gear. Perhaps the largest inventory of sporting goods to be found anywhere.

Paragon Sporting Goods (867 Broadway, New York, NY 10003)
Paragon is the largest sporting goods store in the east, with the most extensive range of warm-up jackets, jogging suits, and running shoes anywhere. There's nothing chic or country gentleman about Paragon, it's rather a huge warehouse with room after room filled to bursting with winterized parkas and Woolrich hiking shirts, golf shoes and ski masks, mountaineering boots, thermal underwear, and basketball sneakers. You can always be assured that they will have your size, and to make matters even better, Paragon sells almost everything at discount.

RIDING

H. Huntsman & Sons (11 Savile Row, London W1)
While there are a number of other excellent tailors in the Savile Row area of London who can put you into perfect kit to chase the fox or amble stylishly through the park, Huntsman has the justifiable reputation for the finest custom-made riding coats and breeches that money can buy. Fittings are done "in the saddle" on a wooden mount to achieve sublimity of form and function. The firm will also be happy to run you up a nice tweed hacking jacket, a pair of cavalry twills with chamois knees, or a fine West-of-England cloth show suit cut to perfection. Prices are commensurate with such perfection.

M. J. Knoud (716 Madison Avenue, New York, NY 10021)
There is no denim in evidence here, nor cowboy hats or Roy Rogers shirts either for that matter, because Knoud specializes in English-style riding appointments. What one does find here are superb tweed and worsted hacking jackets from Pytchley of England, finger-tip-length rubberized riding raincoats, very proper twill jodhpurs, canary and tattersall wool postboy waistcoats with brass buttons, cotton checked rat-catcher shirts with stock collars, rubber-and-canvas Newmarket boots, string gloves, and of course made-to-measure pink hunt coats and show suits.

Shepler's (2500 E. Centennial Boulevard, Arlington, TX 76011)
Shepler's—which has several stores in the west and midwest, as well
as a huge mail-order outlet in Wichita, Kansas—is mecca for cowboys
of the real as well as drugstore variety who want authentic western-
style clothes. The firm stocks more jeans, more ten-gallon hats, more
boots, silver-buckled belts, pearl-studded shirts, chaps, and fancy red
bandanas than there are beans in Boston. See "Mail Order Clothes."

OTHERS:

W. & H. Gidden (15d Clifford Street, London WC1)
For racing silks, rubber estate boots, and riding outercoats.

Herbert Johnson (13 Old Burlington Street, London WC1)
For the finest riding headgear, from plush-bodied top hats and hunt bowlers to canvas polo caps, custom-made riding hats, and even crash helmets.

H. Kauffman & Sons (139 E. 24th Street, New York, NY 10010)
A good general supplier of English and western riding attire.

Henry Maxwell & Co. (11 Savile Row, London W1)
The firm makes what is considered to be the world's best riding boots (a pair of black waxed calf chestnut-topped hunting boots are now priced at about $2,500); Maxwell also stocks the world's largest selection of quality spurs.

Swaine, Adeney, Brigg & Sons (185 Piccadilly, London W1)
Whipmakers, holding a Royal Warrant since 1790, the firm has a small but perfect selection of country shoes, tweed jackets, belts, gloves, scarves, and hats for equestrian pursuits.

E. Vogel (19 Howard Street, New York, NY 10013)
The finest custom-made riding boots in this country, crafted in a dozen different styles.

SHOOTING AND HUNTING

J. C. Cording & Co. (19 Piccadilly, London W1)
For almost a century and a half now Cording has been recognized for its superb, traditional English country clothes. The firm stocks a complete range of Grenfell cloth rainwear (golf jackets, over-trousers, anoraks, full military trench coats, shooting jackets and breeches, and field coats), Harris tweed Inverness capes (the kind Sherlock Holmes wore), tweed shooting jackets that reverse to proofed poplin, stout Norfolk jackets with matching plus fours, the justly famous Barbour game jackets, and a dozen other hunting and shooting jackets, capes, and outercoats in covert cloth, rubberized cotton, and heavy-duty corduroy. The firm is also the supplier of the famous Veldtschoen by Lotus of England, considered by many to be the finest walking shoe ever made.

Hunting World (16 East 53rd Street, New York, NY 10022)
Unlike the ersatz safari-style stuff that seems to be everywhere these last few seasons, Hunting World supplies the Real Thing for the bush and outback: absolutely the finest Egyptian cotton jackets and trousers,

both with a plentiful amount of deep, reinforced pockets; ankle-high rough leather boots, made in Kenya to traverse desert and veldt; Aussie-style broad-brimmed felt hats with puggaree bands to shade a chap from the intense tropical sun; and the most beautiful and tough travel luggage available anywhere. This is the original and authentic gear, the place, one suspects, designers come for inspiration.

OTHERS:

Gokey (84 S. Wabasha Street, Saint Paul, MN 55107)
Snakeproof boots, upland boots, country shoes, camp shoes, and double-soled moccasins, all made of sturdy eight-ounce oil-tanned leather that is very versatile, comfortable, and tough.

Holland & Holland (13 Bruton Street, London W1)
Fine shotgun shell bags, shooting jackets, and other accesories from one of the world's best gunsmiths.

Loden-Plankl (Michaelerplatz 6, Vienna A-1010)
The place for authentic loden cloth shooting capes, hunting jackets, overcoats, and hunting trousers.

Purdey & Sons (57 South Audley Street, London W1)
Purdey shotguns are perhaps the most famous in the world, and the firm stocks excellent cotton shooting jackets with leather gun patches, oil-wool sweaters, and heavy Scottish hand-framed hose so your appearance doesn't detract from the beauty of the gun.

FISHING AND SAILING

C. Farlow (5 Pall Mall, London SW1)
This firm, located in the Royal Opera Arcade, was established in 1840 and is an all-round angling shop. They've got every sort of fishing rod for sea or stream, wet and dry flies, and of course all the multi-pocketed fisherman's vests, waders, creels, and anything else a fisherman would wear. They've also got a Royal Warrant from Prince Charles, who is reputedly an expert angler.

Fulton Supply Co. (23 Fulton Street, New York, NY 10010)
America's Cup yachtsmen and weekend paddle-board pushers alike frequent this eighty-year-old shop across the street from the legendary Fulton Fish Market in this newly refurbished section of lower Manhattan. Fulton Supply carries top quality foul-weather gear in traditional yellow or green-black (sailors never wear white at sea, because then they couldn't be seen in the whitecaps if washed overboard). Full-length slickers, high-chested overalls, real oilskin sou'westers, red canvas sailing trousers, and seaworthy rubber boots are always in stock here.

Goldbergs' Marine (202 Market Street, Philadelphia, PA 19106)
"Where thousands of boaters save millions of dollars" is the subtitle of

their well-known catalogue, and Goldbergs' has everything for boaters—including boats! In the clothing line are a complete range of foul-weather suits in nylon and Gore-Tex, deck boots, wool watch caps and CPO shirts, and flotation jackets. There is also a good range of classic-style navy pea coats, extra-long (42 inches) officers' bridge coats, striped wool Breton sweaters, and even bikini swimsuits. Everything very competitively priced.

Hardy Brothers (61 Pall Mall, London SW1)

Hardy has been a family business since 1872, and while this is not a large shop, everything is best quality, from the Palakona split-cane rods (the finest made) to deep sea reels, nets, tackle, and clothing for the fisherman. The canvas-and-leather bags with snapout rubber liners are perfect, and the fine poplin jackets and hats just the thing for the compleat angler.

OTHERS:

Cambrian Fly Fishers (The Old Vicarage, Trevor, Llangollen, North Wales)

Moleskin trousers and shirts, lightweight waxed fowler jackets, and heavy-cleated estate boots are reasonably priced and high quality; also tweed plus twos, Norfolk jackets, cotton-wool shirts.

Lands' End Merchants (Lands' End Lane, Dodgeville, WI 53595)

Foul weather gear and boots, canvas luggage, and a large selection of poplin and chino shorts, jeans, and deck trousers.

Orvis (10 River Road, Manchester, VT 05254)

Fishing bags of triple-laminated, waterproof cotton duck, tough canvas-and-leather duffel bags, and Gore-Tex rainwear (jackets, pants, hats, outercoats, and even gloves and shoes).

Captain O. M. Watts (45 Albemarle Street, London W1)

"Everything for the Yachtsman and the Yacht," as the sign above the door states, which includes reefer jackets, white duck trousers, bright yellow wellington boots, yachting caps, and of course wet suits.

Hiking and Camping

Hudson's Camping Supplies (105 Third Avenue, New York, NY 10003)
Hudson's is the largest army-navy store in the country and is chock full of work clothes of every conceivable type and material stockpiled in half a dozen enormous rooms. You can count on them for a plentiful supply of army field jackets (with optional insulated liners), jeans (including the original Levi's with the copper button fly), quilted leather flight jackets with mouton collars, down vests, the famous Sorel Canadian snow boots, khaki work shirts, and countless other military and outdoor gear of all sorts.

Kreeger & Son (16 West 46th Street, New York, NY 10021)
Kreeger, ironically located half a block off chic and sophisticated Fifth Avenue, is the backpackiest store imaginable. In the large, woodsy salesroom can be found everything for the hiker: a dozen different styles of hiking boots and shoes (including the full range of Timberlands), thick woolen ragg socks, green felt Maine guide hats, khakis lined in red flannel, corduroy knickers with reinforced seats and knees, and the most extensive range of parkas (double-sized, goose down, flannel-lined, ultra-light, nylon shells, and what have you).

Robert Lawrie (54 Seymour Street, London W1)
Lawrie's is a fitting place to purchase one's climbing boots, since Mr. Lawrie invented the modern, lightweight mountain-climbing boot half a century ago. These were the boots first used on the 1932 assault on Mt. Everest and later on the 1953 expedition headed by Sir Edmund Hillary that finally conquered the peak. It's safe to say they've been on probably every famous climb since then, and Hillary is only one of a host of famous mountaineering clients who come to this serious shop for the best of professional gear.

OTHERS:

Eddie Bauer (Fifth & Union, P.O. Box 3700, Seattle, WA 98124)
The place for goose down coats of all styles from full length to under garments; wool buffalo plaid mackinaws; thermal underwear, mittens, and even goose down kimonos.

Pindisports (13/18 High Holborn, London WC1)
A large sporting goods store specializing in climbing and camping clothing and equipment.

Tricker's (67 Jermyn Street, London SW1)
A sophisticated West End shop that sells very elegant town shoes but also is renowned for their Derby shoe in tan gorse leather with stout, welted sole—an excellent country walking shoe (also made in a boot model).

TENNIS, GOLF, SKIING, RUNNING

Foot Joy (7 East 52nd Street, New York, NY 10021)
While any comfortable sweater and slacks will do nicely for a round of golf, good golfing shoes are imperative. Foot Joy has been making wonderfully functional, comfortable, and good-looking ones for decades and is always sure to have dozens of styles in every size. Whether your mood is for red patent leather, black-and-white calf saddle, green lizard, or plain brown suede, this is the shop.

The Racquet Shop (289 Madison Avenue, New York, NY 10021)
Hang around the Racquet Shop for a while and you're liable to spot most of the Wimbledon finalists, since most of the pros have their racquets strung here. The firm carries all the brand name tennis togs and shoes, warm-up suits, headbands, and everything else fashionable and functional seen on center court (including Tretorn, Lacoste, Fred Perry, Adidas, Head, Bogner). Naturally the shop for the pristine white wool, V-neck tennis sweater.

St. Andrews Golf Centre (St. Mary's Place, St. Andrews, Scotland KY169UY)
St. Andrew's is the home of golf, and this shop stocks superior equipment and quality leisurewear at reasonable prices: Greg Norman rainwear, Ballantyne cashmere pullovers, classic wool checked caps, dress length Argyle hose, beautifully crafted English golf shoes, and natty tartan plaid plus twos create the traditional look on the greens and in the clubhouse. This is, incidentally, the place to buy those famous handmade hickory putters.

Scandinavian Ski Shop (40 West 57th Street, New York, NY 10022)
The evolution of ski wear has been the most radical of any type of
sports clothing in this century. Until the 1940s men were still sliding
down the slopes in suits and sports jackets, warmth provided by awk-
wardly thick thermal underwear and heavy woolen turtleneck sweaters.
Today synthetic fabrics and daring design have given a new freedom
to the skier. The Scandinavian Ski Shop has three floors of the most
innovative equipment and clothes for the slope: a complete selection
by Head, Bogner, Kneissl, Hexcel, Olin, Nordica, Raichle, and Ros-
signol. And the advice of the sales staff here may be trusted with complete assurance, since they have about three decades of experience
behind them.

OTHERS:

Sports Drobny (33 Thurloe Place, London SW7)
Jaroslav Drobny was the men's singles champion at Wimbledon in
1954 and started this shop to provide the best equipment and clothes
to tennis players; limited selection, but quality attire and shoes.

Tennis & Company (211 East 60th Street, New York, NY 10022):
Very sophisticated tennis and jogging clothing; cotton mesh tops striped
in silk, fashion-colored warm-up suits, beautiful shorts, and a full line
of quality court shoes (by Nike, Tretorn, and others).

SUMMER HATS

S ummer hats account for about ten per cent of the total number of hats manufactured and worn. And of course it's not as though hats are thought to be the most essential item in a man's wardrobe these days anyway. But, to look on the brighter side of it, things have been getting better for hatters of late. I don't want to bore you with a lot of facts and figures: allow me to merely give you the most pregnant ones. In 1970, surely the darkest hour before the dawn for hatters everywhere, retail sales were below $200,000,000; by 1980 they had topped (no joke) $900,000,000, and this year promises to be easily better. Perhaps not exactly what we should call a renaissance of headgear, but hat manufacturers, like thirsting men welcoming a mild shower after a devastating drought, are fairly dancing with glee.

The exuberance is indeed newfound. If you peruse photo magazines that were published before World War II, it becomes immediately clear that practically everyone wore hats. Crowd scenes are a sea of felt fedoras, wide brimmed and pinch crowned. But after the war there came a radical change, and hats began a fashion slide from which they are only now just beginning to recover slightly—to phrase it as cautiously as possible. There seem to be two reasons for this deterioration after the war. First, returning soldiers were loath to adjust to the large-brimmed hats hatters were still showing, a fashion from pre-war days. Servicemen had worn small peaked military hats for four years and all those wide, thick-banded gray fedoras had a decided old-fashioned feel. Unlike the ladies, who in 1947 welcomed Christian Dior's "New Look," with its billowing dresses awash in fabric, men were moving towards what today would be called minimalism.

Secondly, and this may sound a bit strange at first, cars came to replace hats—as they in fact came to replace heavy coats, umbrellas, and galoshes. While not long before the war the rallying call had been "A Chicken in Every Pot," the decade after the war saw a prosperity that promised—and delivered—a car for every household. Cars that were warm and dry and that obviated the necessity of walking miles in the rain or standing on a cold and damp street corner waiting twenty minutes for a bus. And so, more and more men started to not wear hats.

Slowly hatters began to realize the market for hats was gone. And then, with relentless pace, came a very popular and very hatless president (hatters often react to the name Kennedy the way some southerners still react to the name Sherman) and long hair and anti-establishment dressing, and hatters were seen weeping in the crossroads. So much for the lack of mass appeal. Hatters made it through the 1960s the way Napoleon made it through Elba. Things were glum.

But now, after a decade of neglect, hats are coming back. They are becoming popular not as a means of protection—despite rising gas costs, cars are still with us, and some not much bigger than pre-war fedoras at that—but as a way of expressing style and personality. One of the more interesting phenomena of hats is that they almost seem to become a part of our personalities, as not a few celebrities have discovered: Telly Savalas and his black Tyrolian; Rex Harrison's English tweed; Tom Landry's velour trilby; Senator Daniel Moynihan's Irish walker; Burt Reynolds's urban cowboy hat all come to mind. And undoubtedly these celebrities and other highly visible personalities have helped to bring about the demi-renaissance for headgear.

There is, of course the utilitarian aspect to summer hats that should not be ignored, particularly with what is now known about the carcinogenic effects of too much sun, but it is this business of personalities and auras that strikes us so forcibly with summer hats. We conjure up images of Newport or the Henley Regatta, of men in trim cut blazers and crisp white ducks wearing boaters banded with club colors. Summer hats evoke Wembley and Wimbledon, gray-and-white seersucker, and white buckskin oxfords. One thinks of wide-brimmed planter's hats in Blue Harbour, Jamaica, or Cap d'Antibes; of Palm Beach and pink button-down shirts; of Noel Coward in Nassau, wearing a white drill mess jacket; or Fred Astaire singing "Let's Face the Music and Dance" in a creamy worsted barathea double-breasted dinner jacket, correspondent slip-ons, and a jauntily set boater.

The Panama and the boater are the two perfect summer hats. One of the nice things about the Panama hat is that it's still woven the way it always has been, by village craftsmen high in the mountains of Ecuador. "Hold on," I can hear my readers mutter, "I could have sworn he said 'Ecuador.' " Absolutely correct. The type of straw traditionally used for this type of hat comes from the jipijapa plant, a palmlike plant with long-stalked, fanlike leaves, and has been woven for more than three centuries in Ecuador ("jipijapa" is in fact the old Spanish word for Ecuador). Because these hats were originally marketed for export from Panama, people mistakenly assumed they had been made there.

Also, the Panama hat (I really don't see any point in trying to force etymological purity at this stage of the game by calling it an Ecuador hat) first attracted national attention in this country when Theodore Roosevelt was photographed sporting one at the Panama Canal construction site—and his was made in Ecuador as well. The vogue for the Panama started then, and industrious sailors on duty in that country bought bales of unblocked straw hats to peddle in American ports when they got home.

These hats are woven by the villagers in their own cottages. The stalks of the jipijapa are first cut and the leaves culled. The youngest and most pliable leaves are reserved for the weaving of hats. There has always been the myth that this work is done under water, to keep the fibers from going brittle. Though the story is apocryphal, there is a small shred of truth to it: to prepare the leaves for weaving they must be split to a desired width—as a rule, the narrower the split leaves the more expensive the hat—and for the job of splitting water is constantly applied to the leaves.

The split leaves are woven into a beehive shape, called a "hood" in the hatter's trade. Usually, when enough hoods have been woven, the villagers will deliver them to a main distribution point, from which they will be exported to hat factories around the world, where the hoods will be formed into hats of various styles. The finest hoods have traditionally come from Montecristi, a town southeast of the capital of Quito having a population of about 4,500; fine hats are often identified with this name. Because several months are required for the weaving of the best quality Panamas ("first grade" hoods are so finely plaited that the texture resembles finely woven linen), the retail price would now be in excess of $300, and therefore it is virtually impossible to find a Panama of this quality on the market today.

At the hat factory the hoods are blocked (that is, given a desired shape) and sized, an inner headband sewn in, and a ribbon outer band attached to the crown. My grandfather used to say that the test for a first-quality Panama was that you could roll it tightly enough to pass it through a wedding ring (which was in fact an old-fashioned designation for these hats because of this test). I've never tried to pass a Panama through a wedding ring, but the point is well taken. The distinguishing feature of a good Panama is its soft and resilient quality, its ability to spring back into shape after being rolled up and stuffed into a suitcase. Good Panamas are often sold in mailing tubes, and these tubes should be kept because they make excellent little traveling cases for the hats.

Whether it be in the large-brimmed "planter" style, or a smaller-brimmed town model, the Panama has a very district-commissioner-retired-from-colonial-service feel about it, the exact thing to wear with a beige pongee suit and white buckskin wing-tip oxfords. The straw boater, that other superb hat of summer, has other connotations: more the regatta set and university crowd, all blazers and old school ties sort of thing.

The boater, as its name indicates, has a nautical origin, and it was the famous British admiral Horatio Lord Nelson himself who first made the hard, round straw hat part of the regulation uniform of his crews. "Sennit," another name for the hat (it's also called a skimmer, but that's easy to understand), is also a term of nautical origin, coming from a naval technique of rope-braiding termed "seven-knit," which the woven straw resembles.

The boater has perhaps the greatest associations with the older public schools of England. In 1886 the headmaster of the King's School, Canterbury, a man named Field, "being a great believer in the value of symbols," as he put it, introduced the first school uniform: a straw boater. This was the only concession made to public school custom at the time, but numerous and thoroughly prescribed ones soon followed. Regarding the student's wearing of the boater, the rule was this: on weekdays the hat was de rigeur for going into town. The ribbon trim indicated the student's year:

> 1st-year: a wide black band
> 2nd-year: a wide colored band
> 3rd-year: a wide colored band
> 4th-year: a narrow colored band
> 5th-year: a narrow black band

At Eton the boater was adopted in honor of Lord Nelson, and every year on Boat Day (June 4th), the boys wear their hats with flowers stuck in the bands. The boaters worn by Harrovians are distinctive in that the brim is slightly wider than is encouraged at other public schools.

The boater's real popularity started after 1870, when a machine for sewing the straw was invented, and young men wore it with their brightly striped blazers "a-punting on the Thames" and other lazy rivers in scenes rescued from time by that whimsical Edwardian writer Jerome K. Jerome. By 1890 it was the most popular hat around. Look at any paintings of public gatherings of the period. My favorite is Renoir's *Le Moulin de la Galette,* a beautiful recreation of late-afternoon Belle Epoch dancing, the ladies in their satin-striped dresses with bustles and lace, holding flirtatious parasols; their partners in more discreet gray-and-black suits and white dress shirts, given a festive air with breezily tilted straw boaters.

It was also significantly popular in another literal way: it defied social rank, and like tweeds worn as sports outfits, it became the great leveler. The New York *Herald of Fashion* observed in the summer of 1894 that the streets of both New York and London were crowded with boaters, and, lest the sociological point be missed, added that "it was only last summer that Londoners began to wear straw hats with any freedom.

Before then it would have been a social crime for any man pretending to fashionable dress, to appear in London streets in any hat other than the high silk hat." The important phrase is "in London streets": the boater, no longer exclusive to seaside and river, had come into the city. Not only popular at cricket matches, picnics, and boating parties, the boater was now seen to accompany traditional business dress—the lounge suit.

Finally, and as a good example of how sportswear tends to infiltrate formal garb, the boater began to appear with the dinner jacket. It made great sense because there had been no summer formal headgear. Fred Astaire looked magnificent in his tropical-weight black tuxedo and boater singing "Something's Gotta Give" to Leslie Caron in *Daddy Long Legs.*

Up until the thirties the Panama and boater continued to be the most popular straw hats, but then more loosely woven straws began to be seen at resorts. The planter's hat in a variety of palm and coconut weaves was introduced by way of Nassau. Then came mesh-weave straws, leghorns (named after Leghorn, Italy, from which the straw—made from wheat fibers—was imported), coarsely woven water palms, raffias (woven from the light-colored leafstalks of the raffia palm), and even hemp weaves. There was the Spanish-style Montego hat, wide-brimmed with a flat crown and narrow band tied on one side. All of these island-style straws were banded usually with cotton or silk puggaree or brightly printed madras. When worn with a white dinner jacket, the puggaree was properly of plain white Indian madras. Occasionally an exotic feather band was seen.

Now of course we must add the urban cowboy hat to the list of straws. There was a TV commercial several years ago in which the actor Tom Selleck wore a straw cowboy hat with a tuxedo, which takes a certain amount of self-confidence to get away with. And since mere protection seems lost to us as an excuse for wearing hats, confidence is what it's all about. Bert Berinsky, the president and award-winning designer of Jay Lord Hatters (not to mention raconteur and general philosophe) told me once that he thought men who are afraid to wear hats are men who don't know themselves, which is an insightful point. In a sense hats are symbolic. I don't mean in a Freudian way, but more generally that they expose the inner personality and reflect what a person thinks of himself, perhaps more easily than any other article of clothing. The psychological reality, truism though it may be, is that the man makes the clothes, the clothes don't make the man.

So, if you know you can do it, by all means wear a straw cowboy hat with your dinner jacket. As the English writer Alison Adburgham said (in *The Bedside Guardian*), "If you are going to wear a hat at all, be decisive, and go the whole hat. In making a courageous choice . . . you have nothing to lose but your head."

TAILORS

"If you will kindly step through, sir?"

I remember the first time I ever heard those magic words. It was my second trip to London. I'd been there once before, when I was a student and had no money to speak of. None to whisper about, for that matter. This time, however, I was determined to have a real Savile Row suit, handmade with all the trimmings: buttonholes on the sleeve, step-lapelled waistcoat, silk linings in the knees, the works. I'd always bought good off-the-rack clothing, worked my way up to "special order" and "made-to-measure" stuff even as a young man in high school, imagining in the back of my mind that someday I'd be ready for THE REAL THING.

And so on that crisp spring morning, half a dozen years out of high school, I turned determinedly into the Row from the Burlington Gardens end, brought my courage to the sticking point, and marched resolutely through the heavy Victorian oak and bevelled glass front door of one of the most reputable bespoke tailoring firms in the world—all the while thinking of the kings and presidents, movie stars and diplomats, Greek shipping magnates, English dukes, and Texas oil millionaires who had done so before me. I was also wondering what I should do once the door closed behind me. Oh, if only one had been born into the Edwardian landed gentry, to have dear aristocratic Dad come along to introduce you to his esteemed tailor, it would have been so much easier.

Not to worry, as the English say. Standing outwardly calm but inwardly quivering like a leaf, I was quickly and quietly approached by a very proper elderly gentleman in a very proper gray, chalk-striped, double-breasted suit, who very properly and politely asked me if he might be of assistance. I wanted a suit, I brightly blurted out. Trust me to say the right thing.

"Of course, sir," he replied, ushering me down the rich but very old and faded oriental carpet, between long oak tables groaning under bolts of the most sybaritic cloth I'd ever seen. And did I prefer town or country suiting, he inquired.

I spent the next forty-five minutes or so going through swatch books, dozens of them—there must have been fifty different patterns of Harris tweed alone—some containing pieces of cloth I thought I'd seen twenty minutes before in another swatch book. My guide stood demurely at my side, offering a word or two of encouragement if I turned to him with a swatch between my fingers.

"Very serviceable piece of worsted that is, sir. Perhaps a bit too heavy, though, for your climate at home, would you think?"

Finally, fearing that I should only become more confused by looking at more samples, and foregoing the other thirty or forty cloths that took my interest, I settled on a handsome lovat-shaded cheviot in a miniature herringbone pattern.

"An excellent choice, sir, if I may say so," my well-upholstered counselor intoned. "You may be interested to know that this particular cloth has been woven for us for almost a hundred years now. Had a suit of it myself when I was younger."And then the magic request.

"And now, sir, if you will kindly step through." His outstretched arm directed me toward the muted elegance of that burnished wood cubicle with the bevelled triplex full-length mirror and malt-colored flannel curtain: THE FITTING ROOM.

There were four of us in the fitting room during the next forty minutes. Not all at one time, actually. First there were myself and my guide—who was in fact a master fitter and cutter, and who would be ultimately responsible for the garments being made—and then, in the

order in which they appeared: the jacket fitter, who took several dozen measurements of my shoulders, neck, arms, waist, chest, seat, and other parts of my upper torso of which I don't know the names; then the trousers fitter, who took only slightly fewer measurements of my legs, waist, and seat. All the while, the master fitter stood by, recording these figures and several indecipherable code terms in a large, leatherbound ledger: my permanent record, a detailed map of my corporeal terrain.

Then we discussed styling. Did I prefer a single-breasted jacket ("I think so, sir, if I may say so, with this type of cloth"), two- or three-button front ("May I suggest a button-two closure for you, sir, as it will give you that bit more height"), slanted or straight pockets on the jacket, ticket pocket, side or center vent, three or four buttons on the sleeve ("We normally prefer four, sir, but if you'd prefer . . ."). Did I use my breast pocket for eyeglasses or just a handkerchief? How many inside jacket pockets would I require? Would I like a change pocket in the trousers ("A safe place to keep your latch key, sir")? Did I think I might be prone to wearing a woollie under the jacket on cold days ("We should like to make allowances for that, sir")?

Well, one could go on and on. The point is that having a suit custom-made is an absolutely unique experience. It should also be an extremely pleasurable one—and unfortunately sometimes isn't. In fact, buying a custom-made suit can be really more of a gamble than buying one off-the-rack because, of course, there at least you have the finished product to examine, while at the tailor's you see nothing but cloth—and sometimes only small swatches of that! Whenever a tailor's name is mentioned, the question that invariably arises among those used to custom-made clothing is, "Can you get what you want?" This may seem like a silly question, since that is what custom-made is supposed to be all about: you tell the tailor what you want, and he does it. Unfortunately that is not what custom-tailoring is all about, and the question is not frivolous. It is in fact the most important question one can ask about a tailor: will he produce the suit I envision?

Theoretically at least, the answer must be, "Probably not." The playwright George S. Kaufman once said that 1937 was a great year for him—memorable anyway—because he got a tailor to deliver a suit as he had requested it. And the point is well taken. I'm not talking about run-of-the-mill, local alterations tailors here, either. I'm talking about the tape-measuring chaps here and in Europe who charge (at the moment) upwards of $1,200 for a suit. These craftsmen—and artisans they all are—tend rather to feel that their clients' bodies will never achieve the perfection of the suit they will have crafted for them. This depressing emotion, that the customer's body betrays the craftman's art, is somewhat mitigated for the tailor by the feeling that he will improve his client's appearance. This explains why tailors are by and large a melancholy group, and there is nothing much to be done for that.

On the other side of it, there's not much point for us to apologise to him about the condition of our bodies, and of course from our point of view—the correct one—it's his clothes that must be made to fit our bodies, not the reverse. But that is still not the answer to the question because fitting us is not the problem. Everyone wants clothes that "fit," but fit is really something of a nonsensical concept. If clothing did indeed conform to our body's shape we should most of us not look our best. The point of clothing is not to "fit" us in the sense of conforming to our individual shapes, but rather to help us conform to some ideal shape more or less culturally determined. We envision how we look, or want to look, and want to wear clothes that help us realize that image in our minds.

But the tailor also has his images. He has his own way of doing and seeing, and no matter that he tells you he is able to make any garment any way you like, he cannot. He, like the rest of us, is hemmed in by habit and training, and more importantly, by imagination. He sees people in a certain way and will transform that vision into cloth at every turn. A tailor may see the ideal man as an American athlete, a French boulevardier, an English m'Lord, or South American businessman—and his clothes will reflect his view. Costume designers understand this concept very well, that's how they are able to help an actor achieve a certain characterization through his appearance. But it's most important when buying clothes—and particularly custom-clothing—to understand that that's how we all work.

The tailor who will produce the suit you want is the man who understands your view of yourself. He must have the same ideas, the same vision. The obvious point to make is that if most competent tailors could indeed make a suit any way we wanted, we could all go to any tailor and be satisfied—which we know is nonsense. What throws us off is the business about fit, when in fact the real problem is one of style. The tailor calls this concept "line," and what he means is the various stylistic attributes that make up the general silhouette of the garment: the height of shoulders, the narrowness of sleeves, the deepness of vents, the broadness of chests and backs, the length of jackets, the width of trousers, that sort of thing. And since good tailors measure in quarter-inches, and every aspect of the garment must "balance," that is, must be in correct proportion to every other aspect, achieving the right line becomes a matter of solving hundreds of minute problems and adjusting dozens of difficult relationships within the garment. It is no easy task.

Technically, what happens is this. After the customer selects his cloth, measurements are taken and details discussed. From those measurements and stylistic details, a paper pattern is then constructed by an expert who is called a "cutter." Once the paper pattern is judged to be correct it is used as the model from which the cloth is cut. The cloth is laid out on a long table, with the various parts of the paper pattern placed on top, and then outlined in chalk. Then the cutter proceeds to actually cut the cloth; this step, which is sometimes called "striking," is usually considered the most important simply because at any other stage adjustments can be made, but if the cloth is cut wrongly (it must be cut to the correct dimensions, of course, but designs in the cloth such as stripes or plaids must line up exactly when the garments are sewn together), you throw it out and start again—and good cloth these days is expensive, too expensive for mistakes.

After the cloth has been cut into the various parts of the pattern, it is passed to the tailor (large shops have specialists for the various garments in a gentleman's wardrobe; of these, vestmakers are usually considered the most skillful), who bastes the garment together using white thread in large stitches. At this point a fitting—referred to as the "first try-on"—is appropriate. At the first fitting corrections are made while the garment is on the customer—jacket sleeves may be ripped off and re-stitched in a moment—and the basted cloth goes back to the tailor, who moves the garment along to the "forward" stage: the garment is actually sewn into permanent shape and the white basting removed;

linings are sewn in, and details take shape. Then a second fitting, a few smaller corrections—get the sleeve and trouser length exact, and make sure the shoulders are perfectly flat—and back to the tailor for finishing: put in the sleeve buttonholes, finish the trouser bottoms, attach the jacket buttons. The suit is completed.

At this stage, if all goes well, both customer and tailor admire the results. On his part, the tailor is prepared to make alterations over the life of the garment—which one can normally expect to be longer than the same garment off-the-rack—and store away the paper pattern against future orders; he hopes to have a client for life (yours or his). On the customer's part, if he is indeed happy with the results, choosing a suit in the future will be much easier since only the final fitting will be necessary. Some satisfied customers have even been known to forego that pleasure and make all their tailoring transactions by phone or mail ("Just send me a suit like the last one I ordered, but in a summer weight. And, oh yes, I put on about five pounds."). Good tailors are accustomed to that sort of thing.

But to return to our question: How to find the right tailor, a man who understands your vision of yourself? The wrong way to go about this is to try to educate the tailor, to try and bring him around to seeing things your way. He is as set in his ways as you are, more so in fact, and cannot be counted on to budge—and you will either end up changing yourself or being very dissatisfied. Better to find a tailor who agrees with you from the onset. One way of course is to ask a friend whose clothes you admire who his tailor is. (Never ask a stranger. My father used to say that anybody who will talk about his tailor in public probably has other nasty habits as well.) Failing that, make the rounds of some better tailors; talk with them, look at their work, discuss your requirements. Communication—that over-used word—is essential: you may assume that he wants to make you happy and will do his best for you—craftsmen are like that—but you must also understand that he does not know you, has no idea what image of yourself you are trying to present to the world through your wardrobe. And you have no idea what is in his mind—one person's ideal man is another person's smarmy gigolo, for example. Some men wear ties that I think would make a self-respecting circus barker cringe, but there you are; it's what makes horse races, isn't it?

And, oh yes, about that first custom-made suit of mine. It is, as it happens, still in my wardrobe. Well, perhaps better to say in my closet rather than wardrobe, since I no longer actually wear it. Not that it isn't wearable. The cloth still has its fine hand and finish; the buttons are as securely fastened as ever; the styling as distinguished as when the suit was first purchased; the jacket, trousers, and vest still holding their shape beautifully—no crinkling of collar, nor bagging of knee.

The trouble is simply that I haven't kept *my* shape nearly so well. I tell myself I really should give the suit to a nephew, it's a shame for it not to be seen in public helping some young man look more sophisticated and knowledgeable. But the truth is that I can't bear to part with it, partly because of the memories I associate with it, and partly—it's difficult for me to reflect that I'm so vain—because I halfway believe one day I'll fit into it again.

And so it hangs in the back of the closet. Every other year or two I take it out, lovingly run finger and thumb along the curve of the lapel, admire the wasp-waisted trousers, and sigh. Then I give it a good brushing and hang it back in the closet.

To make selecting a tailor slightly less risky than a horse race, I've listed a handful of reputable tailors whose art can be counted on. Categorization is necessarily general, but it is provided to give the prospective customer some idea of the favored silhouette at each establishment. A relationship with a tailor is like a marriage in many respects, and as with a wife, you should find one you're compatible with before making the commitment—she's not likely to change afterwards.

THE TAILORS

Anderson & Sheppard (30 Savile Row, London W1)
The doors are opened an hour early so city bankers and businessmen can stop in for a fitting on the way to the office. The most conservative cut, very understated and soft, with almost no padding or interfacings to stiffen the garments. The goal here is propriety, not smartness, and the range of fabrics is said (along with Huntsman) to be the most extensive in London. Although the firm refuses to bandy customers' names

about, it is a well-known secret that Fred Astaire is a long-time customer.

Ferdinando Caraceni (Via San Marco 29, Milan 20121)
Conservative Italian styling, Caraceni's clothes always manage to look fashionable without being trendy. A bit trimmer than an English cut perhaps, and certainly elegant. The sort of clothes a debonair Italian chairman of the board, like Gianni Agnelli, would wear—and does.

Chipp Clothiers (14 East 44th Street, New York, NY 10017)
Chipp is Ivy League custom tailoring. There is simply no one better at making suits and sports jackets in the classic American tradition of natural-shouldered understatement. Simplicity is a virtue here: jackets are about as unconstructed as a jacket can be without becoming a sweater, and the preferred trouser style is plain-fronted and straight-legged.

Cifonelli (Via Quintino Sella 68, Rome 00147)
This Roman institution appeals to those who want to be noticed for their good taste, even though they don't say so. Very stylish and quietly dashing approach to dress. Arms are slim and shoulders straight, in the grand manner.

Davies & Sons (19 Hanover Street, London W1)
The most conservative of tailors, catering mainly to the English gentry. Nothing particularly au courant, certainly nothing showy or flashy. The cut is rather on the loose side, and easy.

J. Dege & Sons (16 Clifford Street, London W1)
Recently granted a Royal Warrant, the firm not only does suits and sports jackets in the classic English shaped manner, but has a reputation for being the great military tailors as well.

Donaldson, Williams & Ward (42 The Burlington Arcade, London W1)
Good, middle-of-the-road styling for the international businessman who wants to be properly dressed without giving the impression of being overly concerned. The firm, begun in 1878, stresses a modern-yet-traditional approach that incorporates medium shaping and flair with a bit fuller chest. Although they tend to eschew fads, they are willing to experiment and in fact do some of the most advanced English styl-

ing as well as conservative. They also like to work with the lighter-weight cloths favored by many Americans.

William Fioravanti (45 West 57th Street, New York, NY 10019)
The firm specializes in what may be called "the power look" for dynamic international executives: lean, straight, and precise. The Fioravanti customer is a knowledgeable, vigorous man and wants his clothes to reflect these abilities. Suits are highly tailored—none of your unconstructed looks here—to be crisp and clean, with no blurred areas. Shoulders are squared, sleeves are trim and must hang perfectly straight, the body of the garment sits close and subtly shaped. Also recommended for sophisticated and fashionable evening attire.

Douglas Hayward (95 Mount Street, London W1)
Mr. Hayward holds the reputation as the discerning artiste's tailor (and his order book reads like a *Who's Who* of the theater and films: Lawrence Olivier, Clint Eastwood, Kirk Douglas, Sean Connery, Michael Caine, and on and on). He blends the contemporary with the classical to produce an elegant yet thoroughly easy and comfortable garment with moderate shaping and build.

H. Huntsman & Sons (11 Savile Row, London W1)
Founded in 1810, Huntsman is the most expensive tailor in London. The styling is what most men think of as traditionally English: jackets are suppressed at the waist and high-vented, armholes are raised and sleeves narrowed, giving a hacking silhouette (which they, more than anyone else, are responsible for popularizing). They stock a superb range of cloth and are considered the best firm for riding breeches and hunt coats in the world—for which one is fit "in the saddle," on a wooden mount.

Kilgour, French & Stanbury (8 Savile Row, London W1)
This is the most highly sophisticated silhouette (along with Fioravanti), grandly elevated with the utmost dash and flair to make a man look like an ambassador (of which the firm has its fair share). Very haute indeed, with much shaping and very definite lines.

Tommy Nutter (18/19 Savile Row, London W1)
The most fashion-conscious of tailors, and the least conservative, Nutter has initiated more than his share of ideas that later were picked up

by less creative designers. He works in traditional English cloths but likes to do things a bit differently. At the moment he is inspired by the Edwardian period and the Art Deco transatlantic 1930s, doing marvelous Prince of Wales checked double-breasted suits and elegant, fancy waistcoats.

Carlo Palazzi (Via Borgognona 7, Rome 00187)
High Italian fashion, Palazzi designs with an eye to the future. There is nothing staid or stuffy about his town or country wear; rather it is the most contemporary and sophisticated styling Italy has to offer.

Henry Poole & Co. (15 Savile Row, London W1)
The firm's name is synonymous with Savile Row—they were the firm that started the tradition—and have made more clothes for royalty than any other tailor in business. Traditional English diplomatic styling: extremes are frowned upon, lapels and trousers are always of moderate width, jacket never anything but properly moderate shaping. This is a silhouette prescribed by tradition.

Vincenzo Sanitate (27 West 55th Street, New York, NY 10019)
Contemporary international styling predominates here, and Mr. Sanitate, a personable man, bends over backwards to accommodate a new idea. He prefers to cut a trim jacket, either side-vented or ventless, with some shaping and straight shoulder-line. Italian cloth, particularly gabardines and silks, are in favor here and are ideal for spring and summer suits and sports jackets with minimalist construction.

TOP HATS

T he top hat is no longer a vital part of a gentleman's wardrobe. It is really no part at all and has thus passed into the realm of history, of costume. It becomes a part of dress now only on special, ceremonial occasions, much the way the Latin language is employed, to enhance the importance of the event. Like Latin, the top hat's vitality is of another era, an era that was born in the days of empire and studied elegance. As a style it was long-lived, and its demise is an event to be pondered, and for some yet living, mourned.

I suppose the handwriting was on the wall when just a few short years ago Brooks Brothers, that formidable upholsterer of the American gentry, decided not to replenish its stock of top hats. Demand was at ground level and the shiny old toppers could no longer pay their own shelf space. Their accustomed spot was given over to fedoras and cloth caps, and in summer, straw casuals.

It was a decade ago (January, 1975, actually) that the Dutch firm Spoorenberg of Eindhoven, the world's largest manufacturer of silk top hats, closed its doors after 160 years in the business. Mark Spoorenberg, the seventh generation of his family to oversee production, was forced to quit because demand had been dropping off drastically in recent years while the cost of production rose rather astronomically. It was a classic textbook case for Economics 101.

Craftsmanship of any kind does not come cheaply these days, let alone the making of silk top hats. And, understandably, young people today are more interested in learning about computers than making hats, so there is virtually no new blood in the profession. Finally, there is the shellac problem.

Yes, the shellac problem. It is little known, and much less cared about, but the essential ingredient that gives the top hat its gloss and characteristic hardness is shellac; and the essential ingredient for the manufacture of this shellac is—and let me put this to you as delicately as possible—certain insect droppings, which must be imported from India. The price of this commodity has more than tripled in the past several years, making the shellac, and the hat which depends on it for its luster, an extremely expensive purchase. Today the shellac, when available, costs well in excess of $5,000 per ton.

The top hat has seen brighter days, to be sure. It began to appear at the end of the eighteenth century. High-crowned, and with a narrow brim, it was designed by the English hunting gentry as a kind of crash helmet to be worn while in pursuit of the fox. It is of course still de rigueur for formal hunting appointments, little changed from the original models.

Actually, the first top hat seems to have been invented by one James Heatherington, and he paid the price all innovators pay for introducing new styles. The newspapers of the period report that on January 16th, 1797, Heatherington, an Englishman, took a stroll through the streets of London wearing his new headgear, and, as the *St. James's Gazette* tells it, was promptly arrested and "arraigned before the Lord Mayor on a charge of breach of the peace and inciting a riot as he appeared on the public highway wearing what he called a silk hat—a tall structure, having a shiny lustre calculated to frighten timid people." Poor Mr. Heatherington had indeed caused something of a riot: an ever-increasing crowd followed him down the street, several women in the throng fainted, dogs barked, horses shied, children screamed and threw things, and at least one lad managed to get his arm broken. Heatherington was bound over to keep the peace and fined £50. Someone strolling down Fifth Avenue today in a space suit could hardly cause more of a sensation.

If Mr. Heatherington did not invent the top hat, he was at least responsible for its first recorded appearance in the town streets, and its value as protective headgear was not lost on the country, fox-hunting gentry. With a chin strap to hold it securely in place, the high, stiff-crowned hat could nicely absorb some of the shock from being thrown from the saddle. And because of the longstanding tendency of the English landed gentry to wear their country clothes to town (and even to court, if it came to that!), the top hat was soon not an unusual sight on Bond

Street and along other fashionable thoroughfares. Beau Brummell and his followers at White's, Almack's, and other Regency London clubs set the style, with anyone pretending to le beau monde swimming close in the slipstream.

In this way the top hat had gone in something less than half a century from outré sporting attire to accepted streetwear. By mid-nineteenth century every gentleman's wardrobe contained a silk topper, worn customarily as everyday streetwear. Then it started to "formalize." Pushed first from the day wardrobe by the bowler, and later, in the Prince of Wales' time (Edward VII), by the homburg and fedora, the top hat was relegated to evening wear and formal occasions. And thus it remained until World War II. The film *Top Hat* (1935)—still the best Astaire-Rogers production—was in fact an unwitting swan song for the style.

Then, in the so-called great casual revolution of the 1950s and 1960s, the top hat abruptly sank into pure costume. It became a period piece, a dead artifact of another world. The last Spoorenberg silk top hat to come into this country was sold in 1974 to a Long Island formal wear rental firm, to be let for weddings, funerals, and other solemn rites of passage.

What the passing of the top hat comes to signify, in its symbolic sense, is the end of the social ideal of gentility. This concept, so much taken up at the end of the eighteenth century, when the democratization of dress replaced the pomp and circumstance of the court circle, was able to stabilize masculine attire for 150 years. But particularly since the end of World War I there has been an almost continuous downward thrust to this process, a movement that reached its most blatant form in the 1960s, when fashion was clearly seen to emanate from the demimonde, the bottom of the social rank. Fashion presented a reverse kind of snobbery, and wealth went wearing denim jeans and work shirts and ranch jackets (which were occasionally lined with ranch mink). John F. Kennedy had, a few years earlier, made a valiant effort to reverse the tide and wore a silk top hat for his inauguration as president, but that was just so much closing the barn door after the horse had wandered away.

Add to this reduction-of-fashion-to-the-lowest-possible-class theory the tendency for both men and women not to wear hats anymore, and one begins to see what the top hat was up against. With the exception of certain types of sports hats, headgear is just seen as non-functional these days (not that fashion is in any way equated with function—we do still have neckties) and worse, as bothersome, which is the very death-knell of style! As protection nowadays hats are quite obsolete, because most men step briskly from home to car to office and back again without being hit by so much as a drop during a downpour. Protective clothing is relegated to the category of dress now called "active sportswear." Every wife knows that if her husband's a really determined golfer, a little thing like a downpour—or monsoon, for that matter—will not keep him off the fairways. So he'll wear his favorite golf hat, that ugly misshapen khaki one with the green and red ribbon band.

Well, there's really no point in weeping at the crossroads for what is passed. The Holy Roman Empire, heavy cream, the top hat . . . things change, and life goes on. But sometimes we sit late at night by ourselves and watch Astaire whirl round and round so effortlessly and elegantly, and wonder.

THE TRENCH COAT

B y almost every account the Crimean War was the one perfectly useless modern war: stupendous blunders, unnecessary losses, and negligible gains. The historian Goldwin Smith has written that in their military orders and strategies "the allied generals were distinguished by their incompetence. Their methods were criminal and their objectives insane." Much of the blame for the mismanagement of the campaign is laid at the feet of two British officers—Lord Raglan and the Earl of Cardigan. How ironic that these two men of such historic importance should now be all but totally forgotten by us except for what they wore. Not a few military men have had something of the dandy about them, but Cardigan in particular seems to have had the keenest interest in dress. As Cecil Woodham-Smith writes in her brilliant book about the Crimean War, *The Reason Why* (New York, 1953), he was not only a stickler on the sartorial deportment of his troops and the officers under his command, but he actually led the Light Brigade into its famous charge in the grandest style:

> He wore the gorgeous uniform of the 11th Hussars and, living as he did on his yacht, he had been able to preserve it in pristine splendour. The bright sunlight lit up the brilliance of cherry colour and royal blue,

the richness of fur and plume and lace; instead of wearing his gold-laced pelisse dangling from his shoulders, he had put it on as a coat, and his figure, slender as a young man's, in spite of his fifty-seven years, was outlined in a blaze of gold.

No cowardly, chameleon-like protective coloration for him! Let the enemy know your true mettle, was his philosophy. Funnily enough, he lived to tell the tale and returned to England a famous man, even though the Russian batteries had handily managed to mow down three-fourths of the troop he led into battle that day. Many of those soldiers had been dressed in knitted woolen over-waistcoats to protect themselves from the fierce cold at Balaclava that winter, and it was this garment that came to be known as a "cardigan" (the Balaclava cap also came into being at this campaign, and for the same reason).

The fact is that modern wars have the dubious distinction of adding many new items to our wardrobes. To name but a few additions: cavalry twill trousers and khaki-colored suits, leather flight jackets and parkas, the duffel coat, field jacket, and of course the trench coat. The proof of this pudding can readily be seen in the popularity of the army-navy surplus shops that do an absolutely thriving business in militaria. When, a few seasons ago, one lower Manhattan store took to dyeing fatigue pants and coats high fashion colors, they quickly became all the rage, and the place was thick with designers from Seventh Avenue taking notes and carrying away merchandise to copy for new collections. Several firms put out mail-order catalogues filled with ghurka shorts, CPO shirts, World War II aviator pants, commando boots, flight suits, Australian troop hats, and Italian army underwear among the other paraphernalia from a variety of standing armed forces past and present.

The classic military garment taken into civilian wear is the trench coat. It has been with us since the trench warfare of 1914, and as rain-protection has proven itself from over a half-century of use. It is the most popular outercoat of this century, specifically designed as protection against the soggier elements. And when one discusses rainwear there are two places to begin: with the Scotsman Charles Macintosh, and with the Englishman Thomas Burberry, both of whom gave their names, and thus a new word, to the English language.

Not that it is a question that crosses one's mind every day, but what did our ancestors wear when it rained? Before the early years of the nineteenth century there was apparently the choice of not going out into it or making do. In colder weather a stout wool cloak or greatcoat offered the best protection. Wool, however, does absorb moisture, making a great coat that much greater and heavier, and the smell of wet wool is a sensation that some have found resistible. But in the nineteenth century we come to those two ingenious chaps, Messrs. Macintosh and Burberry. Charles Macintosh (1766–1843) was a Scotsman, a chemist by trade, who got it into his head to experiment with the concept of rubberized fabric. With many a pub north of the Tweed known as "The Highlandman's Umbrella," it isn't particularly surprising that the idea of protection from rain would hold an eminent place in the Scottish mind. And, to shorten a story that only chemists find thrilling in detail, Macintosh finally, in 1823—an historic watershed, you see—perfected a method of bonding a layer of rubber between two layers of cloth. In fact there had been for some time an oilskin cloth in use—which is, as the name implies, cloth treated with oil to make it water resistant—but it was obvious that Macintosh's approach was superior in that his fabric was waterproof.

Coats made from this bonded fabric soon became synonymous with rainwear, so much so that even today in Britain a raincoat is commonly referred to as a "mac," and when a few years ago a firm brought out a thin, travel raincoat in a pouch, they dubbed it a "Pac-a-Mac." Protective coats were also being made from rubber at this time, but they were decidedly like the atmosphere in a Tennessee Williams play: hot and heavy. These rubber sweat suits gave many people the distinct impression that it was preferable to get wet from the rain. At any rate, Macintosh's bonded fabric, and the outercoats made from it, were popular for many years to come.

The other genius of the early years of rainwear was Thomas Burberry (1835–1926). Born and educated in a small village in Surrey, he first learned the rudiments of the fabric trade as an apprentice to a country draper, and then in 1856 he opened his own shop in Basingstoke, Hampshire. According to his obituary, he first got the idea for the invention of the Burberry raincoat through a conversation he had had when a young man with a physician. The doctor said that he

thought it was better for a man to get wet clear through than to be kept dry in a rubberized garment and "expressed the opinion that the ideal waterproof was one which would withstand wind and rain in a reasonable degree and yet allow air to reach the body." With the help of a neighboring cotton-mill owner, Burberry began experimenting. After trying one method after another, he finally hit upon a combination process that proved very successful in waterproofing cotton fabric: the cotton was chemically treated in the yarn, then tightly woven into fabric, and finally proofed again in the piece before being fashioned into garments. The result was a cloth that was much lighter and cooler than the Macintosh rubberized fabric, but just as waterproof.

He started to specialize in making and selling these terribly durable and protective garments for field sports, at which he himself was an expert, and as he became more and more successful in this venture, moved his shop to London in 1891—it is still there at the original location, No. 30 Haymarket. Burberry himself had definite ideas about the styling of the clothing he sold, concentrating on sports and specialized garments: shooting capes with ingenious pivot sleeves, riding coats that had hidden pleats, a loose-cut outercoat for the new sport of motoring. Additionally, the polar explorers Nassen, Scott, Shackleton, and Amundsen all wore wind- and waterproofed suits designed and made by Burberry. Even the tents that Amundsen left at the South Pole to inform Scott that he'd been there before him were specially designed and made by the firm.

In the first decade of the twentieth century, the uniform department of Burberrys designed a military model of their already classic raincoat that became the famous trench coat of World War I. At the same time the Russo-Japanese War and the Boer War had actually anticipated what was to happen to military dress in 1914. The removal of color and ostentation from uniforms made scarlet jackets, gold braid, and bearskins anachronisms for all but dress parade. World War I—with its new weaponry: the airplane, mustard gas, the tank, and the trench fighting technique—was quite the turning point in the concept of uniforms. The Edwardian era, the last age to emphasize opulence in peace and bravura in war, ended at the Somme and Passchendaele.

The great popularity enjoyed by Burberry weatherproofed coats during the early part of the century, especially among British officers,—

who wore them unofficially—prompted Thomas Burberry to design a pattern for an army officer's raincoat which he submitted to the War Office. The coat, designed as it was for the various miseries of trench warfare, was accepted as the standard pattern for officers' rainwear during World War I. Its success was assured when it was noted that Lord Kitchener, the famous field marshal and Secretary of War, wore one (he was in fact said to be wearing one the day he was killed). During those hostilities of 1914–18 half a million men wore Burberry trench coats. They weren't bulletproof, but they offered formidable protection from rain, wind, mud, and cold.

Since then their cachet has come to us via the film hero, in films such as the old Hitchcock thriller *Foreign Correspondent,* or Dick Powell in *Murder my Sweet,* or Robert Mitchum in *Farewell My Lovely.* It became a trademark for Alan Ladd and Jimmy Cagney, and who can forget Bogart sadly standing on that Paris train station platform in his elegantly disheveled Burberry and fedora, resigned to going on alone without Ingrid Bergman to Casablanca. Even the ladies looked more sultry in trench coats, particularly Marlene Dietrich in *Witness for the Prosecution*—no wonder Tyrone Power couldn't forget her. On the lighter side, Peter Sellers apparently bought two Burberrys before filming every Pink Panther movie, and it only added to the sense of comedy that the authority of the appearance was undercut by the bumbling mannerisms.

Today the authentic version has changed not at all from the days when it was accorded battle-ready status: it is still double-breasted, waterproofed cotton khaki cloth, with epaulets, wrist straps to tighten against the wind and wet, a storm shoulder flap and back yoke, wedge back pleat, large collar and throat latch, and reinforced belt complete with D-rings. These rings were originally meant to hold water bottle, combat knife, hand grenades, and other utensils of military necessity, and while such paraphernalia is frowned upon in civilian life, these loops can still be pressed into service as a fine place to hang a camera or travel umbrella when one needs a free hand.

The reason why the trench coat has become the most popular coat of this century is not only its dashing appearance, of course, but that it works. It is not only a coat for all seasons—get one with a wool removable lining—but for all costumes; as an outercoat, it can accompany the entire spectrum of day and evening wear. It is obviously appropriate with a business suit, blazer, or sports jacket, but it is equally at home with jeans and a turtleneck sweater, and to wear one with a dinner jacket—while it takes a certain aplomb—strikes the perfect note of *sprezzatura*.

UMBRELLAS

I t's a shame that the umbrella is not as popular as it once was—although I've got hopes that it's coming back—because it is a wonderful dress accessory. Umbrellas are functional too, I suppose, but historically they've always been more of a symbol than a utensil. I hate to be dogmatic, but that's the truth of it. The best example is the case of Louis Philippe, that most misunderstood French monarch. Louis came to the throne of France in 1830, after the combined excesses of the French Revolution, Napoleon, and Charles X. When the revolutionary fever of July, 1830 cooled, Louis was chosen "King of the French" by his *concitoyens* in a more democratic manner perhaps than France had ever seen before. Louis appeared on the balcony of the Palais-Royal and sang the "Marseillaise"—off key, the enemies of his regime remarked—and although he was a flaming monarchist at heart, he had to descend to the level of his electors if he were to keep his throne secure. To symbolize this purpose he affected a certain *laisser-aller* attitude in his dress, and foregoing the gold-trimmed uniforms of his predecessors, he chose to wear normal bourgeois clothes of the day. And to further the impression that he was indeed "of the people," instead of a sword he carried an umbrella!

The umbrella became the symbol of the Citizen King—perhaps in much the same way that Carter and Reagan have worn jeans to let the voters know they are real folks—and with it Louis transformed the French court. The whole atmosphere of the Tuileries was different in style from what it had been before his election; even the ushers, who under Charles X had worn the blue and silver uniforms of the ancien regime, were put into black frock coats, which symbolically gave the court an aura of middle-class respectability. To a friend who had questioned him about this shift in dress, Louis confided that he found the Bourbon costume too flashy. In some aristocratic circles he was never forgiven for this *abaissement*. The umbrella became a symbol of pandering to bourgeois power, just as a century later it would become, through the Munich meeting of Neville Chamberlain and Hitler, an embarrassing symbol of appeasement to Nazi power.

Historically it should be noted that while the umbrella is a polychrestic device, that is, being capable of serving numerous purposes, the last thing it was used for—literally—was a rain shield. In Africa and the Far East, from whence it came to Europe and the Americas, the umbrella had for thousands of years been allowed solely as a mark of exalted rank. As such it was used by the aristocracy of ancient Egypt as early as 1200 B.C., as it was by the Assyrians and Persians. The Chinese mandarins had large retinues of umbrella bearers; the Burmese took the Golden Umbrella as their symbol of royalty; the most impressive title of the Ruler of Ava was "Lord of the Twenty-Four Umbrellas," while Buddha, the Indian philosopher and founder of that religion, rates a seven-tiered one.

In antiquity the umbrella was used principally as a protection from the sun—the word deriving from the Latin *umbraculum*, meaning a shady place—and began to be used in Europe in the late sixteenth century exclusively as a sunshade for women. The implications of the alternate, and more effeminate, term "parasol" can clearly be seen in William Frith's famous genre painting *Ramsgate Sands* (exhibited in 1854), picturing a wonderfully sunny day at the seaside, with more than a dozen umbrellas in evidence. While the umbrella was an important article in feminine attire, men who carried them were thought too affected and foppish. In 1756, however, a London philanthropist, author, and general eccentric named Jonas Hanway (there is a street in the Bloomsbury section of London named after him today) justly earned the title of Pioneer of the Umbrella by being the first man to use one of these contrivances on the street—for protection from the rain. When he would hoist his umbrella he not only drew ridicule and aspersions to his masculinity, but even outright hostility from sedan-chair carriers (the eighteenth-century version of taxi drivers), who quite correctly assumed that if others took up this simple rain shield it would prove a considerable threat to their business.

Hanway's pagoda-shaped invention was made of oiled silk with whalebone ribs, and it worked. Its first real success with men was brought about by none other than the very masculine Duke of Wellington, who had someone hold one over him while he inspected his troops. A fashion mania of sorts started with army officers, who began using them to protect their uniforms from inclement weather—even in the throes of battle! Officers were seen on the field of conflict with sword in one hand and colored silk umbrella in the other. The Iron Duke thought this was a bit too much and sent his officers a terse memo from headquarters after the Battle of Bayonne, saying he did "not approve of the use of umbrellas during the enemy's firing and will not allow gentlemen's sons to make themselves ridiculous in the eyes of the army."

Wellington might just as well have saved his breath. There is no stopping fashion, it seems, even by command, and his officers in fact continued to carry their umbrellas. The rage for carrying them into battle eventually ceased, but the umbrella is still very much a part of the British officer's mufti dress. Soon there developed an unwritten rule concerning the proper carriage of the umbrella: the correct way, it was deemed, was to grasp it in the middle, handle back and turned towards the ground, with the opposite end slightly lowered. The distinguishing feature, however, of the gentleman's umbrella was construction: expensive models were made of silk, with green and blue the favored colors; cheaper ones for the less affluent were of cotton gingham (in the nineteenth century "gingham" was a middle and lower class slang expression for an umbrella). The expensive silk ones were slimmer, less bulky and cumbersome than the heavier cotton ones. They were always carried neatly furled, never open; if a gentleman saw rain coming, he used his umbrella to hail a cab, and never, but never, opened it. Correctness meant that it was never to be used for the purpose for which it was intended.

That may tend to strike a strange note, but not only does fashion often take no notice of practicality, it can be rather silly the other way round as well: Nature gave us hair to protect our heads, and then we wear hats to protect our hair; and finally umbrellas to presumably protect our hats. Simply, the reason for both men and women to carry umbrellas is that they add to the physical appearance by providing a larger than normal presence, an outlet for wealth, and something to allow the hands a pose. At the end of the nineteenth century a rather curious configuration occurred for women: wide hats, bustle skirts, and umbrellas all became fashionable at the same time, giving women a decidedly larger-than-life silhouette. The women in Georges Seurat's painting *Sunday Afternoon on the Island of La Grande Jatte* present an appearance of demurely conspicuous consumption. For gentlemen, the umbrella became a fashion replacement for the cane or walking stick that had been popular since the seventeenth century (and had

in turn descended from the riding whip).

It was in large measure the automobile that brought about the demise of the walking stick; it certainly brought about the demise of walking. At first the umbrella was able to defend itself against this mechanical onslaught, but the auto soon replaced the umbrella as a symbol of aristocracy. In his autobiography, A *King's Story*, the Duke of Windsor tells an illuminating anecdote concerning this change:

> Early in my reign I called a meeting of the Duchy Council. The afternoon was rainy; but since it was only a two-minute walk from the Palace to the Duchy offices, I decided not to order the Daimler but to walk instead. So, calling for my bowler hat and umbrella, and accompanied by an old member of my staff, Admiral Sir Lionel Halsey, similarly equipped, I sallied forth. And that for me would have been the end of the episode, but for the chance that a newspaper photographer who had stationed himself at the door of 10 Buckingham Gate for a routine picture of the King disembarking from the Royal motorcar happened to spot the Admiral and me as we came striding across the street.
>
> The result was a scene that must have been repeated ten thousand times that day in London—two men in city clothes, one with a briefcase, the other with upturned collar, striding along under umbrellas on their way to a business appointment. But because one of the two men was the King, the picture was widely published and its informality appeared to please many of my subjects.

Fair enough. Because by then an opened umbrella was a symbol of the middle classes, and thus what we think of as the climate of opinion was with him. But wait a moment. A few days later, at a dinner party, Mrs. Wallis Simpson, soon to be Edward's wife, was cautioned about the king's behavior by a prominent member of parliament who voiced what amounted to gentle contempt:

> That umbrella! Since you know the king won't you ask him to be more careful in the future as to how he is photographed? The monarchy must remain aloof and above the commonplace. We can't have the king doing this kind of thing. He has the Daimler."

The cane had already disappeared as a symbol of the gentleman, with the exception of evening wear, and the more functional umbrella had become a clear sign of those without Daimlers. Funnily enough, as it declined in popularity it improved functionally: nylon covers came in during the 1940s, self-opening devices in the following decade, folding models in the 1960s, plastic campanulate varieties in the 1970s—but these improvements could not salvage the umbrella because they were merely utilitarian. One does see more umbrellas around today than a decade ago, but the reasons to my mind have not strictly been utilitarian, but rather fashion-related. First, as with men's clothing, we are enjoying something of a color revival. While designers are dishing up our gray suits sprinkled with raspberry stripes and mint flecks, the multicolored golf umbrella has left the links and taken to city streets; not only variant color panels, but polka dots, geometric prints, and paisley designs are now strutting their way about town. Second, there is a current nostalgia for the elegance of the past, particularly the 1920s and 1930s, for which the umbrella is a symbol, denoting propriety and sophistication—graces we seem to have lost sight of these past two decades. Third, people in the cities, where more and more of us are spending a sizable portion of our time (the Census Bureau has just reported that half of all Americans live in the thirty-six metropolitan areas with populations of one million or more), are taking to walking more. While we kid ourselves that "it looks like rain," we really carry an umbrella because it feels good, gives us that bit of swagger and makes us all boulevardiers. And we can always use it—if worse comes to worst—if it rains.

If you should be in the market for an umbrella, either of the colorful variety or the more conservative plain black model—my favorite still— I would recommend either James Smith & Sons, 53 New Oxford Street in London, or the Uncle Sam Umbrella Shop, 110 West 45th Street (also at 660 Lexington Avenue, and 161 West 57th Street) in New York City. Smith's is both the oldest and largest purveyor of brollies in Europe, selling well over 10,000 every year, ranging from a plain nylon one with plastic handle at $10 or $15 to ones with ivory grips, gold mounts, and pure silk covers that cost hundreds. They will also make you an umbrella from your own fabric, and with almost any kind of handle imaginable. At its three locations in New York, Uncle Sam's has the largest stock in this country: everything from lacy parasols and huge bright beach umbrellas to the most correct black nylon with bamboo curved grip. The firm even makes umbrellas for two, for those romantic walks in the rain.

Some people now even collect umbrellas and have whole wardrobes of them for display and use. They have city and country umbrellas, ones for day wear and others for evening. It would be a shame not to display a fine collection, perhaps in an old brass Indian bucket or a Peruvian jardiniere or a contemporary lucite-and-chrome stand, somewhat in the way our grandfathers used to display their walking sticks, in the days when no man of quality would have thought of strolling out without his malacca or rosewood cane.

VESTS

Everyone is always talking of comparisons between the stock market and the length of women's skirts and that kind of thing, you know, and so now I am wondering if there is any connection between the social order and the vest. This masculine garment seems to go mysteriously in and out of fashion as regularly as short hemlines do. Not that I take any personal interest in the thing. I happen to like vests—they keep my shirts from billowing out all over the place—but I'm tolerant of folks who don't, and I do agree with those who feel that a vested summer suit or double-breasted one is wretched excess.

Vests do, however, pose a special problem for tailors, in two respects. Since they are the tailored garment that sits closest the body, it calls for considerable technical expertise to get a vest to fit properly: it must touch the torso and lie completely flat, yet it must not bind anywhere. An expert vestmaker is a craftsman of great technical skill, and so there are not many of them about; such talent is not to be found on every street corner. The other reason why there is not an abundance of vest-makers—there are perhaps not a dozen today in New York City—is that when a young man goes into tailoring (and few enough enter the profession at all these days) he doesn't want to become a vestmaker, because you never know if vests are going to be in fashion or not. It's a terrific gamble, and if vests go out of fashion for, say, twenty years, your skill lies fallow. Trousers and jackets are always with us, but vests are in and out. In 1940, when many people were becoming glum over the course of international events, vestmakers were additionally glum over the growing trend towards vestless suits. World War II, with its "utility" restrictions on clothing, in fact, killed off the vest for two decades.

Funnily enough, with all this movement in and out of fashion, the vest has not really been altered in more than a century, unlike women's clothing, which has undergone revolutions. Not only hasn't it changed, but when we consider the vest we find there's nothing here today that wasn't there a hundred years ago: jockey waistcoats, stepped collars, braided borders, rolled lapels, watch-chain bottonholes, post-boy vests, horseshoe fronts, welted pockets. It was all there in 1880. Just let me fill you in on that. But I should like to start by taking two or three steps farther back, helps the old perspective.

Between the fifteenth and sixteenth centuries fell a watershed in Northern Europe which we usually call the Renaissance. It had come to Italy perhaps two centuries before and was a while in making its way north. But when it came it changed everything, not least the way people dressed. The physical appearance of men and women changed considerably. What had happened in dress—it occurred in England somewhere between the Ellesmere Manuscript (c. 1400) and the Holbein portraits of Henry VIII (in the 1530s)—was that tailoring as we know it was invented. Cloth, instead of just being draped around the human form, was cut and sewn to fit the body in stylized ways. The Holbein cartoon of Henry VIII and his father (Henry VII) nicely shows this difference. Henry VII, whose reign had seen the end of the Wars of the Roses and is generally considered the beginning of modern English history, is still wearing the loose-flowing gown (now only seen in academic processions) of a medieval monarch. His son, however, proudly displays in the foreground the doublet and hose of the New Age. Somewhere between the two the first major step had been taken toward clothing in the modern sense: fashion.

For the next three-quarters of a century the doublet (which was merely a padded jacket, close-fitting and worn next to the shirt) began to shrink in volume and length and, in a sense, lost its fight for prominence with the outer garment, the coat. But when an article of clothing begins to shrink in size, as the doublet did, it often makes up for quantity with quality. The doublet, which by the reign of James I (1603–1625) had shrunk to normal waist length and girth, was often richly embroidered, brocaded, and even bejewelled—a sixteenth-century precedent for fancy chest coverings. By the mid-1600s the coat had finally replaced the cloak—which had been the doublet's cold-weather covering—and the doublet itself had begun to lose its stiffness as an over-garment: sometimes longer, then shorter, it gradually began to take on the role of an undergarment, what we think of as functioning perhaps like a vest or pullover of sorts. The transition period (from about 1660 to 1680) from doublet and cloak to waistcoat and coat shows many variations in style, but by 1680 the new fashion of coat, vest, and breeches was established.

Actually, I give the year 1660 as a general date for the beginning of the new fashion only because it's an easily remembered date in round figures. In fact, we can be quite specific here. Indeed, we can be exact: the new style of dress for men, consisting of coat and waistcoat, arrived by official proclamation on October 7th, 1666. The story concerns everyone's favorite monarch, Charles II, who is thought to have been, to use the Earl of Rochester's poetic epitaph, "A great and mighty king / Whose promise none relies on; / He never said a foolish thing, / Nor ever did a wise one." Charles himself had laughingly replied upon hearing the quatrain that the estimate was true because his words were his own while his actions were those of his ministers.

In the sixteenth century, standards of luxury among the aristocracy rose sharply, as explorers and traders to their class brought newfound riches to England. New fabrics were taken up as both male and female silhouette swelled to opulently huge proportions never seen before. This bulky form, so evident in the portraiture of the period, held fashionable sway until Charles I began to favor a slimmer line of dress. For over a hundred years before he had become king, men had worn stiff-ruffed shirts, billowing doublets, and puffy breeches and cloaks. A great deal of credit for changing this old Tudor style is due to Charles himself, often regarded as the founder of taste in England. If we look at early portraits of him (such as the 1615 portrait, when he was Prince

of Wales, attributed to Abraham Blijenberch), and compare them with the later ones by Van Dyck, it's clear that the court of Charles I had thrown off the garish, padded, and burly style of the Tudors for a pared-down, more sophisticated approach. In both the costume and the poetry of the period there is a decidedly rich yet restrained tone—a comparison the Cavalier poets themselves often made!

His son, Charles II, was restored to the throne in 1660, coming home after the turbulent Commonwealth period from what he smilingly referred to as his "travels in France," where he had in truth been exiled at the court of his cousin Louis XIV. He had in those bitter years abroad refined his taste with French fashions in the various arts, but when he was returned to his own throne he had his own mind about how things should be done. And on the 8th of October, 1666, the diarist and diligent bureaucrat in the Navy Office Samuel Pepys heard a council report in which King Charles made an unprecedented declaration:

> The King hath yesterday in Council declared his resolution of setting a fashion for clothes, which he will never alter. It will be a vest, I know not well how. But it is to teach the nobility thrift, and will do good.

Charles, who was wiser than his biographers often credit him, used the excuse "to teach the nobility thrift" for setting the new fashion, but the style had been on the horizon for some time. Styles quite obviously do not spring Minerva-like into the world—despite what some designers and fashion magazines would have us believe—but whether the king was in the forefront of this new fashion movement or merely had caught the changing wind of popular taste in his sail is not really known. We know that there was little resistance to the new style and it became immediately popular. On that famous Monday—October 15, 1666—Pepys went to Westminster Hall to see the king in his new finery:

> This day the King begins to put on his Vest, and I did see several persons of the House of Lords, and the Commons too, great courtiers, who are in it—being a long cassocke close to the body, of black cloth and pinked with white silk under it, and a coat over it, and the legs ruffled with black riband like a pigeon's leg—and upon the whole, I wish the King may keep it, for it is a very fine and handsome garment.

This suit, and we may call it that, was of course different in shape from what we wear today, but on the whole it can be said that all of the ingredients that make up our modern suit were now in place. A thorough description of Charles's costume is given by a contemporary witness named Rugge:

> [In October, 1666] His Majestie and whole court changed the fashion of their clothes—viz., a close coat of Cloath pinkt with a taffety under the cutts this in length reached the calf of the leggs and upon that a sercoat cutt att the brest which hung loose and shorter then the vest six inches, the breeches the Spanish cutt and buskins some of Cloath and som of leather but of the same colour as the vest or Garment, of never in like fashion since William the Conqueror.

Despite the obvious quibble that poor Mr. Rugge had absolutely no true idea of what William the Conqueror actually wore, the point is that by the end of the 1660s the coat and vest had come into general use by the aristocracy and had been given the royal imprimatur. The historically interesting aspect of the new style, which was called "the Persian mode" (which explains its origin; several Englishmen had traveled to Persia in the seventeenth century), is that at this time the vest was *longer* than the coat by some six inches or more as Rugge tells us. It had taken the place of the doublet.

This really all came about because of a new influence—trade with Persia, India, and Arabia. English relations with Persia were close throughout the century, and when Charles received the island of Bombay as part of the marriage dowry of his Portuguese bride Catherine of Braganza, English interest in the East was heightened. It was during this period that men adopted robes and turbans of Oriental influence for negligée. Originally worn at home for leisure, the use finally spread to the counting house, or office, and even to the court. Sir Robert Shirley (who had his portrait painted in a lounging coat and turban by Anthony Van Dyck in 1622), who had traveled much in Persia, became Persian ambassador at the Court of St. James's. Looking at this portrait today, and others like it, it strikes us as being very modern indeed. With our own predilection for peasant dress, caftans, djellabas, kimonos, and fancy lounging robes, we are perfectly used to shopping in Byzantium.

It wasn't long—less than a month—before Pepys himself, shrewd observer and follower of trends that he was, ordered a suit of clothes from his tailor in the new style. It was delivered to him on November 4th, a Sunday—just in time to wear to church:

> Comes my Taylors man in the morning and brings my vest home, and coat to wear with it, and belt and silver-hilted sword. So I rose and dressed myself, and I like myself mightily in it, and so doth my wife. Then being dressed, to church.

In short, what had happened was that the doublet grew shorter and was replaced by the Persian vest, which was in fact longer than the coat worn over it. This vest continued for several decades to resemble and imitate the cut of the outercoat in the first half of the eighteenth century: both became more fitted, figure-following from chest to waist, then flaring out in the skirt section below the hips. But during the second half of the century the vest began to shorten, its skirt ending just above the knee. And very short, almost skirtless vests were sometimes worn with light, fitted coats by young men for sporting occasions (sports and young men and changes in fashion seem to go together). These vests ended at mid-thigh. Often only the waist button was fastened, to show off an exuberant expanse of ruffled shirt front in deliberate deshabille. Sleeves were omitted after 1760. By the following decade, while the coat still reached the knee, the vest had risen to the top of the thigh, and by 1790 it was at the waistline—just where it is today.

By the nineteenth century the vest had become an important part of a gentleman's wardrobe. As it assumed the proportions we should recognize today, that is, as it shrank to the natural waistline and remained sleeveless, it took on a liveliness perhaps only previously seen in some of Henry VIII's fancier doublets. As the vest grew in physical proportions smaller, it became more conspicuous in a refulgent, sprightly way. The Regency dandies, and the Prince of Wales himself (George IV), were inordinately fond of waistcoats. George owned as many as 300 and was often noted at gala balls wearing "a claret-coloured, striped silk coat and breeches and a silver tissue waistcoat, very richly embroidered in silver and stones," or perhaps embroidered cloth of gold; he instituted fancy vests even for day wear, such as "lilac double-breasted," "striped Marseilles quilted," "sprigged marcella," or "fine printed nankeen." His fashion mentor, Beau Brummell, advocated white waistcoats as being the more discreet and proper, but it was the influence of royalty that finally won the day, and as the century continued, the fancy vest became fancier.

Gentlemanly wardrobes contained a dozen or so fancy vests in every conceivable design (tartan checks, spots, embroidered patterns, stripes, and floral prints), color (buff, scarlet, lilac, salmon, pink, peacock blue), and fabric (toilinette, kerseymere, dimity, swansdown, quilted, valencia, moire). In the influential novel *Pelham*, Bulwer-Lytton described the vest as "though apparently the least observable it . . . influences the whole appearance more than anyone not profoundly versed in the habilatory art would suppose." The "ditto" styled suit—coat, trousers, and vest all of the same fabric and color—became increasingly popular after the 1860s for day wear, and there appears to be nothing new in vests since then. Well, actually, there was one other bit of detailing: tailors began to provide a watch-chain hole in the front of the vest from about 1880 on—so let's say there's been nothing really new since then.

In the Edwardian era vests were still very much with us. In summer lightweight and lightly colored linen and canvas were favored materials. For winter wear fancy cloth and—something a bit different—knitted styles. Vests were now increasingly of the same material as the rest of the suit, or, in the case of the frock and morning coat worn with striped trousers, matching the coat. King Edward VII is himself credited with starting the fashion of wearing the bottom button of the vest undone. His grandson, the Duke of Windsor, believed this came about inadvertently—that Edward simply forgot, and in turn the sartorial sycophants in his circle took up the style so as not to embarrass him—but most likely he simply got too corpulent to get the thing fastened properly and still be comfortable. At any rate, he did set the style for leaving the bottom button undone, and in fact even today English tailors cut the vest specifically so that the last button should not be fastened.

The vest, like most other things, was hit hard by the two world wars, particularly the latter one. On both sides of the herring pond the war effort entailed scarcity and austerity. In Britain clothing was rationed from June 1, 1941, and restrictions were not formally lifted until 1948.

One immediate result of the clothing rationing was that the aristocratic habit of dressing for either day or evening was discontinued, and so the business suit became the costume for gentlemen at all hours. A second result was the disappearance of the vest, as the two-piece suit became "de rigueur" in a very real sense. Vests had to some degree begun to be discarded before the war, in sports outfits of flannel and tweed, but the scarcity of cloth in the ensuing years of hostilities accelerated this habit, which persisted even after the controls were withdrawn. In the States the War Productions Board regulations decreed that no vests could be made with double-breasted suits (an idea so sensible one wonders how a government agency could have thought of it). The war years "utility suit" that the board designed was a severe costume: no cuffs, no flaps, no vents, and no vests. The attempt was made to pare down masculine attire to save cloth. For the vest it was all but a death blow.

There were other reasons too why the vest suffered since the war. Better central heating and better insulated housing made layers of heavy clothing unnecessary—at least until the Arab oil boycotts brought the "layered look" back into fashion. Also, there seemed to be less need of pockets, as more men took to wearing their watches on their wrists and carrying other belongings in briefcases; to some extent credit cards obviated the need for almost everything we carried about with us.

But the vest has reached an interesting point of stabilization. Starting in the late 1950s there has been a slow return to both vested suits and sports vests. Today perhaps half of all custom-made and ready-to-wear single-breasted suits are three-piece. Designers have reminded us of bygone styles, particularly those of the 1920s: double-breasted and shawl-collared vests are today included in every collection. And until we move towards a "minimalist" approach to dress—and none is on the horizon—the vest will continue to be with us.